THE HISTORY OF THE INCAS

Joe R. and Teresa Lozano Long Series
in Latin American and Latino Art and Culture

The History of the Incas

BY PEDRO SARMIENTO DE GAMBOA [1572]

TRANSLATED AND EDITED BY
BRIAN S. BAUER AND VANIA SMITH

INTRODUCTION BY BRIAN S. BAUER
AND JEAN-JACQUES DECOSTER

University of Texas Press   Austin

Requests for permission to reproduce material from this work should be sent to:
Permissions
University of Texas Press
P.O. Box 7819
Austin, TX 78713-7819
www.utexas.edu/utpress/about/bpermission.html

♾ The paper used in this book meets the minimum requirements of ANSI/NISO Z39.48-1992 (R1997) (Permanence of Paper).

LIBRARY OF CONGRESS CATALOGING-IN-PUBLICATION DATA

Sarmiento de Gamboa, Pedro, 1532?–1608?
[Historia de los Incas. English]
The history of the Incas / by Pedro Sarmiento de Gamboa ; translated and edited by Brian S. Bauer and Vania Smith ; introduction by Brian S. Bauer and Jean-Jacques Decoster.
p.   cm. — (Joe R. and Teresa Lozano Long series in Latin American and Latino art and culture)
Includes bibliographical references and index.
ISBN-13: 978-0-292-71413-7 ((cl.) : alk. paper)
ISBN-10: 0-292-71413-0
ISBN-13: 978-0-292-71485-4 ((pbk.) : alk. paper)
ISBN-10: 0-292-71485-8
1. Incas—History.   2. Incas—Social life and customs.   3. Peru—History—Conquest, 1522–1548.   4. America—Discovery and exploration—Spanish.   I. Bauer, Brian S.   II. Smith, Vania, 1975–   III. Title.
F3429.S224   2007
985'.02—dc22

                                                          2006023440

This work is dedicated to
JOHN HOWLAND ROWE

So that Your Majesty might be informed, with little effort and much interest, and so that others of differing opinion might be disabused [of their ideas], I was ordered by the viceroy Don Francisco de Toledo, whom I follow and serve in this general inspection, to take charge of this business and to write the history of the lives of the twelve Incas of this land and of the origin of its natives until their end.

PEDRO SARMIENTO DE GAMBOA, CUZCO, 4 MARCH 1572, IN HIS LETTER TO KING PHILIP II OF SPAIN

Contents

LIST OF FIGURES

LIST OF TABLES

BRIAN S. BAUER AND VANIA SMITH

Preface

*T*he goal of this translation is to introduce *The History of the Incas* [1572], by Pedro Sarmiento de Gamboa, to a broad range of individuals interested in the history of the Americas. Sarmiento de Gamboa's manuscript was written in the city of Cuzco, the former capital of the Inca Empire, at a time when the Inca Empire was still remembered by informants who had held important positions of power in it. As such, *The History of the Incas* is an invaluable source of information on the last and largest empire to develop in the indigenous Americas. Inspired by other recent translations of writers such as Bernabé Cobo (1979, 1990), Juan de Betanzos (1996), Pedro de Cieza de León (1998), José de Acosta (2002), and Tito Cusi Yupanqui (2005), we hope that this work will encourage others to explore and understand the Andean past.

During this project we worked primarily with Richard Pietschmann's 1906 transcription of Sarmiento de Gamboa's work, although occasionally we consulted our microfilm of the original document. After the second draft of this translation was completed, we compared it with that done by Clements R. Markham in 1907 and made changes where we felt appropriate. While we have tried to remain true to Sarmiento de Gamboa throughout this translation, we have taken certain liberties to make his document more accessible to a wide readership, particularly to nonspecialists in Andean studies. For example, we have divided many of his excessively long sentences into shorter, more comprehensible lengths, and we have added punctuation where it lends clarity to the text. We have also removed many of the words that Sarmiento de Gamboa habitually uses to begin sentences (And, Therefore, Thus, So, This, etc.). In other sentences we have made grammatical changes, correcting tenses, plurals, and the like. In far fewer places, we have added a word or two to rectify an ambiguous sentence or to clarify confusing pronouns. In a very limited number of cases, we have removed a redundant word to help clarify the meaning of the sentence. As this work is intended for a general readership, we have also attempted to standardize the more common Quechua terms, toponyms, and personal names to match the generalized Hispanic spelling as found in other Spanish chronicles and on modern maps. For example, we use Inca not Inga, Cajamarca not Caxamarca, and Manco Capac not Mango Capac. We have, however, followed Sarmiento de Gamboa's spelling for the more obscure terms, places, and names. Scholars who are interested in the subtleties of Sarmiento de Gamboa's spelling and the orthography of the manuscript should consult microfilms of the document itself. For those who would like to know more about the translation, we provide a Spanish transcription of Chapter 1 and our line-by-line translation in Appendix 1.

Chapters 2 through 5 of Sarmiento de Gamboa's work have not been included in this translation. These chapters, which also were not read to the indigenous leaders of Cuzco, contain little information on the history of the Incas. Instead, they are dedicated to discussing the possible location of Atlantis and the role that it may have played in populating the Americas.[1] Scholars and other specialists interested in these aspects of Sarmiento de Gamboa's work may consult one of the many previously published Spanish editions (Appendix 2).

Acknowledgments

We would like to thank the Office of the Dean (College of Liberal Arts and Science) as well as the Department of Anthropology at the University of Illinois at Chicago for providing financial support for this work. We are especially grateful to Javier Flores Espinoza, Nancy Warrington, and Laura Waterbury, who helped us proofread the entire work. Their suggestions greatly improved the final translation. We would also like to thank Tom Cummins, Bill Hyland, Sabine Hyland, John Monaghan, Joanne Pillsbury, and Jack Scott, who aided us at various stages of the project.

We thank the J. Getty Museum, Los Angeles, for the use of various drawings by Martín de Murúa, as well as the Field Museum for access to their photographic archive.

All photographs are by Brian S. Bauer unless otherwise noted.

THE HISTORY OF THE INCAS

BRIAN S. BAUER AND JEAN-JACQUES DECOSTER

Introduction

PEDRO SARMIENTO DE GAMBOA AND
THE HISTORY OF THE INCAS

The History of the Incas[1] [1572] is one of the most important manuscripts surviving from the Spanish Conquest period of Peru. Written in Cuzco, the capital of the Inca Empire, just forty years after the arrival of the first Spaniards in the city, this document contains extremely detailed descriptions of Inca history and mythology. It was written, on the orders of Viceroy Francisco de Toledo, by the highly educated Pedro Sarmiento de Gamboa, a sea captain and royal cosmographer of the viceroyalty.

The royal sponsorship of the work guaranteed Sarmiento direct access to the highest Spanish officials in Cuzco. It also allowed him to summon influential natives, as well as those who had witnessed the fall of the Inca Empire, so that they could relate their stories. Sarmiento traveled widely and interviewed numerous local leaders and lords (*curacas*), surviving members of the royal Inca families, and the few remaining Spanish conquistadors who still resided in Cuzco. Once the first draft of the history was completed, in an unprecedented effort to establish the unquestionable authenticity of the work, his manuscript was read, chapter by chapter, to forty-two indigenous authorities for their commentary and correction.[2]

After the public reading, which occurred on 29 February and 1 March 1572, the manuscript was entrusted to Jerónimo de Pacheco, a member of the viceroy's personal guard.[3] Pacheco was to take the manuscript to Spain and deliver it to King Philip II, along with four painted cloths showing the history of the Incas and a number of other artifacts and objects that Toledo had collected. However, due to a series of unusual events, this irreplaceable document of Inca history was relegated to obscurity for centuries. Most importantly, a short time after the completion of Sarmiento's *History of the Incas*, Toledo's forces captured the last royal Inca, Tupac Amaru, in the jungles of Vilcabamba to the northwest of Cuzco. For more than forty years, members of the former ruling family had maintained a government in exile in Vilcabamba and had carried out a guerrilla war against the Spaniards. The capture of Tupac Amaru brought an end to the war, and after a hastily arranged trial, Tupac Amaru was beheaded in Cuzco on 24 September 1572. Thus, by the time Sarmiento's document reached the king of Spain, the Inca had already been executed and the long-standing rebellion against Spanish rule in the Andes had been ended.

As a clear violation of the European tradition of the divine right of kings, the killing of Tupac Amaru by Toledo disturbed King Philip II. It is said that when the monarch saw Toledo on his return to Spain nearly ten years later, the king angrily told Toledo that "he had not been sent to Peru to kill kings, but to serve them" (Garcilaso de la Vega 1966:1483 [1609:Pt. 2, Bk. 8, Ch. 20]). Toledo was to die in Spain soon afterward, dishonored and unrewarded after more than a decade of service to the king in Peru.[4] Similarly, it appears that Sarmiento's *History of the Incas*, a product of Toledo's much-criticized administration of Peru, was undervalued, set aside, and subsequently forgotten.[5]

The work resurfaced two hundred years later in 1785 when the private library of Abraham Gronovius was sold to the Göttingen University Library. However, another century passed until the existence of the manuscript was revealed to the world by the librarian Wilhelm Meyer. The historian Richard Pietschmann immediately began editing the manuscript, and in 1906 he published the first transcription of the work.[6] The first English translation was produced by Sir Clements Markham the following year.[7]

SARMIENTO AND HIS GENERAL HISTORY OF PERU

Sarmiento's *History of the Incas* must be seen as the result of the great social and administrative changes that took place during Toledo's monumental term as viceroy of Peru (1569–1581). Francisco de Toledo y Figueroa, the third son of the Count of Oropesa, reached Peru with clear instructions from the Crown and unparalleled powers to carry them out. Philip II had charged the new viceroy with ending the tradition of *encomiendas*[8] in Peru, a highly confrontational task in which one of his predecessors had already failed, resulting in a bloody rebellion against the Crown.[9] Toledo was also told to put an end to the long-standing war with the Incas of Vilcabamba and to completely reorganize the administration of the viceroyalty.

Blessed with notable zeal and formidable energy, Toledo left Lima early in his term to carry out a general inspection of the Andean kingdom of which he was in charge (Table 1). This inspection lasted four years. The viceroy and his entourage left Lima for Cuzco and the highlands of Peru on 23 October 1570. They made various stops along the way to conduct inspections of areas such as Jauja (20 November 1570), where Gabriel de Loarte, president of the court of the Audiencia of Lima, joined the delegation. From Jauja they continued toward Cuzco, inspecting various regions as they traveled, including Guamanga (14 December 1570), Pincos (31 January 1571), Lima-tambo (7 February 1571), Mayo (13 March 1571), and Yucay (19 March 1571). During each of these visits, they met with the eldest and most notable inhabitants, in particular the leaders, *curacas*, and Incas. Through these interviews, they obtained information about the government, economic life, and religious customs of the Incas.[10] Traveling from place to place, Toledo eventually reached Cuzco in late February or early March of 1571, just in time to control the election of the town council (AGI, Lima 110), and to have the formidable Juan Polo de Ondegardo appointed for another term as corregidor of Cuzco.[11] Toledo departed for Collasuyu[12] a little more than a year later, in early October 1572. By 1573 he had reached southern Bolivia, and after a humiliating military defeat at the hands of the indigenous group of that region (the Chiriguanas), Toledo concluded his general inspection and returned to Lima.

One of the most important projects that Toledo initiated during the course of his general inspection was the writing of a historical overview of the regions that he now controlled. This large project was entrusted to Captain Pedro Sarmiento de Gamboa. Toledo had great trust and respect for Sarmiento, who had accompanied the viceroy on his journey across the Andes. He described Sarmiento to the king of Spain as being extremely competent, and he would later personally come to his aid when Sarmiento was imprisoned in Lima.

Although Sarmiento traveled within Toledo's entourage and enjoyed his newly appointed position as royal cosmographer, he was already a controversial figure in Peru.[13] Sarmiento had left Spain in 1555 for Mexico and Guatemala and reached Lima two years later.[14] A great mariner and an excellent geographer, he had already helped discover the Solomon Islands (1567), sailing under the command of Alvaro Mendaña.[15] Later, after the general inspection was completed, Toledo sent him on an unsuccessful mission to capture Sir Francis Drake in 1579. Later still (in 1581), Sarmiento would be given permission by King Philip II to explore the Strait of Magellan to establish a new colony in that remote region.[16] In 1586 he was captured by the English and taken to England, where he remained prisoner for a year before being released.

Sarmiento was also accused of being an astrologer and incurred the wrath of the Holy Office of the Inquisition on two separate occasions. In December of 1564, the archbishop of Lima, Fray Jerónimo de Loayza, imprisoned Sarmiento while a *causa de fe* was initiated against him (Medina 1952:214

TABLE 1. PEDRO SARMIENTO DE GAMBOA AND
THE HISTORY OF THE INCAS

Dec. 1564	The archbishop of Lima, Fray Jerónimo de Loayza, imprisons Sarmiento. He is released six months later, having served time and made penitence.
30 Nov. 1567	Alvaro Mendaña discovers the Solomon Islands. Sarmiento is one of his pilots.
30 Nov. 1569	Francisco de Toledo, the fifth viceroy, arrives in Lima.
23 Oct. 1570	Toledo leaves Lima to begin his general inspection. Within his entourage are Alvaro Ruiz de Navamuel (the king's notary), Pedro Sarmiento de Gamboa (royal cosmographer), and Gonzalo Gómez Jiménez (translator). Numerous interviews concerning the history of the Incas take place along the way.
20 Nov. 1570	Toledo arrives in Jauja and is joined by Gabriel de Loarte.
14 Dec. 1570	Toledo arrives in Guamanga.
Late Feb. 1571	Toledo arrives in the Cuzco region.
June–Sept. 1571	Various interviews are held between Spanish officials and indigenous leaders of Yucay and Cuzco.
Aug. 1571	Juan Polo de Ondegardo begins his second term as corregidor of Cuzco.
4–31 Jan. 1572	A series of interviews are held between Spanish officials and the leaders of different kin groups in Cuzco.
14 Jan. 1572	The painted cloths are presented to various indigenous leaders of Cuzco, many of whom would later hear the reading of *The History of the Incas*.
16 Jan. 1572	The painted cloths are presented to a distinguished group of Spaniards in Cuzco, including Juan de Pancorvo, Alonso de Mesa, Pedro Alonso Carrasco, Mancio Sierra de Leguizamo, and Juan Polo de Ondegardo. Afterward, Ruiz de Navamuel placed his rubric on them, and Sarmiento added wind roses.
22 Feb. 1572	Spanish eyewitnesses to the conquest, including Juan de Pancorvo, Alonso de Mesa, Pedro Alonso Carrasco, and Mancio Sierra de Leguizamo, are interviewed concerning the works and deeds of Pachacuti Inca Yupanqui and Topa Inca Yupanqui.
29 Feb.–1 March 1572	Sarmiento's *History of the Incas* is read to forty-two native leaders of Cuzco and is signed by Ruiz de Navamuel as well as Loarte.
1 March 1572	Toledo writes a letter to King Philip II telling of the completed history and the painted cloths.
2 March 1572	The final transcription of the manuscript, with corrections made during the 29 Feb.–1 March public reading, is approved and signed by Toledo in Cuzco.

TABLE I. CONTINUED

4 March 1572	Having received Toledo's approval of his *History of the Incas*, Sarmiento writes his personal letter to King Philip II as an introduction.
Mid-March 1572	Jerónimo Pacheco leaves Cuzco with *The History of the Incas*, the four painted cloths, and other items to be presented to King Philip II.
8 May 1572	Toledo writes to King Philip II suggesting that all nobles of Cuzco be punished for the current rebellion against the king.
June–Aug. 1572	Tupac Amaru is captured in the remote area of Vilcabamba by forces sent by Toledo.
24 Sept. 1572	Tupac Amaru is executed in Cuzco on orders of Toledo.
Oct. 1572	Toledo departs from Cuzco to continue his general inspection. Polo de Ondegardo leaves the office of corregidor of Cuzco and travels with him. Loarte replaces Polo de Ondegardo as corregidor of Cuzco.
15 May 1573	Two letters are written indicating that Sarmiento continues to collect information.
28 June 1573	Sebastián de Lartaún, the third bishop of Cuzco, arrives in the city.
1575	Sarmiento is briefly arrested by the Holy Office of the Inquisition (Lima) for having supposedly magical amulets in his possession. Toledo argues successfully for his release.
1579	Sarmiento is sent by Toledo on an unsuccessful mission to capture Sir Francis Drake. He returns to Spain via the Strait of Magellan.
1581	Sarmiento is briefly in Spain, where he receives permission to establish a colony in the Strait of Magellan. He also presents a report "about the Incas" to the court.
1582	Toledo returns to Spain and is rebuked by the king.
1586	Sarmiento is captured by the English and taken to England, where he remains for a year.
1734	The painted cloths, housed in the royal palace in Madrid, are destroyed by fire.
1785	The University of Göttingen purchases Sarmiento's *History of the Incas* from Abraham Gronovius.
1906	Sarmiento's *History of the Incas* is transcribed and published for the first time by Richard Pietschmann. Numerous other editions, all based on Pietschmann's work, follow.

[1890]). He was accused by the Holy Office of having magic ink, which no woman, receiving a love letter written in it, could resist, and also of being in possession of two magic rings engraved with Chaldean characters. He was found guilty, in a trial that seems to have been more politically than religiously motivated, and on 8 May 1565 was sentenced, among other things, to hear mass in the cathedral of Lima, "stripped naked and holding a lighted taper in his hand" (Means 1928:463). Ten years later, in 1575, Sarmiento was again brought in front of the Inquisition for having magical amulets in his possession. However, on this occasion, Toledo himself ordered Sarmiento's release so that he could continue his work for the Crown.

But let us return to 1572 and Sarmiento's work in Cuzco. In response to Toledo's orders to write a history of the Andes, Sarmiento developed an ambitious research plan. He envisioned a general history of Peru that was to be divided into three parts. In the first chapter of his *History of the Incas*, he provides a clear outline of what was to be included in each of the parts.

> This general history that I undertook by order of the most excellent Don Francisco de Toledo, viceroy of these kingdoms of Peru, will be divided into three parts. The first will be a natural history of these lands, because it will be a detailed description of them that will include the wondrous works of nature and other things of much benefit and pleasure. (I am now finishing it so that it can be sent to Your Majesty after this [second part], since it should go before.) The second and third parts will tell of the inhabitants of these kingdoms and their deeds, in this manner. In the second part, which is the present one, the first and most ancient settlers of this land will be described in general. Then, moving into particulars, I will write of the terrible and ancient tyranny of the Capac Incas of these kingdoms until the end and death of Huascar, the last of the Incas. The third and last part will be about the times of the Spaniards and their noteworthy deeds during the discoveries and settlements of this kingdom and others adjoining it, divided by the terms of the captains, governors, and viceroys who have served in them until the present year of 1572. (Sarmiento 1906:10 [1572:Ch. 1])

The first part of his general history was to be a geographical description of all the lands of the kingdom.[17] It was to contain the "wondrous works of nature and other things of much benefit and pleasure." A great deal of this work was to be based on the information that was being collected as Toledo and his followers conducted their general inspection of the Andes. However, since Toledo and his party were to move on from Cuzco to the Charcas,

Sarmiento felt that in 1572 the first part of his general history was still incomplete. The work seems to have been well advanced, however, since he tells the king: "I am now finishing it so that it can be sent to Your Majesty after this [second part]."

Sarmiento continued to write Part One as he traveled with Toledo toward modern Bolivia. Catherine Julien (1999:79) notes that there are two letters, both written on the same day (16 May 1575), indicating that Sarmiento continued to research and write a full three years after *The History of the Incas* was completed and sent to Spain. The first of these letters was written by the president of the Royal Audiencia, who notes:

> He [Toledo] has done a very curious thing that will please those who govern this kingdom because he has ordered a good cosmographer to visit all of the provinces and towns, of both Spaniards and Indians, and take the latitude of them and describe them with painting and to write the customs and laws the Inca used to govern them and all of their rites and ancient ceremonies. (Julien 1999:79; translation by Julien)

The second letter was written by the Audiencia of Charcas. It, too, noted the remarkable work of a cosmographer (i.e., Sarmiento):

> ... about the description of all this land that the cosmographer has made and the true history of all that happened in Peru with the information he has taken from those who have been longest in this kingdom, which is something of great importance so that the truth about everything will be known and consent will not be given to circulate in print some false histories. (Julien 1999:79; translation by Julien)

The above letters suggest that Part One of Sarmiento's general history had gone well beyond the "wondrous works of nature" described earlier, to include sections on the customs, laws, rites, and ancient ceremonies of the different regions. In addition, it seems that Toledo expected Sarmiento to use his observational and cartographic skills to paint what he observed so he could illustrate the text of his history. That paintings were created to illustrate the first part of the general history demonstrates that the painted cloths that accompanied the second part, sent to the king, were not a unique initiative.[18] Unfortunately, if in reality the first part of the general history and its accompanying paintings were ever finished, they have not been found and are feared lost.

The second part of Sarmiento's general history, herein referred to as *The*

History of the Incas, tells of the Andean past before the arrival of the Europeans. This portion of the three-part series was largely researched in Cuzco and was completed in early 1572. Its information was primarily gleaned from interviews that Sarmiento conducted with the native authorities of the Inca heartland. It contains very little of the information gathered during Toledo's general inspection between Lima and Cuzco, since that information was to be presented in the first part of the general history.

Fortunately, the king's own copy of Sarmiento's *History of the Incas* has survived in an excellent state of preservation. Written in a clear and steady hand, bound in green leather and red silk, the manuscript can be seen in the library of Göttingen University. Its elegantly plated title page reads: "Second part of the general history called Indica, which by order of the most excellent Don Francisco de Toledo, viceroy, governor, and captain-general of the kingdoms of Peru and steward of the royal house of Castile, written by Captain Pedro Sarmiento de Gamboa" (Figure 1.1).[19]

The third and final part of Sarmiento's general history was to cover the period of Spanish rule in the Andes. It was to begin with the discovery and settlement of South America and include the most notable deeds of the "captains, governors, and viceroys who have served in them until the present year of 1572." Antonio Baptista de Salazar (1867:262–263 [1596]),[20] general assistant to Toledo, appears to have seen parts of this work. This is not surprising, since Salazar had traveled to Cuzco with Sarmiento and Toledo, and may have been in Cuzco for the reading of Sarmiento's completed *History of the Incas*. In a chapter titled "On the investigation that the viceroy ordered made concerning the origin and descendant of the Incas,"[21] Salazar writes:

> Because this city is the ancient court and seat of the Incas, whom they called lords of these kingdoms, and because there are still many of the old Indians and a few of the first conquistadores alive, [the viceroy] ordered investigations and inquiries carried out, in written and painted form, on the genealogy, origins, and ancestry of the Incas before they all die. He confirmed that they were tyrants and not true lords, as had been believed until then. And because of what was written in two printed books, one about the origin of this new discovery and the other about the events of the civil wars that occurred between the Spaniards, [Toledo] ordered all the information known by the old conquistadores [collected] so that both newly corrected histories could be completed, filled with truths about many things that were not told in the other [works]. He assigned this [task] to Pedro Sarmiento de Gamboa, a cosmographer, who has a great

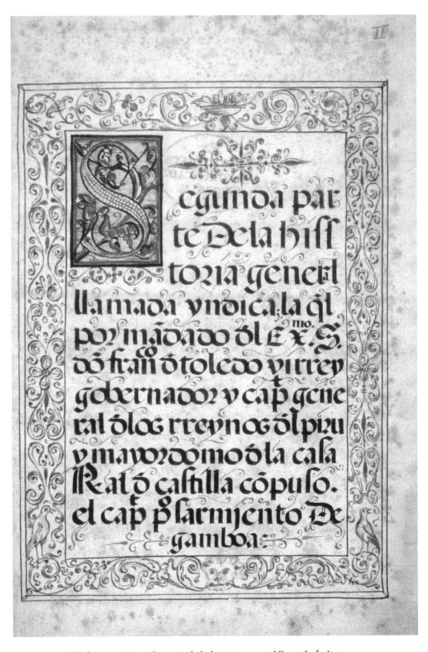

FIGURE I.I. Title page: *Segunda parte de la historia general llamada Índica* . . . (Courtesy of Thomas Cummings.)

capacity for understanding in this, [aided by] a scribe before whom the above-mentioned [people] would give their depositions, and who could swear to everything. I do not know in what state this work was left or what has happened to the papers, which were of great importance and interest.[22]

Salazar confirms much of what we already know about Sarmiento's research on the Incas. Most of the research was conducted in Cuzco and included interviews with the older natives and the few surviving members of Pizarro's forces. Furthermore, the results of Sarmiento's research on the history of the Incas, which took both written and painted forms, supported the view that the Incas were tyrants and not legitimate rulers of the Andes. Salazar also suggests that, while in Cuzco, Sarmiento was working on one, perhaps two other volumes, covering the discovery of the New World and the first decades of Spanish rule in the Andes. Unfortunately, the fates of these works remain unknown.

SARMIENTO'S HISTORY OF THE INCAS (1572)

Sarmiento's 1572 manuscript is composed of a 10-page letter to King Philip II, 262 pages of text, and a final Certificate of Verification that covers 11 pages. It also contains three coats of arms. The cover page displays the coat of arms of Castilla and León (Figure 1.2). This is followed by the ornate title page, which is followed by the royal coat of arms of King Philip II (Figure 1.3). Next is the above-mentioned dedicatory letter to King Philip II, which was signed by Sarmiento in Cuzco on 4 March 1572. The history ends with the coat of arms of the commissioner of the work, Francisco de Toledo (Figure 1.4). The Verification and the final signatures of the witnesses follow this.

In his concluding letter to King Philip II, Sarmiento clearly delineates his sources for his work. He writes:

I have collected this history from the inquests and other investigations that, by order of Your Excellency, have been carried out in the Jauja Valley and in the city of Guamanga and in other areas through which Your Excellency has come inspecting. *But [the history was] principally [collected] in this city of Cuzco, where the Incas had their permanent residence,* and [where] there is more information about their deeds ... (Sarmiento 1906:130 [1572]; emphasis added)

FIGURE 1.2. Coat of arms of Castilla and León. (Courtesy of Thomas Cummings.)

FIGURE I.3. Royal coat of arms of Philip II of Spain. (Courtesy of Thomas Cummings.)

FIGURE 1.4. Coat of arms of Francisco de Toledo. (Courtesy of Thomas Cummings.)

Although informed by his journey through the central Andes, *The History of the Incas* was largely the product of material gathered during his stay in the Cuzco region.

In his cover letter to the king, Sarmiento also reveals the reason why *The History of the Incas* was written. It was to be a true history of the Incas, challenging and discrediting earlier reports that presented the Incas as the rightful and natural lords of the Andes. He emphatically states that since the information provided to earlier authors about the history of the Incas was incorrect, it led them to false conclusions concerning Spain's right to rule the Indies:

> [But as] the information provided to [the scholars] about the deeds [of the Incas] was indirect and not the truth, [the scholars] concluded that these Incas, who were in the kingdoms of Peru, were the true and legitimate kings of these lands and that the *curacas* were and are the true natural lords of this land. These [statements] gave rise to dubiety among strangers to your kingdom. Catholics as well as heretics and other unbelievers discussed and aired their complaints about the rightful pretensions that the Spanish kings had and still have over the Indies. (Sarmiento 1906:4 [1572])

There is no doubt that *The History of the Incas* was written in direct reaction to the works of men such as Bartolomé de Las Casas, whom Sarmiento singles out for specific criticism in his cover letter to the king. The account's purpose was to show that the Incas were not the legitimate kings of the Andes and thus to support Spain's right to rule the kingdom of Peru.

Moreover, the work was written to champion Toledo's massive reforms of Andean culture. Sarmiento also explains this in his cover letter to King Philip:

> [This work is] to give a secure and quiet harbor to Your Royal conscience against the tempests [generated by] your native vassals, theologians, and other learned [individuals] who are misinformed about the events here. Thus, in [Toledo's] general inspection, which he is personally carrying out all across the land, he has examined the sources and spoken with a large number of witnesses. With great diligence and care, he has questioned the most important elders and those of greatest ability and authority in the kingdom, and even those who claim some stake in it because they are kinsmen and descendants of the Incas, about the terrible, deep-seated, and horrendous tyranny of the Incas, who were tyrants in this kingdom

of Peru, and about the specific *curacas* of its towns. [He does this] to disabuse all those in the world of the idea that these Incas were legitimate kings and [that] the *curacas* were natural lords of this land. So that Your Majesty might be informed, with little effort and much interest, and so that others of differing opinion might be disabused [of their ideas], I was ordered by the viceroy Don Francisco de Toledo, whom I follow and serve in this general inspection, to take charge of this business and to write the history of the lives of the twelve Incas of this land and of the origin of its natives until their end. (Sarmiento 1906:7 [1572])

Thus, beneath a thin veil of history, Sarmiento's 1572 work was to play an important role in addressing the mounting criticisms of Spanish rule in the Americas and offset the Black Legend disseminated by Las Casas and his followers. First, his general history was meant to illustrate the illegitimate nature of Inca rule. Sarmiento is relentless in this effort. While recounting the lives of each of the Incas, Sarmiento repeatedly questions their legitimacy. Second, his general history was to show that each of the Incas committed crimes against natural laws and were thus tyrants and unfit to rule. Again, he returns to this point over and over as he describes the lives of each of the Incas. And just in case a reader might have missed his lines of reasoning, Sarmiento presents a summary of the alleged evidence against the rulers of the realm in his penultimate chapter titled "Noting how these Incas were oath-breakers and tyrants against their own, in addition to being against the natives of the land" (Chapter 70). Sarmiento's third political agenda in writing *The History of the Incas* was directed against the *curacas*, the natural (i.e., local) lords of the region. The alleged tyranny and the supposed illegitimacy of the claims to power of the local lords were relevant to the great social reforms that Toledo was introducing into the countryside. These included the creation of *reducciones*, new towns based on Spanish-inspired grid systems and principles of organization. These new settlements were established through the forced abandonment of innumerable villages, and their creation marks one of the largest demographic movements in the Americas. If the *curacas'* power was illegitimate, then they could not invoke their ancient rights in court cases protesting any government changes in local life (Sabine Hyland, pers. comm., 2004). The illegitimacy of the *curacas* is specifically addressed in Chapters 50 and 52, where Sarmiento describes the replacement of all local *curacas* with political appointees. Clearly, Sarmiento's work must be evaluated within the context of the social issues of his time as he attempts to strengthen the moral hand of King Philip II and to justify the broad reforms that were being conducted by Toledo.

This portrayal of Inca history was one that Sarmiento continued to pro-
pound for much of his life. Nine years after the completion of *The History
of the Incas*, Sarmiento was briefly in Spain, where he met with the king
and secured permission to map the Strait of Magellan and establish a new
colony with himself as governor. Apparently, before he left Spain for the
southern tip of South America, Sarmiento submitted another report to the
court providing advice on how the king should continue to protect his control over Peru. Unfortunately, the full contents of this report have not been
described. However, Markham provides a short quote from it. In his 1581
report, Sarmiento writes:

> I left in Lima the eldest son of Titu Cusi Yupanqui, named Quispi Titu.
> He is in the house of a half-caste, his cousin Francisco de Ampuero.[23] I
> advise that the king should order these Incas to be brought to Spain, or
> somewhere away from the people of Peru. The people always retain the
> memory of the Incas in their hearts and adore one of the Inca lineage.
> (Sarmiento, 1581 letter to the king, cited in Markham 1895:xix)

Although we know few details of the 1581 report other than those provided
by Markham,[24] we do know that the report was immediately archived. A
1581 entry by the Council of the Indies reads:

> In terms of Pedro Sarmiento's testimony of what he says of the Inca, the
> Council does not think that there is anything that should cause concern
> because the Indians are more or less without leadership and with less
> strength than ever and the Spaniards with greater presence with all of this
> known by Your Majesty, the viceroy shall be written to, to be warned of
> this and to advise him to understand [this].[25]

According to the opinion of the Council, Sarmiento's 1581 report did not
contain urgent information, since "the Indians are more or less without
leadership." Nevertheless, the Council advised that the viceroy be written
to. The king himself then noted in the margin of the entry, "That is good."

VICEROY TOLEDO AND THE PAINTED CLOTHS

We know from other sources apart from Sarmiento that four painted cloths
were prepared in Cuzco during the time that his *History of the Incas* was
being researched. The painted cloths were ordered by Viceroy Toledo and
were produced by native craftsmen in the house of Juan Maldonado, just off

the central plaza in Cuzco (Iwasaki Cauti 1986:70).[26] On 14 January 1572, Alvaro Ruiz de Navamuel, the king's notary and Toledo's secretary, along with the viceroy himself, presented the painted cloths to thirty-seven representatives of the twelve royal kin groups of Cuzco, many of whom would also be present at the public reading of *The History of the Incas* that would take place a little more than a month later. Also in attendance was Gabriel de Loarte as well as the translator Gonzalo Gómez Jiménez[27] (Ruiz de Navamuel 1882:247 [1572]).

Through Ruiz de Navamuel's report on the public presentation of these painted cloths, we learn that the first cloth contained images of the Tambotoco origin myth of the Incas as well as the Viracocha creation myth. The second and third cloths presented the history of the Inca rulers of Cuzco. Figures of each of the Incas were painted on these in medallions, along with portraits of their wives. Information on their royal kin groups and the history of their reigns was placed around the edges of the cloths. We can speculate that the history of the Inca kings portrayed on these two cloths was evenly divided between the first six and the last six Incas, corresponding to the traditional Hanan (Upper) and Hurin (Lower) divisions of Cuzco. We are also told that Ruiz de Navamuel verified these cloths after their public reading by placing his rubric on each of the cloths. It is also recorded that Sarmiento placed wind roses[28] on these cloths to indicate the location of the towns, but that these were not read to the natives, since they did not understand them (Ruiz de Navamuel 1882:250 [1572]).

The final painted cloth contained a large genealogical tree of the royal kin groups of Cuzco. References to the different sizes of the painted cloths are noted within an inventory of King Philip's estate (Dorta 1975:70). Three of them were almost the same size, and one was considerably longer and narrower. The longer one most likely contained the genealogical record of the royal kin groups (Julien 1999:76–77). While the first three painted cloths appear to have been approved with little comment, the final cloth caused considerable debate, since various individuals attempted to better their own position and that of their family within the royal ranking (Iwasaki Cauti 1986:70).[29] The strongest argument came from María Cusi Huarcay, the recently widowed sister-wife of Sayre Topa, who questioned why Paullu Inca's branch of the family was placed above that of her father, Manco Inca (Levillier 1940 [1570–1572]; Hemming 1970). The answer to this was, of course, because Manco and his sons (including Tito Cusi Yupanqui, who was still in the Vilcabamba area) had rebelled against the king, whereas Paullu's line, which included the current Inca ruler in Cuzco, Don Carlos, had remained loyal to Spain.[30]

Two days after the painted cloths were seen and validated by the native leaders of Cuzco, they were presented to a distinguished group of Spaniards. These included Alonso de Mesa, Mancio Sierra de Leguizamo,[31] Juan de Pancorvo, and Pedro Alonso Carrasco (all early witnesses to the conquest), as well as the current corregidor, Polo de Ondegardo. Each signed a statement indicating that the genealogical tree and histories shown on the cloths were true and accurate. In early March 1572, Toledo sent the cloths and various other items, including Sarmiento's manuscript, to Spain (Levillier 1921, 3:542–544 [1572]). After being presented to the king, the painted cloths were hung for public display in one of the great halls of the treasurer in Madrid.

It is a curious fact that the paintings were received by King Philip and proudly put on public display for years, but the written work that accompanied the cloths disappeared from view and was never mentioned by the Crown. The paintings were considered to be of such authenticity that in 1586, the granddaughter of Hernando de Soto and Leonor Tocto Chimbo[32] used them in a lawsuit to gain lost revenues for the services of her grandfather (Dorta 1975:71–72). It is believed that the cloths were destroyed more than a century later, in 1734, in a fire that swept through the royal palace (Iwasaki Cauti 1986:67).[33]

SARMIENTO DE GAMBOA AS HISTORIAN

Despite the fact that Sarmiento had a clear political agenda for writing his *History of the Incas*, he conducted his research with the utmost care. Realizing that each royal kin group in Cuzco would tell a history that was beneficial to its own social position, Sarmiento went to extremes to collect and compare separate versions of the Inca past. He first met independently with representatives of each of the twelve royal kin groups of Cuzco, listening to them and writing down the most important events of their past. With each group, he then discussed and compared the other versions of the past that he had collected from other rival lineages. Finally, he met publicly with members from all the dynastic groups of Cuzco, and his complete manuscript was read aloud to them in Quechua, the language of the Incas.

Sarmiento describes his methods for researching the history of the Incas in the ninth chapter of his work, as he turns from telling various Inca myths to discussing the legendary first people of the Cuzco Valley.[34] He writes:

> . . . by examining the eldest and wisest in all ranks of life, who are the most credible, I collected and compiled the present history, referring the decla-

rations and statements made by one group to their enemies—that is, the opposite faction, because they divide into factions—I asked each one of them for their own testimony about their lineage and that of their opponent. These testimonies, which are all in my possession, I corroborated and corrected with those of their rivals, and finally I had them ratified in public in the presence of all the factions and *ayllus,* under oath by the authority of a judge; and what is here written was improved with experts in the general language, who were very careful and faithful interpreters also under oath. (Sarmiento 1906:31 [1572:Ch. 9])

At this point in his chronicle, Sarmiento indicates that each royal kin group recorded important events in oral histories as well as in songs that were passed down from one generation to another. Furthermore, the most noteworthy events were recorded on mnemonic devices made of knotted strings called *quipu.* According to Sarmiento:

... these barbarians had a curious method that was very good and accurate to substitute for the lack of letters. It was that from one to another, parents to children, they would recount the ancient things of the past up to their times, repeating them many times, as one who reads a class lesson, making their listeners repeat these history lessons until they remained fixed in their memories. Each one would thus recount his annals to his descendants in this manner, to preserve the histories and feats and antiquities and the numbers of people, towns, and provinces; the days, months, and years; the battles, deaths, destructions, fortresses, and *cinchis.* Finally, they would record (and still do) the most remarkable things, in both kind and quantity, on some cords that they call *quipu,* which is the same as saying *racional,* or "accountant." On the *quipu* they make certain knots that they recognize, through which, and by the use of different colors, they distinguish and record each thing as if with letters. It is remarkable to see the details that they preserve in these cordlets, for which there are masters as there are for writing among us. (Sarmiento 1906:31 [1572:Ch. 9])

Sarmiento also mentions that there were official state historians who painted the most important events of all "on large boards," and that these boards were kept in "a great hall in the Houses of the Sun." These painted boards are also mentioned by Cristóbal de Molina (1989:49–50 [ca. 1575]), who wrote in Cuzco around the same time as Sarmiento.[35]

The careful manner in which Sarmiento organized and gathered his data is truly remarkable. His access to the highest ranks of the surviving Inca nobility and his rigorous collection methods are two of the factors that establish Sarmiento's *History of the Incas* as one of the most important documents written during the conquest period.

VERIFICATION OF THE HISTORY

Sarmiento fully utilized his official position to fulfill his pledge to write a detailed account of Inca history. Other writers, both before and after Sarmiento, also tried to compose the definitive "true" history of the Incas, but what characterizes Sarmiento's work, and makes it especially important, is the public reading of the manuscript in Cuzco. As an epilogue to his history, Sarmiento includes a unique document titled "Fee de la Provanca y Verificacion desta Historia." This epilogue attests to the fact that in Cuzco on 29 February 1572, Sarmiento formally presented the completed manuscript to the royal notary, Alvaro Ruiz de Navamuel, and to Don Francisco de Toledo. After that, in an act recalling the presentation of the painted cloths several weeks before, Gabriel de Loarte summoned representatives of the twelve royal lineages of Cuzco to hear Sarmiento's completed history read to them in Quechua by the translator Gonzalo Gómez Jiménez.

Thirty-six representatives of the royal kin groups assembled for this public event, as well as six additional men. At least nine of these men had also witnessed the presentation of the painted cloths in January. The reading took two days. Ruiz de Navamuel describes the procedure this way:

> They were read [to] and the reading was finished and discussed that same day and the next, from the fable that the Indians tell of their creation until the end of this history of the Incas.[36] As each chapter was read, one by one, it was translated into that language; the Indians [then] talked and conferred among themselves about each of the chapters. Together they all agreed and said through the interpreter that this history was good and true and conformed to what they knew and had heard their fathers and ancestors say and to what they had told their own [kin]. (Sarmiento 1906:133 [1572])

We are told that various minor details of the history, such as the names of persons and locations, were questioned during the public reading and that Ruiz de Navamuel wrote some of the suggested changes in the margin of the document.[37] Other minor changes were made directly to the document itself and hence are more difficult to identify in the manuscript. At the end of the reading, the names and ages of the forty-two witnesses were recorded, and various individuals made their "mark" at the end of the testimony (Figure 1.5).

At the end of the first day of reading, Toledo wrote a letter to King Philip telling him that he would be sending a written history of the Inca along with four painted cloths. On 4 March 1572, having received the viceroy's approval of his history, Sarmiento wrote his letter to the king as an introduction to the history. Soon after that, the envoy, Jerónimo Pacheco, left Cuzco for Spain.

Although Sarmiento's work was read to, and approved by, a large number of indigenous leaders in Cuzco, it still must be read with considerable care. As noted above, Sarmiento specifically states that his goal in writing the history was to document the long-standing tyranny of the Incas and thereby illustrate the Spanish king's right to subsume their territory into his realm. Given the fact that the public reading was held under the auspices of the viceroy, there is little doubt that the acceptance of the final document and its politically charged history was a foregone conclusion.

SARMIENTO DE GAMBOA, HIS INFORMANTS, AND THE AFTERMATH

Sarmiento collected most of the information contained within *The History of the Incas* by interviewing various prominent natives of the Cuzco region from February 1571 to February 1572. These interviews supplemented those conducted on behalf of Toledo during this same period. We do not have transcripts of Sarmiento's interviews; however, many of Toledo's have been preserved. The Toledo interviews included information from a large number of older men, many of whom were leading members of the royal houses of Cuzco.

Although we will never know the full range of Sarmiento's informants, there are several individuals who stand out among those who witnessed the reading of *The History of the Incas*, including Diego Cayo Hualpa, Diego Cayo, and Alonso Tito Atauchi. Short descriptions of these individuals are warranted to illustrate that Sarmiento had access to some of the most important indigenous citizens of Cuzco. Given their high positions in postconquest Cuzco, and the fact that each of their fathers had played important roles in the running of the Inca Empire, one can understand how Sarmiento was able to write such a detailed history.

Among the many noble Incas who were consulted during the preparation of the manuscript was Diego Cayo Hualpa. Cayo Hualpa was a member of

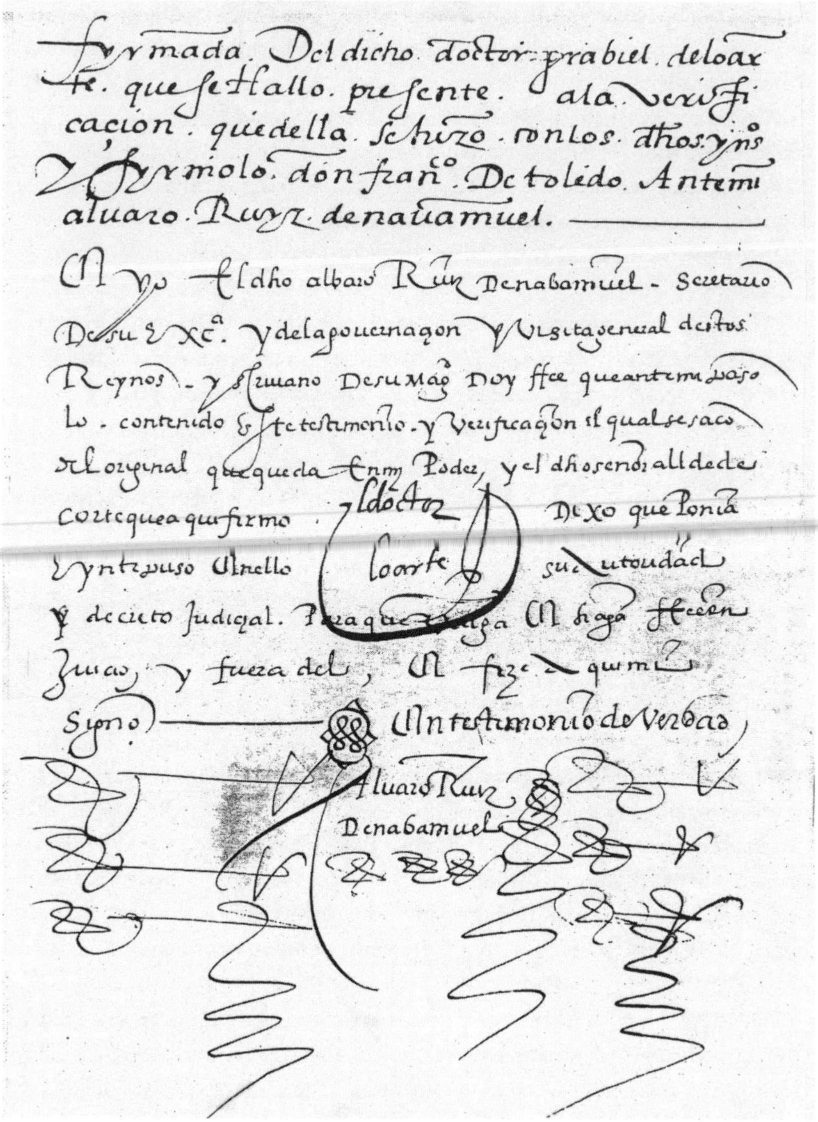

firmada. Del dicho doctor grabiel. deloar
te. que se hallo. presente. ala verifi
cacion. quedella. se hizo. conlos. dhos. y ños
y firmolo. don fran.co De toledo. Antemi
aluaro. Ruyz. denauamuel. _____

El yo el dho albaro Ruiz Denabamuel - secretario
Desu ExCa. y delagouernacion y Visita general destos
Reynos. y scrivano Desu Magd Doy ffee queantemi passo
Lo. contenido destetestimonio. y verificagon el qualsesaco
del original que queda Enmi Poder, y el dhosendi alldedes
corte quea qui firmo. y el doctor Dixo que Ponia
y ynterpuso Olnello loarte su utoridad
y deciero judicial. Paraque valga el hago ffeeen
Juicio, y fuera del, el fize el qui mi
Signo. _____ En testimonio de Verdad

Aluaro Ruiz
Denabamuel

FIGURE 1.5. Last page of the "Fee de la Provanca y Verificacion desta Historia" includes the "marks" of the indigenous leaders to whom Sarmiento's manuscript was read for their approval. Gabriel Loarte's bold signature can be seen in the direct center of the page. Alvaro Ruiz de Navamuel's signature is below it, in the lower center of the page.

Cinchi Roca's kin group and was thought to have been seventy years old[38] at the time that he signed Sarmiento's manuscript. He was also a witness to the painted cloths and he met with Spanish authorities on 18 July 1571 (Levillier 1940:161). In the July interview, we are told that he was a native of Wimbilli (a small village just south of Cuzco where the mummy of Cinchi Roca, the second Inca, was kept), and that Diego Cayo Hualpa's father had been the "*curaca* of the Indians said to be of the Sun."[39]

Diego Cayo (not to be confused with Diego Cayo Hualpa) was also a prominent leader in Cuzco during the immediate postconquest period. He was considered such an important source of information on the Incas that Pedro de Cieza de León had sought to interview him about the empire in 1550, more than twenty years before Sarmiento was in Cuzco (Hemming 1970:284). Cieza de León writes:

> I went to Cuzco . . . where I brought together Cayo Topa [i.e., Diego Cayo],[40] the one living descendent of Huayna Capac, and other *orejones* [noblemen] who looked upon themselves as nobility. And through the best interpreters to be found, I asked these Incas what people they were and of what nation. (Cieza de León 1976:31 [1554:Pt. 2, Ch. 6])

Diego Cayo signed *The History of the Incas* as a member of Pachacuti's descent group (Inaca Panaca[41]) and stated his age as sixty-eight.[42] He is also mentioned within Sarmiento's manuscript as a leader of Inaca Panaca. That year Diego Cayo had already been called upon to give testimonies to Spanish authorities on a number of occasions, including 17 July and 5-6 Sept 1571 (Levillier 1940:151, 168, 173), as well as participating in the verification of the cloths on 14 January 1572.[43] In these interviews, we are told that his father, Alonso Yano, had been a "*segunda persona*" of Huayna Capac.[44] It is also stated that Alonso Yano had been with Huayna Capac during the Collao campaigns and that he had later gone with him to Tomebamba. Accordingly, Diego Cayo is a likely source of information on both Pachacuti and Huayna Capac.

A final example of a witness to Sarmiento's *History of the Incas* is Alonso Tito Atauchi. He signed both the verification of the painted cloths and Sarmiento's history as the sole leader of Huascar's descent group. This is reaffirmed by Sarmiento within the text of *The History of the Incas* in his description of Huascar's death:

> He did not leave a lineage or *ayllu*, although of those who are alive now only one, named Don Alonso Tito Atauchi, the nephew of Huascar, son

of Tito Atauchi, whom they killed along with Huascar,[45] maintains the
name of the *ayllu* of Huascar, called Huascar Ayllu. (Sarmiento 1906:128
[1572:Ch. 69])

As a grandson of Huayna Capac, Alonso Tito Atauchi was interviewed
by Spanish authorities on 5–6 September 1571 (Levillier 1940:167), during
which he stated that his father had at times been in charge of governing the
kingdom when Huayna Capac was away from Cuzco.[46] Given Alonso Tito
Atauchi's high position among the noble houses of Cuzco at the time of the
conquest, and having proved himself loyal to the Crown in battle, he was
given the hereditary title of "Lord Mayor of the Four Quarters" by the king
of Spain. He was even allowed to wear the royal fringe of the Inca and other
prominent signs of nobility (Hemming 1970:342; Decoster 2002).

It is clear that Sarmiento interviewed many members of the Cuzco nobility in preparation for the writing of his *History of the Incas*. During the
course of these interviews, little did the participants realize that in just a few
months the last rebelling Inca, Tupac Amaru, would be captured and, after
a short trial, executed in the plaza of Cuzco.[47] In many ways, this public
execution marked the end of the conquest of Peru.

Although the Inca nobles, and many others, willingly participated in the
various investigations organized by Toledo in the Cuzco region, they did
not necessarily understand that he was considering punishing most of them
to bring the indigenous resistance to Spanish rule to a conclusion. On 8 May
1572 (about a month before Tupac Amaru was captured in the wilds of the
Vilcabamba region), Toledo suggested to the king of Spain that he could
bring the reign of the Incas to an end by destroying the noble bloodlines of
Cuzco. Toledo wrote:

> It would be sufficient to punish all the Incas [for being] involved in this
> plot for rebellion. There would be about three hundred who have kinship
> relations stemming from the Incas, and who preserve their memory and
> ayllus. (Cited in Hemming 1970:451; Levillier 1924:366)

A short time after the completion of *The History of the Incas*, Toledo began
an initial purge of the Inca nobility in Cuzco, and the most prominent elites
were sent to other highland cities or to Lima. Among the unfortunate individuals selected for this removal were Alonso Tito Atauchi and Diego Cayo,
both of whom had worked with Toledo to verify the cloths sent to the king
and with Sarmiento while he was writing *The History of the Incas*.[48]

It is also worth pointing out that Sarmiento was not a passive recorder of Inca history, but was instead an active participant in the widespread reforms initiated by Toledo. This is perhaps most dramatically illustrated in the late-June (1572) attack on the Vilcabamba region by Spanish forces. As troops loyal to Toledo entered and occupied the remote town of Vilcabamba, which had been serving as the capital for the Inca court in exile, it was Sarmiento who planted the royal standard and formally declared possession of the city by Spain (Hemming 1970:433).

THE RELATIONSHIPS BETWEEN SARMIENTO DE GAMBOA'S *HISTORY OF THE INCAS* AND OTHER WRITTEN WORKS

Establishing the exact relationships between various closely related written works is a complex task. This is especially true in the case of works dating to the early Colonial Period in Peru, when not only did many authors share previously written sources, some of which are now lost, but when they also used many of the same native informants. Nevertheless, there has been considerable research into the writings of various early authors of Peru, and the general relationships between them are becoming clearer (Means 1928; Rowe 1985; Porras Barrenechea 1986; Pease 1995; Julien 2000).

Most important to this study are the relationships between Sarmiento de Gamboa's *History of the Incas* and the works of Juan de Betanzos [1557], Bernabé Cobo [1653], Miguel Cabello Balboa [1586], Cristóbal de Molina [ca. 1575], Juan Polo de Ondegardo [1559–1560], and Martín de Murúa [1590]. Although these works were composed in different places and in different years, certain sections within each of them provide similar information. To fully understand Sarmiento's *History of the Incas,* we need to explore the web of written sources and native informants that connects his work to those of other authors who wrote both before and after him.

Juan de Betanzos and Pedro Sarmiento de Gamboa

Juan de Betanzos wrote one of the earliest detailed reports on Inca society. Betanzos was an early settler of Cuzco who married an Inca noblewoman.[49] His mastery of Quechua, his close contacts with members of the former ruling class, and his long stay in Cuzco demand that special attention be paid to his works.[50] In 1557 Betanzos completed his work entitled *Suma y narración de los incas* (Account and narration of the Incas). In the first four chapters of this work, Betanzos recounts several of the Inca origin myths that are also told by Sarmiento (Chapters 6–11), including those describing the creator god's activities in Tiahuanaco, Rachi, and Urcos, as well as the origin of the royal Incas at Pacariqtambo.

A more intriguing overlap of information concerns the death of Pachacuti Inca Yupanqui. Both Betanzos (1987; 1996:138 [1557:Pt. 1, Ch. 32]) and Sarmiento (1906 [1572:Ch. 47]) provide translations of a song that Pachacuti Inca Yupanqui is said to have sung on his deathbed. Betanzos indicates the strength of oral tradition among the Incas, stating that the song "is still sung today in his memory by those of his generation." Furthermore, their descriptions of the battles between Huascar and Atahualpa share striking similarities. Nevertheless, there is no clear evidence that Sarmiento had access to Betanzos' earlier work. These overlaps, and various other ones, can easily be accounted for by widely shared oral traditions in the Inca capital, especially among the members of Pachacuti Inca Yupanqui's kin group.

Bernabé Cobo and Pedro Sarmiento de Gamboa

In 1653, Bernabé Cobo, a Jesuit priest and formidable naturalist, finished one of the last and most important chronicles of Peru, the *Historia del Nuevo Mundo* (History of the New World). Cobo had traveled extensively in Peru, and during the course of his theological training, he had spent several years in Cuzco. Cobo's monumental work is based on his own well-founded inquiries as well as on a series of works written by earlier writers. Cobo used manuscripts stored in secular and ecclesiastical archives of various cities, including Lima, Cuzco, and Arequipa, as well as Juli, the center for Jesuit studies in the Andes. But, like most writers of his time, he was inconsistent in acknowledging his sources. Furthermore, in some sections he mixed information from different sources, and in other places he reproduced entire blocks of data (Rowe 1980:2–3).

In the introduction to Books 12, 13, and 14 of the *Historia del Nuevo Mundo*, Cobo (1979:98–102 [1653:Bk. 12, Ch. 2]) describes the three major sources that he used while writing his overview of Inca history and religion. By citing these three sources, and by stressing that his information was extracted from earlier experts on Inca history and religion, Cobo hoped to give greater credence and authority to his own writings. Cobo states that his most importance source on the Incas was Polo de Ondegardo's 1559 report (i.e., *De los errores y supersticiones de los indios*), which had been written after extensive interviews in Cuzco with *quipu* specialists. In fact, Cobo had the original manuscript with Polo de Ondegardo's own signature that had been sent to Archbishop Jerónimo de Loayza.

In this short section, Cobo also recognizes his debt to Cristóbal de Molina by indicating that he used Molina's "copious account of the rites and fables that the Peruvian Indians practiced in pagan times." This is an unmistakable reference to Molina's *Relación de las fábulas y ritos de los incas* (*Fables and Rites of the Incas*) that had been researched and composed in Cuzco around 1575. But Cobo also states that he made extensive use of a report on the history and government of the Incas written for Viceroy Toledo. Cobo writes:

> ... Viceroy Francisco de Toledo took great care in obtaining a true history of the origin and form of government of the Inca kings, and to this end, since he was in the city of Cuzco himself, he ordered all the old Indians who remained from the time of the Inca kings to be brought together. To insure that the proceedings were conducted with less danger of misunderstanding in an undertaking whose ascertainment was so much desired, each Indian was interrogated separately; they were not allowed to communicate with each other. The person entrusted by the viceroy to make this inquiry, who was one of those working under him on the general inspection, made the same careful inquiry with all the old Incas he found in the provinces of Charcas and Arequipa, and with former Spanish conquistadores who were in this land, not a few of whom still lived at that time. (Cobo 1979:100 [1653:Bk. 12, Ch. 2])

This report on the history of the Incas and their form of government was clearly produced during Toledo's relatively short stay in Cuzco (late February 1571–early October 1572). It is odd, however, that Cobo does not mention Sarmiento by name as the author of this report, since Cobo knew of Sarmiento and he specifically mentions Sarmiento's 1580 service to the Crown elsewhere in his work (Cobo 1979:15 [1653:Bk. 11, Ch. 3]).[51]

There are scattered sections within Sarmiento's and Cobo's work that provide very similar descriptions of events and persons. These sections raise the possibility that Cobo had access to Sarmiento's work and that he extracted information from it to include in his writings. For example, they both provide similar information on the noblewomen who escaped the brutality of Atahualpa after his generals captured Cuzco:

> Among those who escaped were Doña Elvira Chonay, daughter of Cañar Capac; Doña Beatriz Caruamaruay, daughter of the *curaca* [of] Chinchacocha; Doña Juana Tocto; and Doña Catalina Usica, who was the wife of Don Paullu Topa and mother of Don Carlos ... (Sarmiento 1906:123 [1572:Ch. 67])

... also able to escape were some important women, daughters of great lords, who later became Christians; among them were Elvira Quechonay, Beatriz Caruay Mayba, Juana Tocto, Catalina Usoca, mother of Carlos Inca, and many others. (Cobo 1979:169 [1653:Bk. 12, Ch. 19])

Here, and elsewhere in his work, Cobo may have edited Sarmiento's work and reproduced the information in a more condensed form. Alternatively, these textual overlaps could also have occurred if both Sarmiento and Cobo were copying from an earlier account.

Possible Lost Sources Used by Sarmiento de Gamboa and by Other Early Writers

As stated above, there are many passages in Sarmiento's *History of the Incas* and in Cobo's *History of the New World* that suggest that Cobo had access to Sarmiento's work, or that these two authors had access to a shared, but now lost, source of information on the Incas. Additional insights into Sarmiento's and Cobo's works can be gained by comparing these passages with similar ones found in Martín de Murúa's *Historia general del Perú* [1590][52] and in Miguel Cabello Balboa's *Miscelánea antártica* [1586].

As background, it should be noted that Martín de Murúa, a Mercedarian priest and a longtime resident of Cuzco, appears to have been in that city during Toledo's 1572 visit and even witnessed the execution of Tupac Amaru.[53] Murúa finished at least three closely related works on the Incas, the last of which has only recently been published.[54] Miguel Cabello Balboa arrived in the Americas in 1566 and traveled widely, although it is not clear if he arrived in Cuzco. Cabello Balboa was ordained as a priest in Quito in 1571 and started writing his work soon afterward. His *Miscelánea antártica* was completed in Lima some fifteen years later, in 1586.

There are many overlapping sections within the works of Sarmiento de Gamboa, Cabello Balboa, Cobo, and Murúa, but we will draw examples from their descriptions of the lives of Lloqui Yupanqui and Mayta Capac, two relatively minor Inca kings. Consider, for example, Sarmiento's, Cobo's, and Cabello Balboa's descriptions of Lloqui Yupanqui's arranged marriage with Mama Cava, from the town of Oma.[55] Sarmiento states that the marriage was arranged by Manco Sapaca, Lloqui Yupanqui's brother:

Having heard this and having announced to the people what the Sun had told Lloqui Yupanqui, his relatives decided to find him a wife. Moreover, *his brother Manco Sapaca*, understanding the disposition of [his] brother, tried to find him a suitable wife. Finding her in a town called Oma, two leagues from Cuzco, he asked her relatives for her and, this granted, he brought her to Cuzco. Lloqui Yupanqui then married her. This woman was named Mama Cava . . . (Sarmiento 1906:45 [1572:Ch. 16]; emphasis added)

In contrast, Cobo suggests that Pachachulla Viracocha, the lord of the Guaro, had arranged the marriage between Lloqui Yupanqui and Mama Cava:

> Being persuaded by his men, the Inca made up his mind to marry, and to this end, *he had Pachachulla Viracocha called;* he was one of the lords from Guaro who had yielded obedience to him, and the Inca commanded that he go to the town of Oma, little more than two leagues away from Cuzco, and that he ask for the daughter of the lord of that town to be his wife. Upon receiving this message, the lord of Oma was very happy about it, and on the advice of the other lords, they gave her to him. This lady was called Mama Cachua . . . (Cobo 1979:116 [1653:Bk. 11, Ch. 6]; emphasis added)

Yet, in the writing of Cabello Balboa, we find an even more intricate passage indicating that it was Lloqui Yupanqui's brother, Manco Sapaca, who contacted Pachachulla Viracocha (the lord of Guaro), to arrange the marriage:

> *His brother Manco Sacapa* (who felt the lack of [a] nephew [and] heir more than any other) held such great hope in his chest [that] he began searching for a legitimate wife for his brother, the Inca. And having communicated the problem *to the astute Pachachulla Viracocha,* he took charge of it. Well-accompanied, he went to the towns of Oma and he asked their cacique to give his daughter [to] the Inca as [a] wife. She was named Mama Cava and she was granted to him. (Cabello Balboa (1951:283 [1586:Pt. 3, Ch. 12]; emphasis added)[56]

These three passages provide similar, although not identical, accounts of the arranged marriage of Lloqui Yupanqui and Mama Cava. Yet, it is important to note that Cabello Balboa's account is more complete than, and reconciles differences found in, the accounts provided by Sarmiento and Cobo. Because we know that Sarmiento's work was written first [1572], followed by Cabello Balboa's [1586], and then Cobo's [1653], this suggests that all three writers shared a common source. In this case, it appears that Cabello Balboa provides a more complete account of the original source, whereas Sarmiento and Cobo present more fragmentary information.

Additional evidence of a shared source can be found in these authors' descriptions of Lloqui Yupanqui's contact with other leaders in the region surrounding Cuzco. However, in this case, it is Sarmiento and Murúa who provide muddled tellings of the original source, whereas both Cobo and Cabello Balboa offer more complete accounts. Compare the following:

1) He did not leave the area of Cuzco for war, nor did he do anything remarkable, except live like his father, communicating with some provinces called Guaro, [whose cinchi was named] Guamay Samo, Pachachulla Viracocha, the Ayarmacas of Tambocunca, and the Quilliscaches. (Sarmiento 1906:44 [1572:Ch. 16])

2) He lived in great peace and prosperity because many people of different nations came to see him from various places; there was a Guaro named Huamac Samo Pachachulla Viracocha and the Ayarmacas and the Quilescaches. (Murúa 1987:60–61 [1590:Bk. 1, Ch. 7])[57]

3) The first and most noteworthy who came were Guaman Samo (Cacique and Lord of Guaro), Pachachulla Viracocha (a man of great discretion and prudence), and the Ayarmacas nations with their Lords and regents: Tambo vincais and Quiliscochas and other nearby lineages. (Cabello Balboa 1951:283 [1586:Pt. 3, Ch. 12])[58]

4) The first ones to do this were from the Valley of Guaro, six leagues from Cuzco; it had many people, and the lords of the valley were very powerful at that time. The most important ones were called Guama Samo and Pachachulla Viracocha. These were followed by the Ayarmacas of Tambocunca and the Quilliscaches with their caciques. (Cobo 1979:115 [1653:Bk. 11, Ch. 6])

All four of these passages appear to have been derived from the same text or oral tradition; however, they each provide slightly different information.

In a final example, let us turn to descriptions of the life of Mayta Capac, the son of Lloqui Yupanqui, or, more specifically, to an event that is said to have occurred while Mayta Capac was still very young:

1) They say that when Mayta was very young, he played with some youths of the Alcabizas and Culunchimas, natives of Cuzco, and hurt many of them and killed some. One day he broke the leg of a son of the *cinchi* of the Alcabizas after arguing about drinking or drawing water from a foun-

tain, and he chased the rest until they shut themselves in their houses. (Sarmiento 1906:46 [1572:Ch. 17])

2) . . . although his vassals always knew him to be cruel and bloodthirsty, because as a child (playing with others of his age who were native to Cuzco) he would mistreat them, breaking their legs and arms and even killing some of them. On one day in particular he mistreated and badly offended the sons of a certain cacique from Allcayvillas. On that occasion, Culluim Chima . . . (Cabello Balboa 1951:284 [1586:Pt. 3, Ch. 12])[59]

3) He committed some mischievousness during his father's lifetime that made him hated, though feared. It was so much that when he was playing with some boys of his age and with some natives of Cuzco named Alcyvisas and Cullumchima, he killed the boys and broke their legs and he chased and followed them to their houses. (Murúa 1987:63 [1590:Ch. 9])[60]

4) Before he got out of his tutelage, while playing one day with some other boys of his age, there was one who told him to look out for himself and mend his ways. (Cobo 1979:118 [1653:Bk. 12, Ch. 7])

In this case, it is Cobo who provides the barest description, while Sarmiento, Cabello Balboa, and Murúa provide different but overlapping accounts.

The quantity of overlapping descriptions provided by these four authors suggests that they shared one or more sources. This source could have been a written document, a single native informant, a narrative recorded on a *quipu* or on a painted board, a widespread oral tradition, or a complex combination of these sources. Given this conclusion, it is important to note that there are at least two known, but now lost, written sources that all four of these writers may have had access to.

The first possible candidate for the shared information between Sarmiento, Cabello Balboa, Murúa, and Cobo is a work written by Molina concerning the history of the Incas. Molina, in his 1575 report titled "On the Fables and Rites of the Incas" (which was written for the third bishop of Cuzco, Sebastián de Lartaún), summarizes his previous report on the history of the Incas:

The report that I gave to your most illustrious Lordship [Sebastián de Lartaún] described the origin, lives, and customs of the Incas, who were the lords of this land, including: how many [Inca rulers] there were, who were their wives, the laws they made, [the] wars that they waged, and

[the] people and nations that they conquered. In some parts of the report, I discussed the ceremonies and cults that they invented, although not in detail.[61]

Unfortunately, Molina's report on the history of the Incas has been lost. However, Cabello Balboa suggests that it was among those that he used while writing his own overview of Inca history (Cabello Balboa 1951:259–260 [1586:Pt. 3, Ch. 9]). Accordingly, much of Cabello Balboa's information on the history of the Incas, and by extension Murúa's, has been credited to Molina (Loaisa 1943; Julien 2000). There are, however, problems in suggesting that Sarmiento and Cobo also had access to it. First, Cobo specifically states that he had a copy of Molina's *Fables and Rites of the Incas*, but he says nothing of Molina's work on the history of the Incas. Second, although Sebastián de Lartaún, the bishop to whom Molina was reporting, was appointed bishop of Cuzco in 1570, he did not arrive in the city until 28 June 1573 (Esquivel y Navia 1980:232, 246; Urbano 1989:17), a full sixteen months *after* Sarmiento finished his *History of the Incas*. According to this timeline, it seems unlikely that Molina's work was the common source for information found in Sarmiento, Cabello Balboa, Murúa, and Cobo.

Another, more likely source for some of the shared information between these four authors is the 1559 report by Polo de Ondegardo. This report is widely recognized as one of the most important documents produced in Cuzco during the immediate post-Inca period.[62] Cobo notes that he had a copy of the report and that he used it extensively while writing his chronicle. Furthermore, Toledo himself appointed Polo de Ondegardo to his second term as corregidor of Cuzco, during the same period that Sarmiento was in the city conducting his interviews. In fact, Polo de Ondegardo was present for the viewing of the painted cloths (16 January 1572), and there is no doubt that Sarmiento would have had close contact with Polo de Ondegardo during their time in Cuzco. Likewise, Cabello Balboa (1951:257 [1586:Pt. 3, Ch. 9]) indicates that he had both read and admired the works of the "learned and studious Licenciado Polo." And it is clear that Murúa had access to the 1585 abstract of Polo de Ondegardo's 1559 report, published by the Provincial Council of Lima, and he may also have been in Cuzco during Polo de Ondegardo's 1571–1572 term as corregidor. In sum, until further information becomes available, or new documents are found, it seems possible that some of the overlapping information found in Sarmiento, Cabello Balboa, Murúa, and Cobo was originally collected by Polo de Ondegardo.

It is also possible that there is a more complex combination of overlapping

sources. For example, it is possible that both Sarmiento and Cobo incorporated a great deal of information collected by Polo de Ondegardo into their
works, whereas Cabello Balboa and Murúa relied more heavily on Molina's
lost report on the history of the Incas. In this scenario, there would be sub-
stantial overlap between all four authors, since Polo de Ondegardo's and
Molina's works were both based on the oral traditions of the royal families
in Cuzco. Only additional research can untangle this web of lost sources.

SUMMARY

Because no native Andean cultures developed a system of writing, the first
written sources on the Incas and their history were produced during the
establishment of Spanish rule in the Andes. These documents were written by many different people, including state officials,[63] literate soldiers, and
the priests of the many Catholic orders that were quickly established in the
region.[64] There are also several large works written by educated citizens,
including individuals of Spanish, Andean,[65] and mixed descent.[66] Nearly all
of the documents are written in Spanish, although a few are composed in
Quechua.[67]

The earliest chronicles from the Andean region are generally dedicated
to describing the dramatic first encounters between the Spaniards and the
Incas as well as the establishment of Spanish rule.[68] Not surprisingly, these
accounts tend to depict a European view of the events, and they therefore
provide limited information on the indigenous peoples of the Andes or their
histories.

Pedro de Cieza de León's work marks a different direction in Andean his-
toriography. During his extended stay in Peru (1535–1550), Cieza de León
walked almost the entire length of the former Inca Empire, and while in
Cuzco, he sought out various members of the Inca elite to learn of their
history. After his return to Spain, Cieza de León published the first part of
his *Chronicle of Peru*. He was a careful writer, describing what he saw with
little embellishment, and he adds greatly to our understanding of the Incas.
Nevertheless, his time in Cuzco was relatively short, and much of his writing focuses on the power struggles that occurred between various Spaniards
as they fought to maintain their holdings.

Many other writers following Cieza de León composed works on the
Incas. But Sarmiento's work is unique among these, not only because of the
large scale of his investigation and the dramatic public reading of the manuscript, but also because in 1572 there were still former officials in Cuzco who
had held positions of power during the final years of the empire. These men

and women were in their seventies and eighties. More numerous, however, were those of a new generation born after European contact. Within just a few years after Sarmiento completed his *History of the Incas*, the final members of the Inca elite would die. Thus, Sarmiento's work represents one of the largest and last investigations to include members of the Inca elite and their own remembrances of the Inca Empire.

The History of the Incas

Second part of the general history called Indica, which
by order of the most excellent Don Francisco de Toledo,
viceroy, governor, and captain-general of the kingdoms of
Peru and steward of the royal house of Castile, written by
Captain Pedro Sarmiento de Gamboa. [Cuzco:1572]

*T*o H.R.H. King Philip, our liege

Among the [various] qualities, most sovereign and Catholic Philip,[1] that
gloriously decorate princes and place them in the highest esteem, there are
three that are the greatest (as stated by the father of Latin eloquence): largesse, beneficence, and generosity.[2] The consuls of Rome had these on their
coats of arms as their highest praise. Hence in the Plaza of Trajan they
sculpted the following statement in marble from Mount Quirinal: "Generosity is the most powerful attribute in a prince."[3] The kings, who want to
be loved by their own [people] and feared by others, made great efforts to
acquire the fame of generosity. As a result, the following royal sentence was
immortalized: "It is proper for kings to give."[4] Since [giving] was a common
attribute among the Greeks, the prudent Ulysses told Antinuous, king of
the Phaeacians, "You are like a king, and hence it is to your benefit to give,
and in greater amounts than others."[5] Therefore, it is truly favorable and
necessary for kings to practice largesse.

I do not intend with this, most generous monarch, to insinuate to Your
Majesty such unashamed frankness. It would be very wrong of me to try to
persuade you to do something that to Your Majesty is so natural that you
could not live without it. Nor will such a high and generous lord and king
suffer what befell Emperor Titus, who, on remembering one day at dinner
that he had not carried out any act of mercy, lamented, "Oh, friends, I have
lost this day."[6] Your Majesty does not miss a day, not even an hour, in offering benefits and great acts of mercy to all kinds of people. Speaking as one,
all the people will praise Your Majesty in the same way as Virgil sang praises
of Octavius Augustus:

> *It rains all night,*[7]
> *In the morning wondrous sights return.*
> *Caesar holds power shared with Jove.*[8]

What I wish to say is that no other king carries out their obligations of kind-
ness and generosity as well as does Your Majesty. It is necessary, then, [for
you] to have [wealth] and a lot of it, because, as Tullius states, "There is
nothing better for a prince than goods and riches to carry out acts of kind-

ness and generosity." One can also acquire great glory through these acts. It is true, as we read in Salustius, that "in a great empire there is great glory,"[9] for as one becomes greater, the greater amount of deeds one carries out; hence the glory of the king relies on having a large number of vassals and in abating the poverty of the people.

During your life God Almighty has given to Your Majesty, most Christian King, such a great part of this glory that all the enemies of the holy Catholic Church of our Lord Jesus Christ tremble in fear on hearing your name; therefore you are worthy of being called the life of the Church. And the treasures that God made available to your servants have been spent in laudable and holy acts with blessed magnanimity: the eradication of heretics; the expulsion of the accursed Saracens from all of Spain; the building of temples, hospitals, and monasteries; and an infinite number of other charitable and just acts. With dispositions like those of jealous fathers of the country, these servants not only deserve the holy name of Catholics, as they have wholeheartedly served the most benign and almighty God, but they are also rewarded with temporary riches in the current age, because it is true that "he who provides heavenly kingdoms does not take away one's temporary blessings." So these men therefore deserved more than the blessings they received. And [God] gave them an apostolic office, choosing them from among all the kings in the world as the evangelizing nuncios of His divine word in the most remote and unknown lands of these barbaric and blind gentiles, who we now call the Indians of Castile, so that through the ministry of the priests [the natives] could be placed on the road to salvation.

God was the true pilot who made the crossing of the dark and frightening Atlantic Ocean easy, which terrified the ancient Argives, Athenians, Egyptians, and Phoenicians. The arrogant Hercules also marveled on seeing the large expanse of the Atlantic Ocean at Cadiz. He became afraid, and thinking that the earth ended there and that this was the end of the world, he built pillars with these words on them: "*Ultra Gades nil,*"[10] which means, "Beyond Cadiz there is nothing." Since human knowledge about God is ignorance and the force of the earth weakens in His presence, it was easy for your holy grandparents to break and dissolve the mists and difficulties of the mysterious ocean by having the virtue of the most exalted [God] with them. And, mocking Alcides and his coat of arms with good reason, they discovered the Indies[11] well populated by souls to whom the way to Heaven could be taught. There was also a large variety of priceless treasures with which they recovered the great expenses they had incurred [in the exploration of these lands], and they became among the richest princes in the world. They therefore continued their holy and most Christian generosity until death. Due to this very famous voyage and the miraculous and new discovery, the epigraph on the Herculean pillars could be corrected, removing "*Gades nil*" and placing "*Plus*" in front of "*ultra*,"[12] which truly means, "Many lands lie ahead." Hence the wording "*Plus ultra*" remained on the coat of arms and insignia of the Indies of Castile.[13]

Since there are few [people] who do not lust for gold,[14] and since envy feasts on good tidings,[15] the devil moved the hearts of some powerful princes to interfere with this great endeavor. Alexander VI, the curate of Jesus Christ, thought that this [interference] could hinder the preaching of the sacred gospel to these idolatrous barbarians, as well as cause other harm. On his own initiative, and not at the request or petition of the Catholic kings, and under the authority of God Almighty, he decided to give and concede to [the Catholic kings] forevermore the islands and lands that had just been discovered and those to be discovered within the boundaries and demarcations of 180 degrees longitude, which is half the globe,[16] granting them all the dominions, rights, jurisdictions, and belongings thereto and prohibiting navigation and trade in these lands for whatever reason to all other kings, princes, and emperors from the year 1493 onward.

And since the devil saw that this doorway, through which he could have inserted many disputes and difficulties, had closed just as it had started to open, he plotted to wage war using the very soldiers who were fighting against him, the preachers themselves, who now began to question the right and title that the kings of Castile had over these lands. And since your invincible father was so zealous about his conscience, he ordered this issue examined, as much as possible, by learned scholars. [But as] the information provided to [the scholars] about the deeds [of the Incas] was indirect and not the truth, [the scholars] concluded that these Incas, who were in the kingdoms of Peru, were the true and legitimate kings of these lands and that the *curacas*[17] were and are the true natural lords of this land. These [statements] gave rise to doubts among strangers to your kingdom. Catholics as well as heretics and other unbelievers discussed and aired their complaints about the rightful pretensions that the Spanish kings had and still have over the Indies. For this reason, the Emperor Don Carlos,[18] of glorious memory, was on the verge of abandoning [the colonies]. This was exactly what the enemy of Christ's faith sought in order to regain possession of the souls that [the devil] had kept blind for so many centuries. All this occurred because of the lack of attention on the part of the governors of these lands, who did not carry out the necessary steps to inform these souls about the truth, and because of the writings of the bishop of Chiapa.[19] [The bishop] was moved to a passion against some of the conquerors in his bishopric with whom he had very strong disagreements, as I myself learned when I traveled through that province and in Guatemala, where this occurred.[20] Although his zeal seems holy and understandable, he said things about the dominions of this land and against its conquerors that are not supported by the evidence and judicial proofs that we have obtained, and that we who have traveled all over the Indies inquiring about such things, with leisure and without war, now know to be true.

Because this great chaos of ignorance and confusion was spread all over the world and was so entrenched in the opinions of the most learned members of Christianity, God heartened Your Majesty to send Don Francisco de Toledo,[21] steward of Your Royal house, to be the viceroy of these kingdoms. As soon as he arrived in this kingdom, Toledo found many things to do and to solve. Without resting after the immense difficulties of the dangerous and tedious journey across two seas that he had just undergone, Toledo immediately put all the necessary things in order. He reversed the errors of earlier [governments] and he established the new ones in such a way that they will forever bear fruit, as they are based on reasonable and solid foundations, benefiting not only those around him that he was obligated [to serve], but also favoring and helping governors in lands contiguous to this one. He especially aided the wealthy kingdom of Chile [by providing it] with men and munitions, which was a great help to that land, as it was about to be lost. If it had not been for his aid and for his help in the province of Esmeraldas, which was forsaken, all would have been lost. The territories of Yagualsongo and Cumbinama in Santiago de las Montañas, which Juan de Salinas was in charge of, were becoming depopulated due to the disputes between the Spaniards living there. It was Toledo's order that helped to sustain the people and then made them act reasonably and preserve the peace. It was in great part because of this that a good and rich plot of land was populated by Spaniards. As these acts became known across the region, people would come from the farthest reaches of the territory to ask for his assistance. He also gave spiritual and temporal assistance to the provinces of Tucumán, Juries, and Diaguitas. While aiding and providing the territory of Santa Cruz de la Sierra, he gave stability to a province where stability had seemed impossible. He put a stop to and punished the Chiriguanas, [who are] cannibals, who were infesting Your kingdom of Peru in the region of the Charcas. The goods that now come out of these provinces, and the stability in which the provinces have remained, are only thanks to Don Francisco de Toledo. He fixed these lands and, what is most important to consider and respect, he provided work for a large group of idle and immoral people. All of this was carried out with extreme diligence.

In addition, he did not want to enjoy the pleasures of Lima, where his predecessors had lived in contentment. Instead, through his immense and vivid fervor to serve Your Majesty, he carried out new and greater efforts that no previous viceroy or governor had dared or even thought to do. He traveled this extremely rugged land to conduct a general inspection, though he has not finished it yet.[22] He has truly fixed many faults and major abuses that existed in the teaching and ministering of the Christian doctrine. He gave religious and political instruction to the ministers so that they would carry out their tasks in the service of God and in the discharge of Your Royal conscience in a suitable fashion. He removed people from cliffs and rough terrain, where they could not be cured or indoctrinated, to towns he created in healthy and accessible places.[23] Before this they used to live and die like wild beasts, participating in idolatry as in the times of the Inca tyrants and their blind followers. He took away the public drunkenness, the living in sin, and the funeral mounds of their idols and devils. He also compensated them and freed them from the tyranny of their *curacas*. Finally, he gave them rationality, which they lacked and [thus] acted like brutes. This viceroy's labors have been so effective that the Indians are completely regenerated and they openly call him their protector and procurer. And they call Your Majesty, who sent him to them, their father. The benefits of these changes to these natives have been so celebrated that the warring infidel Indians of many regional provinces, knowing for certain to be under his word and authority, have come out to see and speak with him and have given spontaneous obedience to Your Majesty. This was also done by the Andes of Jauja on the boundary of Pilcoconi, the Mañaries to the east of Cuzco, and the Chunchos, among others. They were sent back to their lands grateful and obligated to Your Royal service by the gifts given to them and the memory of their good reception.

Among Christians it is of utmost importance to have a good name, and the one that Your Majesty has in these parts (although you are the holiest and most exalted king in the world) has been harmed. This has happened, as I mentioned previously, in the hearts of the learned as well as in others due to a lack of truthful information. Toledo proposed to do the greatest of services for Your Majesty, among all the great services that are included in his duties. [This work is] to give a secure and quiet harbor to Your Royal conscience against the tempests [generated by] your native vassals, theologians, and other learned [individuals] who are misinformed about the events here. Thus, in [Toledo's] general inspection, which he is personally carrying out all across the land, he has examined the sources and spoken with a large number of witnesses. With great diligence and care, he has questioned the most important elders and those of greatest ability and authority in the kingdom, and even those who claim some stake in it because they are kinsmen and descendants of the Incas, about the terrible, deep-seated, and horrendous tyranny of the Incas, who were tyrants in this kingdom of Peru, and about the specific *curacas* of its towns. [He does this] to disabuse all those in the world of the idea that these Incas were legitimate kings and [that] the *curacas* were natural lords of this land. So that Your Majesty might be informed, with little effort and much interest, and so that others of differing opinion might be disabused [of their ideas], I was ordered by the viceroy Don Francisco de Toledo, whom I follow and serve in this general inspection, to take charge of this business and to write the history of the lives of the twelve Incas of this land and of the origin of its natives until their end.

I carried out this task with curiosity and diligence both in the process and in the ratification of the witnesses, as Your Majesty will see. I can truly testify to the terrible and most inhumane tyranny of these Incas and of their *curacas*, who are not, and never were, true lords of this place. Instead, they were appointed by Topa Inca Yupanqui, the greatest, most horrendous, and most damaging tyrant of them all.[24] And the *curacas*, who were and are now the greatest tyrants, were named by other great and violent tyrants, as will be clearly and undoubtedly shown in the history. They perpetrated their tyranny even though they were foreigners in Cuzco. They imposed violence on all the natives of the Cuzco Valley and all the others from Quito to Chile through the use of weapons. Then, without the consent or election of the natives, they proclaimed themselves to be Incas.

In addition, their tyrannical laws and customs explain the true and holy title that Your Majesty has to this kingdom and kingdoms of Peru because Your Majesty and His most holy royal ancestors have forbidden the sacrifice of innocent people and the eating of human flesh, the unspeakable sin, as well as the casual copulation with sisters and mothers, the abominable use of beasts, and [all of] their nefarious and damned customs. God banished each of these [sins] from his realm, and the [punishment of the people] will therefore primarily belong to the princes and especially to Your Majesty. Therefore, war may be declared and waged on the tyrants, even if they were the native and true lords of the land, and men could be sent and a new principality established.

[The natives] can be punished and penalized because of these sins against nature. This can be done even if the native peoples of these lands do not contradict such customs and [even] if they do not want to be considered the innocent ones avenged by the Spanish. This is because they do not have the right to deliver themselves or their children unto death. Furthermore, as the archbishop of Florence and Pope Innocent teach, the natives can be forced to follow the laws of nature. Friar Francisco de Victoria[25] confirms this in the account he made of [Your] titles over the Indies.[26] Hence, through this title alone, and without any others, Your Majesty has the most supreme and most legitimate right to all the Indies that any prince in the world would have to any feudal estate. This general breaking of the laws of nature has been found (to a greater or lesser degree) in practically all of your Majesty's lands that have been discovered across the North and South seas.

And because of this right, Your Majesty can without hesitation send conquerors to the islands of the Nombre de Jesús Archipelago,[27] which are commonly known as the Solomon Islands, although they are not actually so. I personally discovered them and provided news of them in 1567, although General Alvaro de Mendaña, along with others, was also in that southern sea.[28] I offer my services to Your Majesty to explore and populate [this archipelago],[29] finding and facilitating all the sea voyages necessary to the enterprise of surveying and, with God's help, also taking [ships] along a shorter route. I sincerely offer my services and I trust the Lord Almighty, in whose grace I plan to carry out all my actions while in Your Royal service. And it is because of the abilities that God gave me that I aspire to such worthy deeds and because he does not demand a strict account of me. I believe I will comply with all that is required, as I have never wanted to achieve anything with more fervor. I hope Your Majesty will see this fervor and will bless it with good fortune so that you do not lose what other kings desire [to obtain]. I have spoken openly and freely about the desire I have of perishing in your service, a wish I have had since childhood.

Understanding that [writing] the present history was no minor service but in fact was greater than all the rest, I obeyed your viceroy, who ordered me to write it in this way. I hope Your Majesty reads it many times because, not only is it enjoyable to read, but it is also of great importance to Your Majesty's conscience. Please take note of all the things that are included in it as well as their substance. I call this the second part because it will be preceded by the first part, which will be the descriptive geography of these lands that will provide great clarity and information for setting up governments, establishing bishoprics, founding new towns, and carrying out new discoveries. This knowledge will prevent the problems that, for lack of it, occurred in earlier times. Although the [first] part should precede this [second] part in time, it will not be sent to Your Majesty at present because it has not yet been finished. Much of its information will be obtained during [Toledo's] general inspection. It will suffice for it to be first in quality, although not in time. And after this second part the third part will be sent, which concerns the period of evangelization.[30] All of these are being written by order of your viceroy Don Francisco de Toledo. Your Majesty, please receive this work with the greatest and most willing purpose in all things to do with our Lord God's and Your Majesty's service and in the benefit of our nation. May our Lord watch over the Holy Catholic Royal Personage of Your Majesty for the restoration and growth of the Catholic Church of Jesus Christ.

Cuzco, 4 March 1572
S. C. R. M.
Humble vassal of Your Majesty
the Captain
Pedro Sarmiento de Gamboa

[1]

DIVISION OF THE HISTORY

*T*his general history that I undertook by order of the most excellent Don Francisco de Toledo, viceroy of these kingdoms of Peru, will be divided into three parts. The first will be a natural history of these lands, because it will be a detailed description of them that will include the wondrous works of nature and other things of much benefit and pleasure. (I am now finishing it so that it can be sent to Your Majesty after this [second part], since it should go before.)[31] The second and third parts will tell of the inhabitants of these kingdoms and their deeds, in this manner. In the second part, which is the present one, the first and most ancient settlers of this land will be described in general. Then, moving into particulars, I will write of the terrible and ancient tyranny of the Capac Incas of these kingdoms until the end and death of Huascar, the last of the Incas. The third and last part will be about the times of the Spaniards and their noteworthy deeds during the discoveries and settlements of this kingdom and others adjoining it, divided by the terms of the captains, governors, and viceroys who have served in them until the present year of 1572.

[6]

THE ORIGIN FABLE OF THESE BARBAROUS INDIANS OF PERU, ACCORDING TO THEIR BLIND OPINIONS

*S*ince these barbarous Indian nations always lacked writing, they had no means to preserve the monuments and memories of their times, ages, and ancestors in a truthful and organized manner. And since the devil, who always endeavors to harm the human race, saw that these unfortunates were easily fooled and timid in obedience, he introduced many illusions, lies, and frauds to them. He made them believe that he had created them in the beginning, and that he had afterward destroyed them with the flood because of their wickedness and sins, and had then created them anew and given them food and a means of subsistence. And it so happens that they had previously had some information, which had been passed down by word of mouth from their ancestors, concerning the truth about the past. They combined this with the devil's stories and with other things that they altered, invented, and added, as is often done in all nations, and made a mixture that, although jumbled, is noteworthy in some respects for the curious who know how to think about and discuss human matters.

One point among many that must be made is that the things that are here described as fables—which they are—these people hold to be as true as we hold those of our faith. As such, they state and confirm them unanimously and swear by them. However, through God's mercy, some of them are now opening their eyes and learning what is true and what is false in these matters. But since we must write down what they say and not what we understand in this regard, let us hear what they believe about their first ages. Then we will move on to the ancient and cruel tyranny of the Inca tyrants, who oppressed these kingdoms of Peru for so long. By order of the most excellent Don Francisco de Toledo, viceroy of these kingdoms, I have researched all of this with the utmost diligence and in such a way that this history may well be called a proof attested to by all [the people] of the kingdom: elders and youths, Incas and tributary Indians.

The natives of this land say that in the beginning, or before the world was created, there was one [being they] called Viracocha. He created a dark world without sun or moon or stars, and because of this creation, they called him Viracocha Pachayachachi, which means "creator of all things." After creating the world, he formed a race of large, misshapen giants, painted or sculpted, to see if it would be good to make people of that size (Figure 6.1). As he found them to be much larger than himself, he said: "It is not good for people to be so large; it would be better if they were my size." Thus he created men in his likeness as they are now. And they lived in darkness.

Viracocha ordered these people to live in harmony and to know and serve him. He gave them a certain commandment, which they were to keep on pain of being thrown into confusion should they break it. They kept this commandment—though they never say what it was—for some time. But as the vices of pride and greed arose among them, they broke the commandment of Viracocha Pachayachachi, and, as they fell victim to his indignation through this sin, he confounded them and cursed them. Some were then turned into stones and others into other forms; others were swallowed by the earth and others by the sea; and above all he sent them a universal flood that they call *unu pachacuti*, which means "water that overturned the world." They say that it rained for sixty days and sixty nights, and that all that had been created was drowned. Only a few vestiges remained of those who had been turned into stones as a memorial of this event and as an example for posterity, in the buildings of Pucara, which is sixty leagues from Cuzco (Figure 6.2).

Some nations other than the Cuzcos also say that they were saved from this flood to populate the coming age. Each nation has a particular fable that they tell about how their forefathers were saved from the waters after the flood. So it can be seen what form their blindness took, I will describe only one from the nation of the Cañaris, in the land of Quito and Tomebamba, more than four hundred leagues from Cuzco.[32]

They say that in the time of the *unu pachacuti* flood there was a hill called Huasano in a town called Tomebamba in the province of Quito. Today the natives of that land [still] point it out. Two Cañari men climbed this hill; one of them was named Ataorupagui and the other Cusicayo. As the waters kept rising, the mountain swam and floated in such a way that it was never covered by the floodwaters. Thus the two Cañaris escaped. The two of them, who were brethren, sowed [fields] after the flood ceased and the waters receded. One day they went to work, and on returning to their hut in the afternoon, they found some small loaves of bread in it and a jug of *chicha* (which is the beverage drunk in this land instead of wine, made

FIGURE 6.1. The large statues of Tiahuanaco (ca. AD 500–1100) were interpreted by the Incas to be the remains of a race of giants created by their creator god, Viracocha. (Photograph by Luis Gismondi, private collection.)

FIGURE 6.2. Like those of Tiahuanaco, the ruins of Pucara were associated by the Incas with the activities of their creator god, Viracocha.

from maize boiled in water). They did not know who had brought this, but they gave thanks to the Creator and ate and drank the provisions. The next day the same rations were sent to them. They were so astonished by this mystery, and so eager to know who brought them the meals, that they hid one day to spy on those who brought the food. While hiding, they saw two Cañari women arrive, cook the food, and put it in the usual place. As they were leaving, the men tried to seize them, but the women slipped away from them and fled. The Cañaris, understanding the mistake they had made in frightening those who helped them so much, became sad. They prayed to Viracocha for forgiveness for their error, and they pleaded with him to send those women back again to give them the food they used to give. The Creator granted them this, and, upon returning again, the women said to the Cañaris: "The Creator has thought it would be good for us to return to you so that you do not die of hunger." And they made their meals and served them. The women became friendly with the Cañari brothers, one of whom had sexual intercourse with one of the women. After the older brother drowned in a nearby lake, the one who remained alive married one of the [women] and kept the other as his mistress. With them he had ten sons, whom he divided into two groups of five each. He settled them and he called one side Hanansaya, which is the same as saying "the upper side," and [he called] the other Hurinsaya, which means "the lower side." All the Cañaris who now exist descended from these.[33]

The other nations have similar fables of how some of the [people] from their nations, from whom they trace their origin and descent, were saved. But the Incas and most of the Cuzcos, and the people who are thought here to be the wisest, say that no one escaped from the flood. Instead, Viracocha [went back to] making and creating people anew, as I will describe below. However, one thing is believed among all the nations of these parts: they all believe and frequently speak about the universal flood in the same way, and that is why they called it *unu pachacuti*. From this we can clearly see that if in these lands there is a memory of the great universal flood, then in the first age of the world this great mass of floating islands, which were later called the Atlantic Islands and are now called the Indies of Castile, or America, were [first] populated. And they began to be populated anew immediately after the flood, although they tell this in different terms than what the true Scriptures teach us. This must have occurred by an act of divine providence [that brought] the first people who traveled across the land of the Atlantic Island, which was connected to this one, as was stated above.[34] Since the natives, although barbarous, explain their ancient settlement [by] referring to the flood, writers need not exhaust themselves drawing conjectures from [outside] authorities concerning their origins. However, since we are tracing what these people tell about the second age after the flood, we will relate that in the next chapter.

[7]

THE FABLE ABOUT THE SECOND AGE AND THE CREATION OF THESE BARBAROUS INDIANS, ACCORDING TO THEIR ACCOUNT

I have already said how everything was destroyed by the *unu pachacuti* flood. Now it should be known that when Viracocha Pachayachachi destroyed this land, as has been related, he kept three men with him, one of whom was named Taguapaca, so that they would serve and help him create the new people he was to make in the second age after the flood, which he did in this manner. With the flood over and the land dry, Viracocha decided to populate it a second time. And to do it much better [than before] he decided to create luminaries to provide light. To do this he went with his servants to a great lake that is in the Collao. In the lake there is an island called Titicaca, which means "lead mountains,"[35] which is discussed in the first part.[36] Viracocha went to this island and ordered the sun, moon, and stars to emerge and rise up into the sky to give light to the world, and so it was done. They say that he made the moon much brighter than the sun and that because of this the jealous sun threw a handful of ash into its face as they were about to rise into the sky. From then onward [the moon] has the darkened color that it has now. This lake is near Chucuito, a town in the Collao, fifty-seven leagues to the south of Cuzco. But [when] Viracocha ordered his servants to do some things, Taguapaca disobeyed his orders. Furious with Taguapaca because of this, he ordered the other two to seize him. They bound him hand and foot, and he was cast into the lake in a boat (Figure 7.1). So it was done. While Taguapaca was cursing Viracocha for what he had done and swearing that he would return one day to take revenge on him, he was carried by the water to the drainage of the lake and was not seen again for a long time. This done, Viracocha built a most solemn *huaca* as a shrine in that spot as a sign of what he had made and created there (Figure 7.2).

Leaving the island, he passed over the lake to the mainland, and taking

FIGURE 7.1. The inhabitants of the Lake Titicaca region have long traveled in reed boats. (Photograph by Luis Gismondi, ca. 1920, private collection.)

FIGURE 7.2. According to Inca legends, the sun first emerged from this rock on the Island of Titicaca, in Lake Titicaca.

with him the two servants he had kept, he went to a place now called Tiahuanaco, which is in the province of Collasuyu. In this place, he [took] some
large stone slabs and sculpted and drew all the nations that he planned to
create. This done, he ordered his two servants to memorize the names that
he was telling them of the people that he had painted there, and the names
of the valleys and provinces and places from which these people were to
emerge, which were scattered across the land. He ordered each of them to
take a different road, calling the people and ordering them to emerge, procreate, and populate the land. His servants, obeying the order of Viracocha,
started on their journey and work. One went by the highlands, or the *cor-
dillera* as they call it, that form the headwaters above the coast of the South
Sea. The other [went] by the highlands that overlook the fear-inspiring
mountains that we call the Andes, located to the east of that sea. They
walked along these highlands, calling out in loud voices: "Oh you people
and nations, hear and obey the order of Ticci Viracocha Pachayachachi, who
orders you to come forth, multiply, and populate the land!" Viracocha himself did the same in the lands between those of his two servants, naming
all the nations and provinces through which he passed. Every place obeyed
the summons, and so some [people] came forth from lakes, others from
springs, valleys, caves, trees, caverns, rocks, and hills, populating the land
and forming the nations that are now Peru.

Others state that Viracocha performed this creation at the site of Tiahuanaco, where, having first formed some figures of giants, he found them
too large and remade them of his own height. (Viracocha was, they say,
of medium height, as we are.) When [they were] formed, he gave them
life, and from there they left to populate the land. Before they departed,
they spoke one language, and they constructed the buildings in Tiahuanaco
as the house of Viracocha, their Creator, the ruins of which can now be
seen (Figure 7.3). Upon departing, they changed their languages, copying
the cries of wild beasts. [They changed them] so much that on meeting up
again later, those who had been relatives and neighbors before could not
understand one another.

Be that as it may, in the end all agree that the creation of these people was
the work of Viracocha. They report that he was a man of medium height,
white, and dressed in white clothing, secured around his body like an alb,
and [that] he carried a staff and a book in his hands.

After this they tell of a strange event. After Viracocha created all the
people, he was walking along and reached a place where many of the people
he had created had congregated. This place is now called the town of Cacha
(Figure 7.4).[37] When Viracocha arrived there, the inhabitants did not rec-

Ruinas de Tiaguanaco. Bolivia.

FIGURE 7.3 The Incas believed that the ruins of Tiahuanaco were the remains of a town built for the creator god, Viracocha. (Anonymous photograph, ca. 1900, private collection.)

ognize his clothing or his manner, so they whispered about him and proposed to kill him [by] throwing him from a nearby hill. They took up their weapons for this, but Viracocha perceived their wicked intentions. He knelt on the ground on a plain and, raising his hands and face to the sky, [brought] fire down from above onto those who were on the mountain and burned the entire area. The land and stones burned like straw. Since those wicked people feared the terrifying fire, they came down the mountain and threw themselves at the feet of Viracocha, asking him for forgiveness for their sin. Moved to compassion, Viracocha went to the fire and extinguished it with his staff. However, the hill was scorched in such a way that the stones on it were made so light from the blaze that a large stone that a cart [normally] cannot move, can easily be picked up by a man. This can be seen today. It is a marvelous thing to see that place and mountain, which measures about a quarter of a league, completely scorched.[38] It is in the Collao (Figure 7.5).[39]

Continuing his journey after this, Viracocha arrived at the town of Urcos, six leagues south of Cuzco. Remaining there for a few days, he was well served by the natives of that place. When he left, they made a celebrated *huaca* or statue of him [for them] to worship and offer gifts to (Figure 7.6).[40] Later, the Incas offered many valuable items of gold and other metals to this statue. Above all [they offered] a golden bench, which later, when the

FIGURE 7.4. Parts of the Temple of Viracocha are still well preserved.

FIGURE 7.5. The cone of an extinct volcano near Rachi

FIGURE 7.6. A shrine to Viracocha was located on top of the mountain now called Viracochan, just outside Urcos.

Spaniards entered Cuzco, was found and divided among them. It was worth 17,000 pesos. The marquis Don Francisco Pizarro took it for himself as his prize.

Returning to the subject of the fable, Viracocha continued his journey, carrying out his deeds and teaching the people he created. In this way he arrived at the region where Puerto Viejo and Manta now are, on the equator, where he was joined by his servants. Wishing to leave the land of Peru, he spoke to those he had created, telling them of things that would befall them. He told them that people would come, some of whom would say that they were Viracocha, their Creator, and that they should not believe them. Moreover, in times to come, he would send his messengers to protect and teach them. This said, he and his two servants entered the sea, and they walked over the water, as if on land, without sinking. Because they walked over the water like foam, they called him Viracocha, which is the same thing as saying "grease" or "foam of the sea." And some time after Viracocha left, they say that Taguapaca, whom Viracocha had ordered thrown into Lake Titicaca in Collao, as was described above, came back and, aided by others, began to preach that he was Viracocha. Although at first the people were fooled, [Taguapaca and the others] were finally seen to be false and were ridiculed.

These barbarians have this ridiculous fable of their creation, and they state it and believe in it as if they had actually seen it happen and take place.

[8]

ANCIENT TRIBES OF THE PROVINCES OF PERU AND ITS REGIONS

*I*t is worth noting that these barbarous Indians know nothing more about what happened since the second creation, which was brought about by Viracocha, until the times of the Incas than what has been described above. But it may be assumed that, although the land was settled and full of people before the Incas, it had no civilized government, nor did they have natural lords elected by common consent who would govern and rule, and whom the commoners respected, obeyed, and paid taxes to. Previously all nations, which were disorganized and scattered, lived in general freedom, each individual being the sole lord of his house and fields. And in each settlement there were two groups. They called one Hanansaya, which means "the upper side," and the other one Hurinsaya, which means "the lower side." They still have this usage today. This division had no other purpose than for them to accurately count themselves, although later on it served, and still serves, more useful purposes, as will be told in its place.

When disagreements arose among them, they sought a certain kind of militia for their defense in the following way. When a nation learned that some other people from other parts were coming to wage war on them, they would seek one of their natives, or even a foreigner to their homeland, who was a valiant warrior. Many times such a man would voluntarily offer to protect them and fight for them against their enemies. They would follow and obey this man and carry out his orders throughout the war. Once it was over, he would remain as poor as before and like the rest of the people. Neither before nor afterward would they render him tribute, or any form of taxes. At that time the people called these men *cinchi*, and they still call them this today, which is the same as "valiant." They would also call them "*cinchicona*," which means "valiant now," which is to say: "Now, while the war lasts, you will be our valiant [leader], but not afterward."[41] Or in another translation, it means "valiant men," because *cona* is an adverb of time and it also denotes plurality. Whatever the meaning, it was appropriate for these temporary captains, who existed in the times of the tribes[42] and general freedom. In this way, all the natives of these kingdoms lived without recognizing a natural or elected lord[43] from the [time of the] universal flood that they report until the advent of the Incas, which was 3,519 years. They were able to exist, as is said, in a simple state of freedom, living in huts, caves, and small humble houses. This title of *cinchis*, which served them for leaders in war only, lasted throughout the land until the time of Topa Inca Yupanqui, the tenth Inca, who established the *curacas* and other officials in the way that will be extensively described below in the life of Topa Inca himself.[44] Even now they have this manner and custom of governing themselves in the provinces of Chile and in other parts of the forests of Peru to the east of Quito and Chachapoyas, where they do not obey any lord longer than the war lasts. And the one they obey is not always the same individual, but the one they know to be the smartest, bravest, and most daring in war. But the reader should be forewarned that, although all the land was tribal in terms of the dominion of the lords, there were clearly nations in each province that had their own ways and specific customs, as is seen among the natives of the Cuzco Valley and other parts. We will speak of each in its place.

[9]

FIRST SETTLERS OF THE CUZCO VALLEY

I have told how, although in ancient times the populations of these lands were maintained and organized into tribes, they also had their own homelands, nations, and customs. Since many of these are known, they will be dealt with elsewhere.[45] Here I will present the origins of the native inhabitants of the valley where the city of Cuzco is now, because from here we will trace the origin of the tyranny of the Incas, who always had their seat in the Cuzco Valley.

First of all, it should be known that the Cuzco Valley is at latitude 13°15' from the equatorial line toward the South Pole. Because it had fertile fields, this valley was populated in ancient times by three nations or groups: the first were called Sauaseras, ~~the second Antasayas~~,[46] and the third Huallas. They settled separately but close to one another because of the arable lands, which was what in those times they primarily wanted and valued, and still do today. The natives of this valley lived here peacefully, cultivating their farms for many centuries.

It is told that some time before the Incas, three *cinchis* foreign to this valley (the first was named Alcabiza, the second Copalimayta, and the third Culunchima) gathered certain companies and came to the Cuzco Valley, where they settled and populated with the consent of its natives. They became brothers and companions of those most ancient natives already mentioned. Thus these six groups, three natives and three outsiders, lived in peace and harmony for a long time. And they say that the outsiders came from where the Incas [later] emerged, as will be told below,[47] and that the outsiders call themselves their kin. This point is essential for what will come later.

But before entering into the full history of the Incas, I would like to warn or, more accurately speaking, to address an issue that may arise among those who have not been in these lands. Some may say that this history, made from the accounts that these barbarians give, cannot be true because without writing, the natives could not memorize so many details of such ancient times as are told here. To this one replies that these barbarians had a curious method that was very good and accurate to substitute for the lack of letters. It was that from one to another, parents to children, they would recount the ancient things of the past up to their times, repeating them many times, as one who reads a class lesson, making their listeners repeat these history lessons until they remained fixed in their memories. Each one would thus recount his annals to his descendants in this manner, to preserve the histories and feats and antiquities and the numbers of people, towns, and provinces; the days, months, and years; the battles, deaths, destructions, fortresses, and *cinchis*. Finally, they would record (and still do) the most remarkable things, in both kind and quantity, on some cords that they call *quipu*, which is the same as saying *racional*,[48] or "accountant." On the *quipu* they make certain knots that they recognize, through which, and by the use of different colors, they distinguish and record each thing as if with letters (Figure 9.1). It is remarkable to see the details that they preserve in these cordlets, for which there are masters as there are for writing among us.

Besides this there were, and still are, special historians of these nations, which was an occupation that was inherited from father to son. The great diligence of Pachacuti Inca Yupanqui, the ninth Inca, was turned to this matter; he issued a general summons to all the old historians of all the provinces

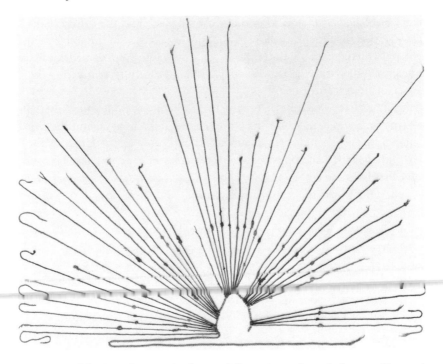

FIGURE 9.1. The Incas kept track of many different items through the use of knotted cords called *quipu*. (Courtesy of the Field Museum, negative A81973.)

that he subjugated, as well as many others throughout these kingdoms. He had them in the city of Cuzco for a long time, questioning them about the antiquities, origins, and remarkable deeds of his forebears in these kingdoms. After he was fully informed of the most noteworthy events of their histories, he ordered it all painted on large boards. He established a great hall in the Houses of the Sun where these boards, which were adorned with gold, were kept as in our libraries, and he appointed learned men who knew how to interpret and explain them.[49] And no one could enter [the room] where these boards were kept, except the Inca or the historians, without the express permission of the Inca.

In this way, everything about their ancestors came to be learned and could be learned by all kinds of people, so that today the lesser and greater Indians generally know it, although in some things they may hold different opinions due to vested interests. Thus, by examining the eldest and wisest in all ranks of life, who are the most credible, I collected and compiled the present history, referring the declarations and statements made by one group to their enemies — that is, the opposite faction, because they divide into factions—I asked each of them for their own testimony about their lineage and that of their opponent. These testimonies, which are all in my possession,[50] I corroborated and corrected with those of their rivals, and finally I had them ratified in public in the presence of all the factions and *ayllus*, under oath by the authority of a judge; and what is here written was improved with experts in the general language, who were very careful and faithful interpreters also under oath. This was done with such diligence because it is the basis of the truth of this great endeavor, which is to learn about the tyranny of the cruel Incas of this land so that all the nations of the world can understand the juridical and more-than-legitimate right that the king of Castile has to these Indies and to other neighboring lands, and particularly to these kingdoms of Peru. Since all the histories and past events were recorded in the inquest, which in this case was carried out so carefully and faithfully by the order and diligence of the most excellent viceroy Don Francisco de Toledo, no one can doubt that everything that is in this volume has been most fully investigated and verified, leaving no room for argument or contradiction. I have made this digression because, while writing this history, I heard many of the above-stated doubts, and I wished to satisfy all of them at once.[51]

[10]

HOW THE INCAS BEGAN TO TYRANNIZE THE LANDS OF THE TRIBES

*H*aving said that in ancient times all this land was tribal, it is necessary to explain how the Incas began their tyranny. Although all lived in simple freedom, without recognizing a lord, there were always some valiant men among them who, aspiring to superiority, would inflict violence on their compatriots and on other foreign peoples to subjugate them and to bring them to obedience and place them under their rule so they could make use of them and make them tributaries. Thus groups from some regions would leave and go to others to engage in wars and thefts and murders and to usurp the lands of others.

As these groups raided many areas and many nations, each one seeking to subjugate its neighbor, it so happened that six leagues from the Cuzco Valley, in a place that they call Pacariqtambo, there were four men and four sisters of fierce spirits and wicked intentions, although of lofty ideas. As they were of greater ability than the others and they understood the pusillanimity of the natives of these regions and the ease with which the natives believed anything that was proposed to them with any authority or force, they agreed among themselves that they could become lords of many lands by force and deception. Thus the eight siblings, four men and four women, joined together and discussed how they could tyrannize the other people beyond the place where they were, and they proposed to carry this out with violence. Understanding that most of these natives are ignorant, and easily believe what is told to them, particularly if it is proposed with some roughness, rigor, and authority, to which they cannot object or resist, because they are naturally timid, the siblings invented certain fables about their birth so that they would be respected and feared. They said they were children of Viracocha Pachayachachi, their Creator, and that they had emerged from some windows[52] to rule the rest. As they were fierce, they made themselves be believed, feared, and taken to be more than men and even worshiped as gods. Thus they introduced the religion they wanted. The following is the account and fable they give of this beginning.

[11]

THE ORIGIN FABLE OF THE INCAS OF CUZCO

All the native Indians of this land generally recount and affirm that the Capac Incas had the following origin.[53] Six leagues from Cuzco to the south-southwest, along the road that the Incas made, is a place called Pacariqtambo, which means "house of production," where there is a hill called Tambotoco, which means "house of windows." And it is true: in this hill there are three windows, one called Marastoco and the other Sutictoco, and the one that is between these two is called Capactoco, which means "rich window," because they say that it was adorned with gold and other riches. A nation of Indians called Maras emerged from the Marastoco window, without being created by parents, and there are some of them in Cuzco today. From the Sutictoco window emerged some Indians called Tambos, who settled in the area around that same hill, and members of this lineage are found in Cuzco today. From the largest window, Capactoco, emerged four

FIGURE 11.1. The rock outcrop called Puma Orco marks the location called Tambotoco by the Incas.

men and four women who called themselves siblings. They have no known father or mother other than what they say: that they emerged and were produced from that window by command of Ticci Viracocha. They themselves said that Viracocha had created them to be lords. Thus, for this reason, they took the name "Inca," which is the same as saying "lord." Since they had emerged from the Capactoco window, they took "Capac" as their surname, which means "wealthy," although they later used this term to denote the paramount lord of many (Figure 11.1).

These are the names of the eight siblings: The eldest of the men and the one with the most authority was called Manco Capac; the second, Ayar Auca; the third, Ayar Cache; and the fourth, Ayar Uchu. The eldest of the women was called Mama Ocllo; the second, Mama Huaco; the third, Mama Ipacura or, as others say, Mama Cura; and the fourth, Mama Raua.

These eight siblings called Incas said: "Since we are born strong and wise, and with the people we will gather here we will be powerful, let us leave this place and seek out fertile lands. Where we find them, let us subjugate the people who are there and take their lands and wage war on all those who do not receive us as lords." They say this was said by Mama Huaco, one of the women, who was fierce and cruel, and also by Manco Capac, her brother, who was just as cruel and atrocious. Once this was agreed upon by the eight, they began to move the people who were in the area of the hill, telling them that as a reward they would make them rich and would give them the lands and estates of those whom they conquered and subjugated. Hence, ten factions or *ayllus*—which among these barbarians means "lineage" or "group"—moved out of greed; their names are as follows:[54]

Chavin Cuzco Ayllu: Of the lineage of Ayar Cache; in Cuzco today there are some of this group, the heads of which are Martín Chucumbi and Don Diego Guaman Paucar.

Arayraca Ayllu Cuzco-callan: Of this *ayllu* today there are Juan Pizarro Yupanqui,[55] Don Francisco Quispe,[56] and Alonso Tarma Yupanqui of the lineage of Ayar Uchu.

Tarpuntay Ayllu: There are some from this *ayllu* in Cuzco now.

Guacaytaqui Ayllu: A few of these now live in Cuzco.

Sañoc Ayllu: There are some of these in Cuzco.

These five groups are Hanan Cuzcos, which means "the group from Upper Cuzco."

Sutictoco Ayllu: This is the lineage that emerged from the window called Sutictoco, as is mentioned above. There are some of these in Cuzco now, and their leaders are Don Francisco Auca Micho Auri Sutic and Don Alonso Hualpa.

Maras Ayllu: These are the ones who they say emerged from the Marastoco window. There are some of these in Cuzco, but the most important ones are Don Alonso Llama Oca and Don Gonzalo Ampura Llama Oca.[57]

Cuycusa Ayllu: There are some of these in Cuzco, and the head is Cristóbal Acllari.

Masca Ayllu: Of this lineage in Cuzco there is Juan Quispe.

Oro Ayllu: From this lineage today there is Don Pedro Yucay.

I say that all these lineages have remained in such a way that the memory of them has not been lost. Since there are more people than those mentioned above, I list only their leaders, who are the protectors and headmen of the lineage and the ones through whom they are being preserved. Each one of these headmen has the duty and obligation to protect the rest and to know the things and deeds of their ancestors. Although I say that these people now live in Cuzco, the truth is that they are in a suburb of the city that the Indians call Cayocache and we call Belén, from the patroness of the church of that parish, which is called Our Lady of Belén.[58]

Returning, then, to our subject, all the above-named groups moved with Manco Capac and the other siblings in search of lands and to tyrannize those who did them no harm, nor gave them cause for war, or with any other right or title other than what has been mentioned. In preparation for war, they chose Manco Capac and Mama Huaco as leaders, and with this purpose, these companies left the hill of Tambotoco to put their plan into effect.

[12]

THE ROUTE THAT THESE COMPANIES OF THE INCAS TOOK TO THE CUZCO VALLEY AND THE FABLES THAT THEY MIX WITH THE HISTORY

*T*he Incas and the rest of the mentioned companies or *ayllus* left the place of Tambotoco in good numbers, taking with them their belongings, servants, and weapons. They formed a good squadron, taking as leaders the aforementioned Mama Huaco and Manco Capac (Figure 12.1).[59] Manco Capac had with him a falconlike bird called *inti*, which everyone venerated and feared as a sacred thing or, as others say, an enchanted thing. They thought that it made Manco Capac lord and made the people follow him. This was what Manco Capac led them to believe, and he had them fooled, always keeping it with much care in a small, boxlike straw case. Afterward he left it to his son as an heirloom, and the Incas possessed it until Inca Yupanqui. Manco Capac also carried a gold staff with him in his hand, to test the lands where he went.

Traveling together, they all arrived at a place called Huaynacancha,[60] four leagues from the Cuzco Valley, where they spent some time sowing and searching for fertile land. In this town, Manco Capac had sexual relations with his sister Mama Ocllo, whom he impregnated. As this place was barren and did not seem capable of supporting them, they went to another town called Tamboquiro, where Mama Ocllo gave birth to a son whom they

FIGURE 12.1. Manco Capac, by Martín de Murúa [1590:f. 21v]. (Courtesy of The J. Getty Museum, Los Angeles, copyright © The J. Paul Getty Museum.)

named Cinchi Roca. After holding the festivities for the birth of the infant, they left in search of fertile land and went to another nearby town called Pallata, which is almost adjacent to Tamboquiro. They remained there for some years.

Unsatisfied with the land, they came to another town called Haysquisrro,[61] a quarter of a league from the previous town. Here they discussed what they should do on their journey and how to get rid of Ayar Cache, one of the four Inca brothers. As he was fierce and strong and very skilled with a sling, Ayar Cache had committed great mischief and inflicted great cruelties, both in the towns that they passed through and on the companions. The other siblings feared that due to the misbehavior and mischief of Ayar Cache, the companies of people they had with them would disband and they would be left alone. As Manco Capac was prudent, he agreed with the others to isolate their brother Ayar Cache through trickery. To do this they called Ayar Cache and told him: "Brother, know that in Capactoco we forgot the gold vessels called *topacusi*, and certain seeds,[62] and the *napa*, which is our paramount insignia of royalty." (The *napa* is a white sheep[63] native to this land, which wore a red body cloth, gold earspools, and an insignia of red shells on its chest that the wealthy and powerful Incas took with them when they left their house. In front went a pole with a banner with a cross of feathers that they call *sunturpaucar*.) "It is for the good of all that you return there and bring them." When Ayar Cache refused to go back, his sister Mama Huaco stood up and, reprimanding him with fierce words, said: "How can such cowardice exist in such a strong youth as you! Prepare for the journey and do not fail to go to Tambotoco and do what you are ordered!" Shamed by these words, Ayar Cache obeyed and left to do so. They gave him as companion one of the [men] who traveled with them, named Tambo Chacay, to whom they secretly entrusted that he make sure any way that he could that Ayar Cache died in Tambotoco, so that Ayar Cache did not return with him. Thus they returned together to Tambotoco with this order. They had scarcely arrived when Ayar Cache entered the window or cave of Capactoco to get the things he had been sent for. Once Ayar Cache was inside, Tambo Chacay quickly placed a boulder over the opening of the window and sat on top of it so that Ayar Cache would remain inside and die. When Ayar Cache returned to the opening and found it closed, he understood the betrayal that the traitorous Tambo Chacay had committed against him, and he decided to escape, if he could, to take revenge on him. He used such force to open the cave and screamed so loudly that he made the mountain tremble, but being unable to open it and knowing that his death was certain, he cursed Tambo Chacay in a loud voice: "Traitor, you have done me great harm. You think you will take news of my mortal imprisonment, but that will never happen! Because of your treason, you will remain out there turned into stone!" And so it happened. To this day they show [a rock] on one side of the Capactoco window [as Tambo Chacay].

We now return to the seven siblings who had remained at Haysquisrro. When they learned of the death of Ayar Cache, they were distressed with what they had done because he was valiant and they missed not having him with them when they waged war on others. Thus they mourned him. This Ayar Cache was so skilled with a sling and so strong that he would demolish a mountain and would form a ravine with each throw of a stone. Thus they say that the ravines that are now in the places where they traveled were made by Ayar Cache with stone throws.

The seven Incas left that town with their companions and arrived at a town called Quirirmanta, at the foot of a hill that they later called Huanacauri. In this town they discussed how they would divide the tasks of their journey among themselves so that there would be distinctions between them. They agreed that since Manco Capac had had an offspring with his sister, he would marry her and procreate with her to preserve their lineage, and that he would be the head of them all, and that Ayar Uchu would remain a *huaca*[64] for their religion. Ayar Auca, from where he was sent, would go and take possession of the land wherever they would settle.

Leaving this place, they came to the hill that is about two leagues away from the Cuzco area. Climbing to the summit, they saw over it a rainbow, which the natives call *huanacauri*. Taking this to be a good sign, Manco Capac said: "Take this as a sign that the world will never again be destroyed by water![65] Let us go there, and from there we will choose where we will found our town!" And casting lots, they saw that the [signs] were good for doing so and for exploring the land that could be ruled from there. Before they reached the summit where the rainbow was, they saw a *huaca* (which is a shrine) in the shape of a person near the rainbow. They decided to seize it and remove it from there. Ayar Uchu offered himself for the task because they said that its [removal] would be good for them. When Ayar Uchu reached the statue or *huaca*, he sat atop it with great courage, asking it what it was doing there. At these words the *huaca* turned its head to see who addressed it, but it was unable to see Ayar Uchu because his weight bore down on it. Ayar Uchu then wanted to move but could not do so because he found himself stuck by the soles of his feet to the back of the *huaca*. Seeing that he was captive, the six siblings went to help him. But Ayar Uchu, seeing himself transforming and realizing that the siblings could not free

FIGURE 12.2. The mountain of Huanacauri is located on the south side of the Cuzco Valley. The ruins of a small Inca complex can be seen near its summit.

him, said to them in parting: "Siblings, you have wrought an evil deed on me. Because of you, I came to where I will remain forever removed from your company! Go! Go! Blissful siblings! I announce to you that you will be great lords. Hence, siblings, I beseech you that in payment for the willingness that I always had to please you, you will remember to honor me and venerate me in all your festivities and ceremonies, and that I be the first to whom you make offerings, because I remain here for your sake. When you celebrate the *guarachico* (which is to arm the sons as knights), you will adore me as your father, who remains here for all." Manco Capac replied that they would do so, since this was his will and his command. Ayar Uchu promised them that in return he would give them gifts and the status of nobility and knighthood, and with these last words, he was turned into stone. They made him a *huaca* of the Incas and gave him the name Ayar Uchu Huanacauri. Thus it always was the most solemn *huaca* and the one that received the most offerings of any in the kingdom, until the time of the Spaniards. The Incas went there to arm knights until about twenty years ago, more or less, when the Christians abolished this ceremony. This was virtuously done because there they committed many idolatries and abuses that were offensive and contrary to God our Lord (Figure 12.2).

[13]

THE ENTRY OF THE INCAS INTO THE CUZCO VALLEY AND THE FABLES THAT THEY TELL ABOUT IT THERE

The six siblings were sad because Ayar Uchu had left them, and also because of the death of Ayar Cache. Because of this, ever after and to this day, those of the Inca lineage are always fearful of traveling to Tambotoco, because they say that they will remain there like Ayar Cache. They went down to the foot of the hill, and from there they began to enter the Cuzco Valley. They arrived at a place called Matagua,[66] where they settled and built huts to stay for a while. Here they armed the son of Manco Capac and Mama Ocllo, called Cinchi Roca, as a knight and pierced his ears. They call this act guarachico,[67] which is the insignia of knighthood and nobility, as a privilege or noble house is known among us. Because of this they rejoiced greatly and drank continuously for many days. And at intervals they mourned having abandoned their brother Ayar Uchu. Here they invented how to mourn the dead, imitating the cooing of doves. They then performed the dances called *capac raymi*,[68] which is a festivity of the rich or royal lords that they perform with long, purple robes; and the ceremonies that they call *quicochico*, which is when a women has her first period; and the *guarachico*, which is when they pierce the ears of the Incas; and the *rutuchico*,[69] which is when they cut the hair of the Inca for the first time; and the *ayuscay*, which is when a child is born and they drink continuously for four or five days.

After this, they remained in Matagua for two years, intending to go to the upper valley in search of good and fertile land. Mama Huaco, who was very strong and skilled, took two gold staffs and threw them toward the north.[70] One covered a distance of about two shots of a harquebus [and entered] a fallow field called Colcabamba.[71] It did not sink in well because the earth was loose and not terraced. In this way they knew that the land was not fertile. The other one reached farther toward Cuzco and sank well into the territory they call Huanaypata,[72] and so they knew the land was fertile. Others say that Manco Capac conducted this test with the gold staff he carried with him. They knew the land was fertile when he sank it with one thrust into an area called Huanaypata, two shots of a harquebus from Cuzco. Because the topsoil of the land was thick and dense, it stuck to the staff in such a way that he could not pull it out.[73]

Be that as it may, all agree that they came searching for land, testing it with a stick or a staff and smelling it until they arrived at Huanaypata, which satisfied them. Realizing its fertility—because on sowing it continually, it always yields the same way; the more they sow it, the more it gives, and it dries up if not sown—they decided to usurp the fields and region for themselves by force in spite of their owners and the natives [of] that place. They returned to Matagua to discuss how they would do this.

From there Manco Capac saw a stone boundary marker that was close to where the monastery of Santo Domingo of Cuzco is now. Pointing it out to his brother Ayar Auca, he said to him: "Brother! Do you remember how we agreed that you should go to take possession of the land where we are to settle? So now look at that rock!" Showing him the boundary marker, he said, "Fly over there" (because they say that he had grown wings), "and sit there and take possession of the very place where that boundary marker is so that we can then go to settle and live there!" Hearing the words of his brother, Ayar Auca lifted himself up with his wings and went to the place that Manco Capac had ordered him to. Sitting there, he then turned into stone and became a territorial boundary marker, which in the ancient language of this valley is called *cozco*. It is from this that this place retains the name Cuzco even today. Hence the Incas have a proverb that says: *Ayar Auca cuzco huanca*, which means: "Ayar Auca: boundary marker of marble." Others say that Manco Capac gave it the name of Cuzco because he cried in the place where he buried his brother Ayar Cache. Because of this and because of the fertility of the place, he gave it this name, which in the ancient language of that time means "sad and fertile." But the first is more believable, because Ayar Cache was not buried in Cuzco, [since] he had died earlier in Capactoco, as was told above. This is generally known among the Incas and the natives.

Thus, of the four Inca brothers, only Manco Capac remained, as well as the four women (Figure 13.1). They then decided to leave for Huanaypata and where Ayar Auca had gone to take possession. To do this, Manco Capac first gave to his son, Cinchi Roca, a wife called Mama Coca, from the *ayllus* of the nation of Saño.[74] She was the daughter of a *cinchi* called Siticguaman, and Cinchi Roca later had a son with her called Sapaca.[75] He also instituted the sacrifice called *capac cocha*,[76] which is to sacrifice two children, one male and one female, to the idol Huanacauri when the Incas were armed as knights. This arranged, Manco Capac ordered the companies to follow him, and he marched to where Ayar Auca was.[77]

Reaching the lands of Huanaypata, which is near where the Arco de la Plata[78] is now, on the road to Charcas, he found settled there a nation

FIGURE 13.1. Manco Capac and the founding of Cuzco, by Martín de Murúa [1590:f. 19]. (Courtesy of The J. Getty Museum, Los Angeles, copyright © The J. Paul Getty Museum.)

of native Indians called Huaylas, who were described above. Manco Capac and Mama Huaco began to settle there and to take the Huaylas' lands and waters against their will. In addition, they did them much harm and damage, and because the Huaylas therefore defended their lives and lands, Mama Huaco and Manco Capac inflicted many cruelties upon them. They say that Mama Huaco was so fierce that in killing a Huaylas Indian, she cut him into pieces, tore out his entrails, and put the heart and lungs into her mouth. And with a *haybinto* (which is a stone tied on a rope, with which she fought) in her hands, she fought against the Huaylas with diabolical determination. When the Huaylas saw this horrid and inhuman spectacle, they feared that she would do the same to them, and being simple and timid, they fled. Thus they abandoned their native land. Seeing the cruelty they had done, and fearing that they would therefore be branded as tyrants, Mama Huaco decided to kill all the Huaylas, believing that the affair would thus be forgotten. They therefore killed as many as they could lay their hands on and tore out the babies from the wombs of pregnant women so that no memory would remain of those poor Huaylas.[79]

This done, Manco Capac pressed ahead. When he was about a mile southeast of Cuzco, a *cinchi* called Copalimayta came out to meet [him]. Previously we mentioned that although he was an outsider, he had been naturalized by consent of the natives of the valley and had been incorporated into the nation of Sauaseray Panaca, natives of the Santo Domingo area in Cuzco.[80] Since the Sauaseras saw these tyrannizing foreigners enter their lands and had seen the cruelties they had inflicted on the Huaylas, they chose Copalimayta as their *cinchi*. He, as was told, came out to resist them, telling them not to enter his lands and those of the natives. Through his efforts, Manco Capac and his companions were forced to retreat. Thus they returned to Huanaypata, the land they had usurped from the Huaylas. They found a great abundance of cereals in the fields they had sown and therefore called those lands by this name, which means "something precious."

A few months later, they returned to attack and enter the settlements of the Sauaseras and tyrannize their lands. Thus they assaulted the town of the Sauaseras, and they attacked so swiftly that they captured Copalimayta, killing many of the Sauaseras with great cruelty. Seeing himself captive, and fearing death, Copalimayta fled in desperation and abandoned his estates so they would let him go. He was never seen again, and Mama Huaco and Manco Capac usurped his houses, estates, and people. In this way, Manco Capac, Mama Huaco, Cinchi Roca, and Manco Sapaca settled the area between the two rivers and built the House of the Sun, which they called Inti-

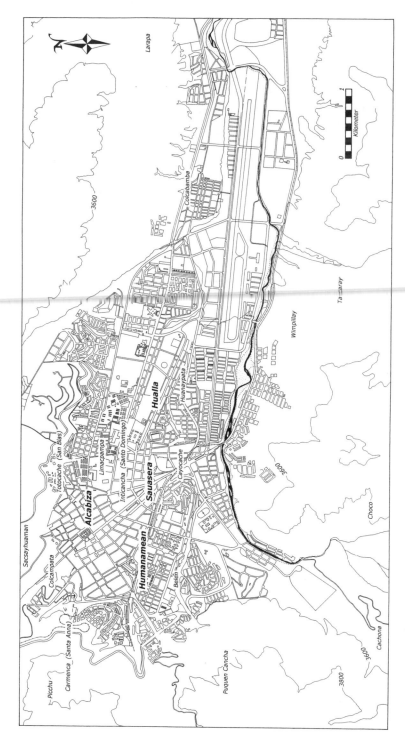

FIGURE 13.2. Map of Cuzco, including many of the locations mentioned by Sarmiento in the origin myth of the Incas

cancha.[81] They divided the entire area, from Santo Domingo to the junction of the rivers, into four neighborhoods or quarters, which they call *cancha* (Figure 13.2). They called one Quinticancha, the second Chumbicancha, the third Sayricancha, and the fourth Yarambuycancha. They divided [these *canchas*] among themselves.[82] Thus they settled the city, which was called Cuzco because of the boundary marker of Ayar Auca.

[14]

THE DISAGREEMENTS BETWEEN MANCO CAPAC AND THE ALCABIZAS OVER THE FIELDS

It is said that the Alcabizas were and are one of the native nations of the Cuzco Valley. At the time that Manco Capac settled in Inticancha and seized the goods of the Sauaseras and of the Huaylas, the Alcabizas lived in the area from about half a harquebus shot from Inticancha to the area where Santa Clara is now.[83] Because Manco Capac wanted to build up his forces so that his tyrannical intentions could not be stopped, he sought to obtain followers among the free[84] and the idle by giving them gifts from the spoils. To maintain them, he would seize the lands of anyone, without distinction. And since he had taken those of the Huaylas and those of the Sauaseras, he also wanted to seize those of the Alcabizas. Although the latter had [already] given him some lands, Manco Capac wanted to take them all or nearly all, and tried to do so. When the Alcabizas saw that [Manco Capac] would seize even their houses, they said, "These are warlike and unreasonable men! They take our lands! Let us go and set up markers on the ones that we still have!" And this they did. But Mama Huaco said to Manco Capac: "Let us take all the water from the Alcabizas, and thus they will be forced to give us the lands that we want!" So they took their water. They fought over this, and as the warriors of Manco Capac were more numerous and more skilled, they forced the Alcabizas to give up the lands they wanted and made them serve them as if they were lords. However, the Alcabizas never served Manco Capac of their own will, nor held him as lord. Instead, they always went about saying to the people of Manco Capac in loud voices: "Get out! Get out of our land!" Manco Capac therefore tried all the more to break them and tyrannically oppress them.

Aside from these, there were other groups native to the Cuzco Valley that Manco Capac and Mama Huaco utterly destroyed, as we said above (Figure 14.1). Above all, they destroyed one group, called the Humanamean, that lived on the block nearest to Inticancha. They lived between Inticancha and Cayocache, where another native *cinchi* called Culunchima dwelled. Manco Capac seized the houses and estates of all the natives, especially of the Alcabizas, and imprisoned their *cinchi* for life. He banished the rest to Cayocache and forced them to pay him tribute. But one or another group always sought to free itself from the tyranny, such as we will tell later of the Alcabizas.

Manco Capac was very old by the time he finished defeating these natives and tyrannizing their goods and persons. Finding himself close to death, he feared that because of the evil he had wrought it was possible that his son and successors would be unable to preserve what he had tyrannized and what future generations would tyrannize. So to leave his son, Cinchi Roca, securely as lord and ruler, he ordered that the ten *ayllus* that had come with him from Tambotoco, along with the rest of his lineage, were to form themselves into a guardlike garrison (Figure 14.2). They were to always assist his son and the rest of their descendants. They would elect the successor [of the Inca] after he had been chosen by his father or had succeeded at the death of the father. For Manco Capac did not trust that the natives would name him or elect him, as he knew the harm and destruction that he had done to them. As Manco Capac was dying, he left the locked-up bird, *inti*, the *topayauri* (which is a scepter), the *napa*, and the *sunturpaucar*—the regalia of a prince even though [he was] a tyrant—for his son, Cinchi Roca, so that he would take his place—and this without the consent or election of any native.

Those of his *ayllu* and lineage state that Manco Capac died at the age of 144. [The years] were distributed in this manner: when he left Pacariqtambo or Tambotoco he was 36. He spent 8 years stopping at the towns between Pacariqtambo and the Cuzco Valley while he was searching for fertile lands, because in one place he would spend 1 year and in others 2 years and in others more or less [time], until he reached Cuzco. Here he lived all the rest of the time, which was 100 years, during which he was *capac*, which among them means "supreme" or "wealthy monarch."

They say that he was a tall man, thin, rustic, cruel, although frank, and that on dying he turned into a stone one yard high. He was preserved in Inticancha with much reverence until the year 1559, when Licentiate Polo de Ondegardo, the chief magistrate in Cuzco at that time, discovered him

FIGURE 14.1. Mama Huaco, by Martín de Murúa [1590:f. 23]. (Courtesy of
The J. Getty Museum, Los Angeles, copyright © The J. Paul Getty Museum.)

cinchiroca

FIGURE 14.2. Cinchi Roca with his father, Manco Capac, by Martín de Murúa [1590:f. 21]. (Courtesy of The J. Getty Museum, Los Angeles, copyright © The J. Paul Getty Museum.)

and removed him from where he was worshiped and venerated by all the Incas in the town of Bimbilla,[85] near Cuzco (Appendixes 3 and 4).[86]

The ten *ayllus* named above originated from this Manco Capac. He began the [tradition of] *guauquis,* which were idols or demons that each Inca selected for his companion and [that] would act as oracles and give answers. The bird *inti,* which was mentioned above, was his *guauqui* idol. Manco Capac ordered the following for the preservation of his memory: that his eldest son by his legitimate wife, who was his sister, was to succeed to the state. If there was a second son, he was to be entrusted with the duty of being in charge of and protecting all the other children and kin, and they were to recognize him as their leader. They would take his last name, and he had the duty of helping them and supporting them, and Manco Capac left them estates for this. He called this group, faction, or lineage "*ayllu,*" which is the same as "lineage." If there was no second son, and even if there was but he was incapable of governing, it would be entrusted to the nearest and most skilled relative. So that future generations would follow his example, he made the first *ayllu* and called it Chima Panaca Ayllu, which means "lineage that descends from Chima," because the first to whom he entrusted his lineage, or *ayllu,* was called Chima. And "Panaca" means "to descend." It is noteworthy that those of this *ayllu* always worshiped the statue of Manco Capac and not the statues of the other Incas, whereas the *ayllus* of the other Incas always worshiped this statue and the others. It is not known what was done with his body; we only know about the statue.[87] They would carry it to war, believing that it gave them the victories they won, and they took it to Huanacauri when they performed the *guarachicos* on the Incas. Huayna Capac took it with him to the Quitos and Cayambes. They returned it to Cuzco later, when they returned the dead body of Huayna Capac. There are some of this lineage in Cuzco now who preserve the memory and deeds of Manco Capac. The principal leaders are: Don Diego Checo and Don Juan Guargua Chima. They are Hurin Cuzcos. Manco Capac died in the year 665 after the birth of Christ our Lord, when Loyba the Goth was reigning in Spain and Constantine IV was emperor.[88] Manco Capac lived in Inticancha, the House of the Sun.

[15]

THE LIFE OF CINCHI ROCA,
THE SECOND INCA, BEGINS

*I*t has been told how Manco Capac, the first Inca, who tyrannized the natives and peoples of the Cuzco Valley, only subjugated the Huaylas, Alcabizas, Sauaseras, Culunchima, Copalimayta, and the others mentioned above, who were all located around what is now the city of Cuzco. This Manco Capac was succeeded by his son Cinchi Roca, also the son of Mama Ocllo, his mother and aunt, by appointment of his father and under the care of the *ayllus*, who then all lived together. But he was not chosen by the natives because at that time they were all fleeing, imprisoned, wounded, or banished, and, ultimately, they were all his mortal enemies due to his father, Manco Capac, who had inflicted so many cruelties, robberies, and killings on them. Cinchi Roca was not a warrior, and thus no noteworthy deeds of arms are told of him, nor did he leave the Cuzco area, either by himself or with his captains. He added nothing to what his father had tyrannically dominated, and simply maintained himself and his *ayllus* by keeping oppressed those whom his father had left in ruin (Figure 15.1). He had Mama Coca from the town of Saño[89] as his wife, with whom he begot a son called Lloqui Yupanqui, which means "left," because he was left-handed. He left behind his *ayllu* called Raura Panaca Ayllu; they are of the Hurin Cuzco side. Some of this *ayllu* remain, and the leaders are named Don Alonso Puscón[90] and Don Diego Quispe.[91] These men have the duty of learning and maintaining the memories and deeds of Cinchi Roca. He lived in Inticancha, the House of the Sun; he reached the age of 127 years; he succeeded at 108 years and was *capac* for 19 years. He died in the year 675 after the birth of our Lord Jesus Christ, when Bamba was king of Spain and Leo IV was emperor[92] and Donus [was the] pope.[93] He left a fish-shaped stone idol called *guanachiri amaru*, which was his *guauqui* idol during his lifetime. This idol was found with the body of Cinchi Roca in the town of Bimbilla, between some copper bars, by Licentiate Polo [de Ondegardo], [who] was the chief magistrate of Cuzco.[94] The idol had servants and agricultural fields for its service.

figura al natural de Cinchiroca
ya Inga y Señor primero

armas que añadio este
Inga

FIGURE 15.1. Cinchi Roca, by Martín de Murúa [1590:f. 24v]. (Courtesy of The J. Getty Museum, Los Angeles, copyright © The J. Paul Getty Museum.)

[16]

THE LIFE OF LLOQUI YUPANQUI,
THE THIRD INCA

*W*ith Cinchi Roca dead, Lloqui Yupanqui, the son of Cinchi Roca and his wife, Mama Coca, took over the Incaship. It is to be noted that although Manco Capac had ordered that the first son should succeed, this Inca broke his grandfather's command, because he had an elder brother named Manco Sapaca, as was told above. But Lloqui Yupanqui did not accept his succession to the state, and the Indians do not state whether he was appointed by his father. From this I believe that Lloqui Yupanqui was not appointed by his father, but rather Manco Sapaca, as the eldest son, was, for he also was not appointed by the natives nor approved by them. This being so, a tyranny was imposed on the natives, and the blood relations were betrayed with the help of the warrior *ayllus*, with whose support they did whatever they wanted and got away with it. Thus Lloqui Yupanqui lived in Inticancha. He did not leave the area of Cuzco for war, nor did he do anything remarkable, except live like his father, communicating with some provinces called Guaro,[95] [whose *cinchi* was named] Guamay Samo, Pachachulla Viracocha,[96] the Ayarmacas of Tambocunca,[97] and the Quilliscaches.[98]

They say that one day, when Lloqui Yupanqui was very sad and anguished, the Sun appeared before him in the shape of a person and consoled him saying, "Do not feel sorrow, Lloqui Yupanqui, because great lords shall descend from you!" and that he should be assured that he would have a male offspring. Because it so happened that Lloqui Yupanqui was very old, and he did not have a son, nor did he expect to have one. Having heard this and having announced to the people what the Sun had told Lloqui Yupanqui, his relatives decided to find him a wife. Moreover, his brother Manco Sapaca, understanding the disposition of [his] brother, tried to find him a suitable wife. Finding her in a town called Oma,[99] two leagues from Cuzco, he asked her relatives for her and, this granted, he brought her to Cuzco. Lloqui Yupanqui then married her. This woman was named Mama Cava, and Lloqui Yupanqui had a son with her named Mayta Capac.[100]

This Lloqui did nothing worthy of remembrance. He carried with him an idol—his *guauqui*—called *apu mayta*. His *ayllu* was named Avayni Panaca Ayllu, because the first to whom this lineage was entrusted was called Avayni. Lloqui Yupanqui lived and died in Inticancha. He was 132 years old; he succeeded at 21 and was *capac* for 111 years. He died in the year 786, when Alfonso the Chaste was king of Spain and Leo IV was the supreme pontiff.[101] There are some of this *ayllu* alive who live in Cuzco. The principal ones among them are named Putizoc Tito Avcaylli, Tito Rimache, Don Felipe Tito Conde Mayta, Don Agustín Conde Mayta,[102] and Juan Baptista Quispe Conde Mayta. They are Hurin Cuzcos. Licentiate Polo [de Ondegardo] found ~~the body and idol of this Inca~~ figure[103] of this Inca [together] with the other ones mentioned.[104]

[17]

THE LIFE OF MAYTA CAPAC, THE FOURTH INCA

Mayta Capac, the fourth Inca, son of Lloqui Yupanqui and of his wife, Mama Cava, is to these Indians what the birth and deeds of Hercules are to us, because they tell strange things about him (Figure 17.1). In terms of his birth, the Indians of his lineage and everyone else in general say that when his father conceived him, he was so old and weak that everyone believed him to be impotent. Thus they believed the conception was a miracle. Concerning his deeds, everyone claims that his mother gave birth to him three months after she became pregnant, and he was born strong and with teeth. He grew so fast that when he was one he had the body and strength of a boy of eight or older. As a two-year-old, he fought with much bigger boys and would hurt them and do them much harm. All this seems as though it could be included with the other fables, but I write what the natives believe about themselves and about their elders. They hold this to be so true that they would kill anyone who claims otherwise.

They say that when Mayta was very young, he played with some youths of the Alcabizas and Culunchimas, natives of Cuzco, and hurt many of them and killed some. One day he broke the leg of a son of the *cinchi* of the Alcabizas after arguing about drinking or drawing water from a fountain, and he chased the rest until they shut themselves in their houses. There the Alcabizas lived without doing any harm to the Incas.

But the Alcabizas, unable to endure Mayta Capac's mischief (which he inflicted on them with the approval of Lloqui Yupanqui and the *ayllus* who guarded him), decided to risk their lives in order to regain their freedom.

FIGURE 17.1. Mayta Capac, by Martín de Murúa [1590:f. 28v]. (Courtesy of The J. Getty Museum, Los Angeles, copyright © The J. Paul Getty Museum.)

Thus they chose ten determined Indians, who went to the House of the Sun where Lloqui Yupanqui and his son Mayta Capac lived, and they entered, determined to kill them. Mayta Capac was then in the courtyard of the House [of the Sun], playing ball with some other boys. When he saw his enemies enter his house with arms, he seized a ball he was playing with and struck one of them and killed him with it, and then another, and he chased the others, making them flee. Although they escaped from him, it was with many wounds. And they reached their *cinchis*, Culunchima and Alcabiza, in this condition.[105]

The *cinchis* pondered the harm that Mayta Capac had done to them, though he was still a boy, and feared that when he grew up, he would utterly destroy them. They therefore decided to die for their freedom. Thus all the natives of the Cuzco Valley who had remained after the destruction wrought by Manco Capac joined together to wage war on the Incas. This thoroughly alarmed Lloqui Yupanqui, and he [thought] himself lost. Reprimanding his son, Mayta Capac, he told him this: "Son! Why have you been so harmful to the natives of this land? Do you want me to die at the hands of our enemies at the end of my days?" But since the garrison of *ayllus* who were with Lloqui Yupanqui lived off pillaging, and enjoyed themselves more with disturbances and robberies than with peace, they answered for Mayta Capac and told Lloqui Yupanqui to be silent and to let his son be. Thus Lloqui Yupanqui did not reprimand his son anymore. The Alcabizas and Culunchimas prepared their people, and Mayta Capac organized his *ayllus*. They fought each other and, although the battle long hung in the balance, without either side gaining an advantage, in the end, after each side had fought hard to win, the Alcabizas and Culunchimas were defeated by Mayta Capac's people.

This, however, did not dishearten the Alcabizas; instead, they reformed and returned with more courage, attacking the House of the Sun from three sides. Mayta Capac, who knew nothing of this and had already retired to his home, came out to the courtyard, where he fought a long battle with his enemies and finally made them reel in confusion and defeated them. Afterward he performed the *guarachico* and armed himself as a knight.

But this did not make the Alcabizas give up their cause, which was to free themselves and exact revenge. Far from it, they once again called Mayta Capac to battle, which he accepted. While they were fighting, they say that it hailed so much on the Alcabizas that it caused them to be defeated for a third time, and they were completely destroyed. And Mayta Capac kept their *cinchi* in prison until he died.

Mayta Capac married Mama Taucaray, a native of the town of Taucaray, and had with her a legitimate son named Capac Yupanqui, as well as four others named Tarco Guaman,[106] Apu Conde Mayta, Queco Avcaylli, and Roca Yupanqui.

This Mayta Capac was valiant and the first to distinguish himself with arms since Mama Huaco and Manco Capac. They say that the successors of Manco Capac and the predecessors of Mayta Capac had always kept the bird *inti*, which Manco Capac had brought from Tambotoco, locked in a chest or box of straw, which they did not dare open—such was the fear that they had of it. But Mayta Capac, who was more daring than all of them, was anxious to see what it was that his ancestors had kept so guarded. So he opened the chest and saw the bird *inti* and spoke with it, for they say that it gave oracles. And from this conversation Mayta Capac grew very wise and understood what he had to do and what would happen to him.

But even so he did not leave the Cuzco Valley, although some nations came to visit him from afar. He lived in Inticancha, the House of the Sun. He left a lineage called Usca Mayta Panaca Ayllu, and there are some of them alive in Cuzco now, the leaders of which are Don Juan Tambo[107] Usca Mayta[108] and Don Baltasar Quizo Mayta. They live in Cuzco. They are of the Hurin Cuzco side. Mayta Capac died at the age of 112. He died in the year 896 of the birth of our Lord Jesus Christ. Licentiate Polo [de Ondegardo] also found the body of this Inca and his *guauqui* idol with the others.[109]

[18]

THE LIFE OF CAPAC YUPANQUI, THE FIFTH INCA

At the time that Mayta Capac died, he appointed Capac Yupanqui, his son by his wife, Mama Taucaray, as his successor (Figure 18.1). After he succeeded to the Incaship, Capac Yupanqui made his brothers swear that they wanted him to be *capac*. They did so out of fear, because he was haughty and cruel. At first he lived in great quietude in Inticancha. But it is to be noted that although Capac Yupanqui succeeded his father, he was not the eldest of the sons. Before him came Conde Mayta, another brother of his, who was ugly, which is why his father [had] disinherited him from the Incaship and named Capac Yupanqui as successor to the Incaship. And [he named] Apu Conde Mayta as the high priest. For this reason, Capac Yupanqui did not

FIGURE 18.1. Capac Yupanqui, by Martín de Murúa [1590:f. 30v]. (Courtesy of The J. Getty Museum, Los Angeles, copyright © The J. Paul Getty Museum.)

FIGURE 18.2. The site of Ancasmarca

hold himself to be the legitimate lord, even within his tyranny, and made his brothers swear that they would be loyal to him.

It is said that Capac Yupanqui was the first who left to conquer outside the Cuzco Valley, because he subjected the towns of Cuyumarca[110] and Ancasmarca,[111] four leagues from Cuzco, by force (Figures 18.2). Out of fear, a wealthy *cinchi* Indian of the Ayarmacas sent Capac Yupanqui one of his daughters as a gift; she was named Curihilpay. Others say that she was a native of Cuzco. Capac Yupanqui took her as a wife and with her had a son named Inca Roca Inca, besides five other sons that he had with other women. The first of these sons was named Apu Calla, the second Humpiri, the third Apu Saca, the fourth Apu Chimachaui, and the fifth Uchuncuna Scallarando. Apu Saca had a son named Apu Mayta, an extremely valiant and famed captain who, along with Vicaquirao, another esteemed captain, accomplished very remarkable feats in war in the time of Inca Roca Inca and of Viracocha Inca. Besides these, Capac Yupanqui had another son named Apu Urco Guaranga. Capac Yupanqui lived 104 years; [he] was *capac* for 89 years, having succeeded at the age of 15. He died [in the] year 985 of the birth of our Redeemer Jesus Christ. His *ayllu* and lineage was called, and is now called, Apu Mayta Panaca Ayllu. At present there are some of this lineage alive, including its four major leaders: Don Cristóbal Cusigualpa, Don Antonio Picuy, Don Francisco Cocazaca, and Don Alonso Rupaca. They are of the Hurin Cuzco side and are in Cuzco and its suburbs. The body of this [Inca] and his *guauqui* idol were also discovered by the licentiate Polo [de Ondegardo], who hid them with the others to prevent their idolatries and their heathen ceremonies.

[19]

THE LIFE OF INCA ROCA, THE SIXTH INCA

*W*hen Capac Yupanqui died, Inca Roca Inca, his son by his wife, Curi-hilpay, succeeded him by appointment [of his father] and of the custodian *ayllus*. At the beginning of his Incaship, Inca Roca showed spirit and valor, because he conquered with much violence and cruelty the towns called Mohina and Pinahua,[112] a little over four leagues to the south-southeast of Cuzco (Figure 19.1). He killed their *cinchis*, Mohina Pongo and Vaman-topa—although they say that Vamantopa fled and was never seen again. Inca Roca did this with the help of Apu Mayta, his nephew and the grand-

FIGURE 19.1. The site of Chokepukio was the central village of the Pinahua ethnic group.

son of Capac Yupanqui. Thus Inca Roca conquered Caytomarca,[113] four leagues from Cuzco, and discovered and channeled the waters of Hurinchacan and those of Hananchacan, which is like saying "the waters above" and "the waters below" Cuzco. Even today these irrigate the fields of Cuzco. Thus his sons and descendants still possess and own them.[114]

But Inca Roca Inca later devoted himself to pleasures and banquets and preferred to live in idleness. He loved his sons so much that, because of them, he forgot the people and even himself. He married a noblewoman called Mama Micay from the town of Patahuayllacan,[115] the daughter of the *cinchi* of that town named Soma Inca. Later, the wars between Tocay Capac and the Cuzcos took place because of this, as will be told later. Inca Roca Inca had a son with this woman called Tito Cusi Hualpa, who was also known as Yahuar Huacac. Besides this legitimate and eldest son, Inca Roca had four other famous sons,[116] the first named Inca Paucar Inca, the second Guaman Taysi Inca, the third Vicaquirao Inca, who was a strong and great warrior and was companion-in-arms to Apu Mayta. These two captains were the ones who attained great victories for Viracocha Inca and Inca Yupanqui, and who won many provinces for them and were the founders of the great power that the Incas afterward attained.

Since what occurred between Inca Roca and the Ayarmacas will be told in [the account of] the life of his son, here we will say nothing more about this Inca except that, seeing that his predecessors the Incas had always lived in the lower part of Cuzco and were therefore called Hurin Cuzcos, he ordered that henceforth those who descended from him should form another group or faction and should call themselves Hanan Cuzcos, which means "the Cuzcos from the Upper Side." Thus with this Inca began the side of the Hanan Cuzcos, because he and his successors then left their home in the House of the Sun and built houses outside of it where they lived in the upper areas of the town.[117]

And it is to be noted that each Inca built a special palace in which to dwell. Not wanting to live in the houses in which his father had lived before, the son would leave them in the state they were in at the death of his father, with their retainers, kin, and *ayllu* and estate holdings, so that they could support themselves and the buildings could be maintained. The Incas and the *ayllus* of Inca Roca were and still are Hanan Cuzcos, although these *ayllus* were later reorganized in the time of Pachacuti. Some therefore say these two divisions, so famous in these parts, were created then.

Inca Roca Inca named his son Vicaquirao as head of his lineage, and thus this group was called, and is now still called, Vicaquirao Panaca Ayllu. There are some of this lineage who live in Cuzco today. The principal ones

who protect and preserve this *ayllu* are the following: Don Francisco Guaman Rimache Hachacoma[118] and Don Antonio Guaman Mayta. They are
Hanan Cuzcos. Inca Roca Inca lived 123 years; he succeeded at 20 years
and was *capac* for 103 years. He died in the year 1088 of the birth of our
Lord. The licentiate Polo [de Ondegardo] found his body in a town called
Rarapa,[119] [where it was kept] with much authority and veneration according to their rites.[120]

[20]

THE LIFE OF TITO CUSI HUALPA, WHOM
THEY COMMONLY CALL YAHUAR HUACAC

*T*ito Cusi Hualpa Inca, the eldest son of Inca Roca Inca and his wife,
Mama Micay, had a strange childhood, which is why these natives recount
his life from his infancy. And in the course of this they tell some things
about his father and about other neighboring groups of Cuzco in this manner. It has been told how Inca Roca Inca married Mama Micay according
to their rites. It should be known that the people of the town of Huayllacan
had promised to give Mama Micay, who was a native [from there] and very
beautiful, as wife to Tocay Capac, the *cinchi* of the Ayarmacas, who were
Indians from the neighboring region. The Ayarmacas were offended when
they saw that the Huayllacan had broken their word to them, and they declared themselves their enemies, waging war on them. The Huayllacan in
turn defended themselves and offended the Ayarmacas. Both sides committed cruel deeds, murders, and robberies, causing great damage to one
another. While these things were happening between these two peoples,
Mama Micay gave birth to Tito Cusi Hualpa. The wars continued some
years after his birth, and taking into account that they were destroying one
another, both sides decided to come to terms to avoid further destruction.
The Ayarmacas, who were superior to the Huayllacan, then asked them
to deliver the child Tito Cusi Hualpa into their hands so they could do
with him as they pleased; then they would put down their arms. If the
Huayllacan did not do so, the Ayarmacas promised not to desist from their
goal, which was to wage deadly war on them until they were completely
destroyed. Being fearful and finding themselves too inferior to resist, the
Huayllacan accepted the condition, even though they were the uncles and

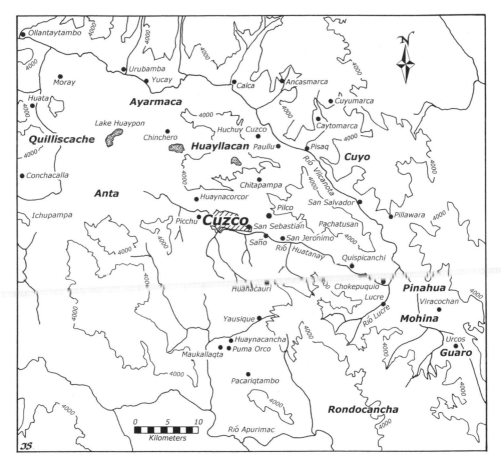

FIGURE 20.1. The Inca heartland and many of the places mentioned by
Sarmiento de Gamboa

kin of the child. To put the agreement into effect, they arranged for Inca
Roca Inca to be tricked in this manner. A brother of Inca Roca and uncle of
Tito Cusi Hualpa who was named Inca Paucar was in the town of Paullu.
He went, or sent his messengers, to plead with Inca Roca to consider sending his nephew Tito Cusi Hualpa to his town of Paullu, because he [Inca
Paucar] wanted to pamper him while he was still a child and to have him
meet his relatives on his mother's side and see their estates, for they wanted
to make him the heir of their estates while they were still alive. Trusting
these words, Inca Roca Inca allowed them to take his son to Paullu or to the
town of Micaocancha.[121] Once they had the child in their town, the Huay-

llacan held great festivities for Tito Cusi Hualpa, who was then about eight years old. His father had sent some Incas from Cuzco to guard him. With the festivities over, the Huayllacan sent word to the Ayarmacas that while they were busy cultivating some fields, or as they say, *chacaras,* they could descend upon the town and take the boy to their land and do with him whatever they wished, as had been agreed. Notified, the Ayarmacas came down at the agreed time and place, and finding the town empty, they stole the child Tito Cusi Hualpa (Figure 20.1).

Others say that this treason occurred in this way: Because the boy's uncle presented him with and gave him many things, the sons of Inca Paucar, his cousins, were jealous. They therefore conspired with Tocay Capac that they would deliver the boy into his hands, and with their information, To-cay Capac entered [the area of the Huayllacan]. Tocay Capac, the enemy of Inca Roca, was told when Inca Paucar left to present his nephew Tito Cusi Hualpa with certain estates and a herd of livestock, and he attacked those who carried the boy. The person carrying him fled, and the child was seized and taken by Tocay Capac.

One way or another, the result was that the Ayarmacas kidnapped Tito Cusi Hualpa from the custody of Inca Paucar in the town of Paullu. Inca Paucar and the other Huayllacan sent news of this to Inca Roca on the one hand, and on the other, they took up arms to go after the Ayarmacas.

[21]

WHAT HAPPENED AFTER THE AYARMACAS
KIDNAPPED TITO CUSI HUALPA

*W*hen the Ayarmacas and their *cinchi,* Tocay Capac, kidnapped the son of Inca Roca, they marched off with him. The Huayllacan of Paullupampa named Inca Paucar as their *cinchi* and took up their weapons and went after them. They caught up with them in the town of Amaru,[122] the home of the Ayarmacas. The two sides clashed, one side trying to recover the boy and the other to defend their prize. Because those of Paullu, so they say, only fought to save face and to have an excuse to give Inca Roca, the Ayarmacas prevailed in the end, and the Huayllacan returned fleeing and injured. They say that all the noblemen who had come from Cuzco as part of the boy's guard were killed during this encounter and when he had been kidnapped. The Ayarmacas took the kidnapped child to the main town of their province that was called Aguayrocancha.[123]

Many say that Tocay Capac was not present during this theft, but rather that he sent the Ayarmacas, who, after they arrived at the town of Aguay-rocancha, presented the boy Tito Cusi Hualpa to him, saying: "Look here, Tocay Capac, at the prize that we bring you!" The *cinchi* was greatly satisfied by this and asked in a loud voice if this was the son of Mama Micay, the one who was going to be his wife. Although a child, Tito Cusi Hualpa boldly replied that he was the son of Mama Micay, his mother, and of Inca Roca Inca, his father. Tocay, indignant on hearing these words, ordered those who had brought Tito Cusi Hualpa prisoner to have him killed. The boy, who heard the sentence pronounced upon him, was filled with such grief and anger that tears of blood burst from his eyes as he began to cry from fear of death. And with an indignation beyond his years, he uttered a curse against Tocay and the Ayarmacas: "Verily I tell you that if you kill me, such a curse will come upon you and your descendants that you will all come to an end, and no memory shall remain of your nation!" Then the Ayarmacas and Tocay carefully pondered the boy's curse and the tears of blood, and they said that this was a great mystery that such a young child should say such weighty words and that the fear [of death] should make such an impression on him that he [would] weep blood. They were perplexed, and guessing that he would become a great man, they revoked the death sentence and named him Yahuar Huacac, which means "cried tears of blood," because of what had happened to him. But although by then they did not want to kill him with their own hands, they ordered that Yahuar Huacac should be treated in such a way that he would eventually starve to death. But before this, they all ordered the boy to turn his face toward Cuzco and weep over it so that the curse that he had cast would be turned against the inhabitants of Cuzco. And so he did.

This done, they delivered him to the most valiant Indians that were there and ordered them to take him to one of their herding ranches. There they should guard him, giving him very little food so that he would start being consumed by hunger until he died. Yahuar Huacac was there for a year without leaving that place, and thus it was not known in Cuzco, nor anywhere else save there, if he was dead or alive. As nothing certain was known of his son during this time, Inca Roca did not want to wage war on the Ayarmacas so that they would not kill Yahuar Huacac if he was alive. Thus he did nothing besides prepare his warriors and lie low, inquiring about his son through all possible avenues.

[22]

HOW IT BECAME KNOWN THAT
YAHUAR HUACAC WAS ALIVE

*S*ince young Yahuar Huacac had spent a year among the shepherds, without leaving the herders' huts that served as a prison for him, nobody knew anything of his whereabouts, because he did not leave there and was closely watched by the shepherds and other guards. But it so happened that in that town there was a woman named Chimbo Orma, a native of the town of Anta, three leagues from Cuzco. She was the mistress of the *cinchi*, Tocay Capac, and for this reason she was free to wander about and enter any area that she wanted. Once when entering where Yahuar Huacac was, she saw him and was astonished to see such an attractive and graceful young man. That gave her the opportunity to ask him about his father and life, and the youth gave her an account of all that she asked and told of his misfortune, imprisonment, and hunger. When the woman understood whose son he was, moved by compassion, she consoled him, telling him that she would try to pass by there many times and that he should make sure to continue using that path so as to meet up with her. Thus she would always bring him some food, with which he could maintain himself. In addition, she became determined to free him.

She sustained him in this way for some time, with much caution so that the guards would not see her. And as the woman had already conceived a plan to free Yahuar Huacac, she told him about it. He thanked her and begged her to do so. She, who was the daughter of a *cinchi* of Anta, told her father and brothers and other relatives of this, and persuaded them to free Yahuar Huacac. They agreed to do so on a given day. With the instructions that Chimbo Orma gave, her father and relatives freed Yahuar Huacac. They placed themselves behind a hill on a day when Yahuar Huacac had for this very reason organized a game with the other boys, to see who could climb a hill the fastest. When Yahuar Huacac reached the top, those of Anta, who were hidden there, took him in their arms and quickly began to walk to their town of Anta. When the [other] youths saw him taken this way, they told the valiant men who guarded him, and they went after those of Anta. They overtook them at Lake Huaypon, where they fought a very fierce battle. In the end, the Ayarmacas fared the worst, as almost all were wounded or killed. Those of Anta continued on their journey to their town, where they gave many gifts and made many services to young Yahuar Huacac, whom they had freed from the deadly prison in which Tocay Capac had held him. They had him in the town of Anta for a year, serving him with much love and esteem, yet so secretly that in all this time his father, Inca Roca, did not learn about the freed youth. At the end of this time, the people of Anta decided to send their messengers to Inca Roca to beseech him to show them his firstborn son who was to succeed him, because they wanted to know and serve him. The messengers went to Inca Roca, and [having] delivered the message, received the reply that he had heard nothing of him except that the Ayarmacas had stolen him. When they asked him again and again, Inca Roca rose from his throne and questioned the messengers, urging them to tell him something about his son, since they would not ask him so many times without a reason. Finding themselves so sharply interrogated by Inca Roca, the messengers told him what had happened and how his son was free in Anta, served and feted by their *cinchi*, who had freed him. Inca Roca thanked them and promised them rewards and [then] dismissed them, remaining much indebted to their town and *cinchi*. Because of this, Inca Roca Inca greatly rejoiced and held many celebrations.

Not fully trusting what the messengers had just told him, Inca Roca sent after them a poor man, who in the guise of asking for alms, was to inquire in the town of Anta whether [the story] was true. The poor man went and learned for certain that Yahuar Huacac was free, and he returned with the news to Inca Roca; and on account of this they held new celebrations in Cuzco. Then Inca Roca sent many headmen from Cuzco with gifts of gold, silver, and textiles to the Anta, pleading with them to accept the gifts and to send him his son. The people of Anta replied that they had no need of his gifts, which they returned to him, for they preferred to have Yahuar Huacac with them and to serve him and his father as well, because they dearly loved the young man. And if Inca Roca wanted his son, it would be on condition that from then on the noblemen of Cuzco would call the Antas their relatives. When Inca Roca learned this, he went to the town of Anta and granted its people and their *cinchi* what they asked. From then on, those of Anta called themselves kin of the Cuzcos because of this.

Inca Roca brought his son Yahuar Huacac Inca Yupanqui to Cuzco and then appointed him as successor of the Incaship. And the noblemen and *ayllus* received him in custody as such. And when Inca Roca died two years later, Yahuar Huacac Inca Yupanqui, who before had been named Tito Cusi Hualpa, was now the sole [Inca]. Before Inca Roca died, he befriended Tocay Capac through Mama Chicya, the daughter of Tocay Capac, who mar-

FIGURE 22.1. Yahuar Huacac, by Martín de Murúa [1590:f. 34v]. (Courtesy of The J. Getty Museum, Los Angeles, copyright © The J. Paul Getty Museum.)

ried Yahuar Huacac. [In turn], Inca Roca gave one of his daughters, named Curi Ocllo, as wife to Tocay Capac (Figure 22.1).[124]

[23]

YAHUAR HUACAC INCA YUPANQUI, THE SEVENTH INCA, BEGINS THE INCASHIP ONLY AFTER THE DEATH OF HIS FATHER

*W*hen Yahuar Huacac saw that he was free and that he alone ruled, he recalled the treason that the Huayllacan had done to him in selling him and delivering him to his enemies the Ayarmacas, and he proposed to inflict an exemplary punishment on them. When the Huayllacan learned this, they humbled themselves before Yahuar Huacac, asking him to forgive the wickedness they had committed against him. Taking into consideration that they were his relatives, Yahuar Huacac forgave them. He then sent men against the Mohina and Pinahua, four leagues from Cuzco, and he appointed as his captain-general his brother Vicaquirao, who conquered those towns. He perpetrated many cruelties on them for no other reason than because they did not come to obey him voluntarily. This would have been about twenty-three years after having returned to stay in Cuzco. Some years later, he went to subjugate and conquer the people of Mollaca,[125] near Cuzco, by force of arms.

Yahuar Huacac Inca had three legitimate sons with his wife, Mama Chicya (Figure 23.1). The eldest was named Paucar Ayllu. They had appointed the second, Pahuac Hualpa Mayta, as successor to his father, even though he was the second. The third and youngest was named Viracocha, who later became Inca because of the death of his brother. Besides these, Yahuar Huacac Inca had three other illegitimate sons; the first was called Vicchu Topa because he conquered the town of Vicchu.[126] The second one was called Marcayuto, and the third, Inca Roca Inca. The Huayllacan wanted Marcayuto to succeed Yahuar Huacac because he was their relative, so they decided to kill Pahuac Hualpa Mayta, who was appointed [heir]. To do this they asked Pahuac Hualpa Mayta's father to take him to Paullu. Forgetting the past treason, he gave his [son] to his grandfather Soma Inca, sending forty noblemen from the *ayllus* of Cuzco to guard him. Once they had Pahuac Hualpa Mayta in their town, they killed him. His father there-

y Pa hua co Coya

FIGURE 23.I. Mama Chicya, by Martín de Murúa [1590:f. 35v]. (Courtesy of
The J. Getty Museum, Los Angeles, copyright © The J. Paul Getty Museum.)

fore greatly punished the Huayllacan, killing some and banishing others. Hence very few of them remained.

Then Yahuar Huacac went to conquer Pillauya,[127] three leagues from Cuzco, in the Pisaq Valley, and then to the nearby town of Choyca[128] and the town of Yuco.[129] He then forcefully and cruelly oppressed the people of Chillincay[130] and Taocamarca[131] and the Cabiñas,[132]and he made them give tribute. In this way, Yahuar Huacac Inca conquered ten nations by himself and with his sons and captains, although some attributed his conquests to his son Viracocha Inca.

Yahuar Huacac was a gentle man with a very beautiful face. He lived 115 years; he succeeded his father at 19 and was *capac* for 96 years. He died in the year [. . .][133] of the birth of our Lord. He left his *ayllu* called Aucaylli Panaca, some of whom live today in Cuzco. The most principal ones who maintain it are Don Juan Concha Yupanqui,[134] Don Martín Tito Yupanqui,[135] and Don Gonzalo Paucar Aucaylli.[136] They are Hanan Cuzcos. His body has not been found. It is believed that those of the town of Paullu have it, together with its *guauqui* idol.[137]

[24]

THE LIFE OF VIRACOCHA, THE EIGHTH INCA

*W*hen the Huayllacan, as has been said, killed Pahuac Hualpa Mayta, who was to succeed his father, Yahuar Huacac, Viracocha Inca, who was called Atun Topa Inca as a child [and was the] youngest legitimate son of Yahuar Huacac and Mama Chicya, was named to succeed. He married Mama Rondocaya, a native of the town of Anta. Once, when Atun Topa Inca [was] in Urcos, a town that is a little over five leagues to the south-southeast of Cuzco, where the sumptuous *huaca* of Ticci Viracocha was,[138] this deity appeared to him at night. In the morning, gathering his noblemen and among them one [named] Hualpa Rimache, his governor, he told them how Viracocha had appeared to him that night and had informed him of great good fortune for him and his descendants. Congratulating him, Hualpa Rimache saluted him, saying, "Oh Viracocha Inca!" The others joined in and applauded this name Viracocha, and it remained with him for the rest of his life. Others say that he took this name because when they armed him as a knight and pierced his ears, he took Ticci Viracocha as godfather of his knighthood. However it may have occurred, all that is certain is that when he was a child, and before he succeeded his father, he was named Atun Topa Inca, and then for the rest of his life he was called Viracocha Inca.

After Viracocha appeared to him in Urcos, he returned to Cuzco and conceived [a plan] to begin to conquer and tyrannize the areas surrounding Cuzco. It should be known that although his father and grandfather had conquered and robbed the above-mentioned nations, as they did no more than rob and spill blood, they did not place garrisons in the towns they subjugated. Thus, on seeing an opportunity, or at the death of the Inca who had defeated them, the nations then sought their liberty anew, and therefore would take up arms and rebel. This is why we repeatedly say that [the same] nation was subjugated by different Incas, such as the Mohina and Pinahua, who, although banished and subjugated by Inca Roca, were also oppressed by Yahuar Huacac, and then subsequently by Viracocha and his son Inca Yupanqui. Each nation fought for its freedom so fiercely, with and without their *cinchis*, who each tried to subjugate the other. This was especially true in the time of the Incas, for even inside Cuzco itself, those of a suburb called Carmenca [139] waged war on those of another suburb called Cayocache. Thus, it has to be understood that although the seven Incas preceding Viracocha Inca kept the people of Cuzco and others very close to Cuzco in great fear, because of the strength that the *ayllus* gave them, these people only served the Incas while there was a spear held over them. But when the opportunity presented itself, they would rise up in arms, calling for their freedom, something they defended at great risk and with [many] deaths, even those within Cuzco, until the time of Viracocha Inca.

Viracocha Inca, proposing to subjugate all those he could through force and cruelty, chose two valiant noble Indians from the lineage of Inca Roca Inca as his captains; the first was Apu Mayta and the other Vicaquirao. With these captains, who were cruel and pitiless, Viracocha Inca began to subdue first of all the people of Cuzco who were not Inca noblemen, inflicting many deaths and great cruelties on them. At this time, many nations and provinces in the regions surrounding Cuzco were already up in arms, defending themselves against the Inca noblemen of Cuzco who had waged war on them to tyrannize them. At the same time, others strove to attain the same as the Incas, which was to subjugate these nations—if their forces were sufficient. Thus, they elected some *cinchis* and were in such a state of confusion and tribalism that they decimated one another, and each particu-

FIGURE 24.1. Mama Rondocaya, by Martín de Murúa [1590:f. 37v]. (Courtesy of The J. Getty Museum, Los Angeles, copyright © The J. Paul Getty Museum.)

lar little nation was left with few people and was bereft of help from others. Viracocha Inca was aware of this opportunity, and it encouraged him to spread his tyranny beyond Cuzco.

Before discussing the towns that Viracocha Inca conquered, let us list his sons. With Mama Rondocaya,[140] his legitimate wife, he had four sons (Figure 24.1). The first and eldest was Inca Roca Inca. The second was Topa Yupanqui; the third, Inca Yupanqui; and the fourth was Capac Yupanqui. He had two sons with another beautiful Indian woman, named Curichulpa, of the Ayavilla[141] nation in the Cuzco Valley; the first [was] Inca Urcon, and the other was Inca Sucsu. Although the descendants of Inca Urcon say that he was legitimate, everyone else says that he was a bastard.

[25]

THE PROVINCES AND TOWNS THAT VIRACOCHA INCA, THE EIGHTH INCA, CONQUERED AND TYRANNIZED

*W*hen Viracocha had appointed Apu Mayta and Vicaquirao as his captains and had mustered his men, he sent them to conquer the area beyond Cuzco (Figure 25.1). Thus they went to the town of Pacaycancha[142] in the Pisaq Valley, three and a half leagues from Cuzco. Because the [inhabitants] did not come to pay obeisance, he ravaged the town, killing the inhabitants and their *cinchi* named Acamaqui. He then turned on the towns of Mohina and Pinahua, Casacancha[143] and Rondocancha,[144] five short leagues from Cuzco, that had already freed themselves even though Yahuar Huacac had wreaked havoc upon them. He defeated them and killed most of the natives and their *cinchis*, who at that time were also named Muyna Pongo and Guaman Topa. He waged this war and inflicted these cruelties on them because they said that they were a free people and would not serve him or be his vassals.

At this time, Inca Roca, his eldest son, was already a man and showed signs of being courageous. Viracocha Inca therefore made him his captain-general and gave him as companions Apu Mayta and Vicaquirao, who brought with them Inca Yupanqui, of whom there was also great hope because of the valor he had shown during his flourishing adolescence. Thus

FIGURE 25.1. Viracocha Inca, by Martín de Murúa [1590:f. 36v]. (Courtesy of The J. Getty Museum, Los Angeles, copyright © The J. Paul Getty Museum.)

Viracocha Inca continued his conquest with these captains and destroyed the Guayparmarca[145] people and the Ayarmacas, and he killed their *cinchis*, Tocay Capac and Chiguay Capac, who had their seats near Cuzco. They subjugated the town of Mollaca and destroyed the town of Cayto,[146] four leagues from Cuzco, and killed their *cinchi* named Capac Chani. They ravaged the towns of Socma[147] and Chiraques[148] and killed their *cinchis* named Poma Lloqui and Illacumbi, who were very warlike *cinchis* at that time and who very valiantly resisted the previous Incas so that they could not leave Cuzco to pillage. In this same way, Viracocha Inca conquered Calca and Caquia Xaquixaguana,[149] three leagues from Cuzco, and the towns of Collocte[150] and Camal.[151] He subjugated the towns that lay between Cuzco and Quiquiguana, and [in] their surroundings, and the Papres, and the other people in this region, all within seven or eight leagues, at most, around Cuzco. In these conquests he committed very great cruelties, robberies, murders, and destruction of towns, burning them and razing them along the roads without leaving memory of some of them.

Because he loved Inca Urcon's mother so much, when he was very old, Viracocha Inca named Inca Urcon, his bastard son, as successor to the Incaship, departing from the rule for the order of succession. Inca Urcon was valiant and arrogant and contemptuous of others. He thus aroused the anger of the warriors, especially of the legitimate sons, and of Inca Roca, who was the eldest, as well as that of the valiant captains Apu Mayta and Vicaquirao. For this reason, they agreed that he should not succeed to the Incaship, and that they would instead elect one of the other brothers, the most fitting one and one who would treat them well and honorably, as they deserved. Thus they secretly set their eyes on the third legitimate son, named Cusi, who was later called [Pachacuti] Inca Yupanqui, because they knew that he was straightforward and affable and besides this he showed signs of spirit and high ideals. Apu Mayta sought this more forcefully than the others, as he wanted someone to shield him from the fury of Viracocha Inca, who he believed wanted him killed because Apu Mayta had had sexual intercourse with a woman called Cacchon Chicya, a wife of the Inca. Apu Mayta told his companion Vicaquirao of his plan and of his devotion to Cusi. They were seeing how they would arrange this when it came to pass that the Chancas of Andahuaylas — [which is] thirty leagues from Cuzco — came upon Cuzco, as will be recounted in the life of Inca Yupanqui. Viracocha Inca fled Cuzco out of fear of them and went to a town called Caquia Xaquixaguana, where he shut himself away out of fear of the Chancas. He died there some years later, dispossessed of the city of Cuzco, because his son Cusi held it during much of his father's lifetime. Thus Viracocha Inca was the one who conquered the most outside of Cuzco, and we can say that he even tyrannized Cuzco anew, as was said above.

Viracocha Inca lived 119 years. He succeeded at 18, was *capac* 101 years, and died in the year [. . .]¹⁵² of the birth of our Lord. He founded the *ayllu* Sucsu Panaca Ayllu, which he left for the continuation of his lineage, some of whom now live in Cuzco. Their principal leaders are these: Amaru Tito,¹⁵³ Don Francisco Chalco Yupanqui,¹⁵⁴ and Don Francisco Anti Hualpa.¹⁵⁵ They are Hanan Cuzcos.

This Inca was industrious and an inventor of textiles and embroidered work, which they call in their language "Viracochatocapo," which is like brocade among us. He was wealthy because he stole a lot, and he made gold and silver vessels. He was buried in Caquia Xaquixaguana. Gonzalo Pizarro, having heard that a treasure was [buried] with him, searched for it and took out the body, [along] with a large quantity of treasure. He burned the body, but the natives took the ashes anew and hid them in a small earthen jar.¹⁵⁶ Licentiate Polo [de Ondegardo] discovered this jar with its *guauqui* idol called inca amaru while he was chief magistrate of Cuzco.

[26]

THE LIFE OF INCA YUPANQUI, OR PACHACUTI INCA YUPANQUI, THE NINTH INCA

*I*t is said that Viracocha Inca had four legitimate sons during his life. The third was named Cusi and had the title of Inca Yupanqui Inca. For their own reasons, Apu Mayta and Vicaquirao, [who were] famous captains, and the other legitimate sons of Viracocha sought to raise him as Inca against the will of their father. While they were going about putting this [plan] into effect, the passage of time gave them the opportunity to attain their goal — which they had been unable to achieve — with the coming of the Chancas against Cuzco. It happened in this manner.

Thirty leagues to the west of Cuzco is a province called Andahuaylas, whose natives are called Chancas (Figure 26.1). In this province there were two *cinchis*, named Uscovilca and Ancovilca, [who were] thieves and cruel tyrants. They came pillaging with certain bands of thieves from the area of Guamanga.¹⁵⁷ They had come to settle in the Andahuaylas Valley and

FIGURE 26.1. The Andahuaylas Valley, heartland of the Chancas

had formed two groups there. They were brothers, and Uscovilca, who was the eldest and most important, founded one of the groups and called it Hanan Chancas, which means "the upper Chancas." Ancovilca formed the other group and named it Hurin Chanca, which means "the lower Chancas." These *cinchis* were embalmed after they died. Because they were feared for their cruelties while alive, the remaining members of their companies carried the statue of Uscovilca with them in war and on raids. For this reason, although they had with them other *cinchis*, their deeds were always attributed to the statue of Uscovilca, [who was] called by the name Anco Ayllu.

The remaining people and companies of Uscovilca had multiplied greatly by the time of the Incaship of Viracocha Inca. Believing themselves to be so powerful that no one on earth could equal them, they decided to leave Andahuaylas to plunder and conquer Cuzco. To do so, they elected two *cinchis* to lead them in their enterprise and expedition; the first one was called Astoyguaraca, and the other, Tomayguaraca. One [was] from the group of Hanan Chanca, and the other was from Hurin Chanca. These Chancas and *cinchis* were proud and insolent. Leaving Andahuaylas, they marched toward Cuzco and settled in a place called Ichupampa, five leagues to the west of Cuzco, where they remained some days, terrorizing the region and preparing to enter Cuzco (Figure 26.2).

The Cuzco noblemen were so terrified when they learned of this that they made Viracocha Inca, who was inside [the city] and was by then very old and tired, doubt himself. Not sure he could hold Cuzco, he called his sons and captains to council, whereupon Apu Mayta and Vicaquirao told

FIGURE 26.2. The area of Ichupampa, west of Cuzco, played an important role in the legendary attack of the Chancas.

him: "Viracocha Inca! We understand that you are asking us about what you should do at this juncture. After careful consideration, we think that as you are so old and tired from the many labors that you have suffered in past wars, it is not wise for you to now attempt such a large and dangerous deed of so doubtful result as that which now comes before you. Rather, the wisest advice that you can take for your safety is that there is no other solution but to leave Cuzco at once, Lord, and go to the town of Chita,[158] and from there to Caquia Xaquixaguana, which is a fortified site, from where you can come to terms with the Chancas." They say that Apu Mayta and Vicaquirao counseled Viracocha Inca in this way to get him out of Cuzco and to have a good opportunity to put their plan, which was to proclaim Cusi Inca Yupanqui as Inca, into effect without hindrance.

Be that as it may, it is true that Viracocha Inca accepted the advice and that he decided to leave Cuzco for Chita, as had been suggested to him. When Cusi Inca Yupanqui saw his father determined to leave Cuzco, they say that he told him: "How, father? How has it entered your heart to accept such infamous advice as to leave Cuzco, the city of the Sun and of Viracocha, whose name you have taken, and whose promise you have that you shall be a great lord, you and your descendants?" Although a youth, he said this with the daring spirit of a man of much honor. The father replied that Inca Yupanqui was young and, as such, he spoke unknowingly, and that those words should leave this place. Inca Yupanqui replied that Viracocha Inca could go where he wanted, [but] that he would not think of leaving Cuzco or of abandoning the city of the Sun. They say that all of this must have been planned by the captains of Viracocha Inca, Apu Mayta and Vicaquirao, to throw off their guard those who might have been suspicious about Inca Yupanqui staying behind. Thus Viracocha left Cuzco and went to Chita, taking with him Inca Urcon and Inca Sucsu, his two bastard sons. His son Inca Yupanqui remained in Cuzco, determined to defend Cuzco or die [in its defense]. Seven others remained with him. These were: Inca Roca, his legitimate and elder brother; Apu Mayta; Vicaquirao; Quilliscache Urco Guaranga;[159] Chima Chaui Pata Yupanqui; Viracocha Inca Paucar; and Mircoymana, Inca Yupanqui's tutor.

[27]

THE CHANCAS ATTACK CUZCO

*A*t the time that Viracocha Inca was leaving Cuzco, Astoyguaraca and Tomayguaraca departed from Ichupampa, first making their sacrifices and blowing into the lungs of an animal, [a ritual] that they call *calpa*.[160] From what happened to them afterward, [it is clear] that they did not understand this [prophecy] well. Marching toward Cuzco, they arrived at a town called Conchacalla, where they captured an Indian from whom they learned what was happening in Cuzco. He offered to lead them secretly into the city; and so he took them half the way there. But the Indian guide, considering the wickedness he was doing, fled from them and went to warn Cuzco that the Chancas were advancing determinedly. The news provided by this Indian, a Quilliscache from Cuzco, made Viracocha hasten his departure or flight to Chita, where the Chancas sent him their messengers demanding his surrender and threatening him with war if he did not do so. Others say that they did not go as messengers but were disguised as scouts instead. And as they were recognized by Viracocha Inca, he told them that he already knew that they were Chanca spies, that he did not want to kill them, and that they should leave and tell their people that if they wanted something from him, he was there. Thus they left, and some of them fell and died while jumping over a canal. This greatly distressed the Chancas, and they said that they were killed by Quequo Mayta, a captain of the Inca, on the orders of Viracocha Inca.

While this was happening with the Chanca messengers, and while the Chancas were drawing closer to Cuzco, Inca Yupanqui fasted greatly in honor of Viracocha and the Sun, pleading with them to protect his city. And one day when he was in Susurpuquiu,[161] in great pain, reflecting upon how he would face his enemies, a being like the Sun appeared to him in the air, consoling him and calling him to battle. He showed Inca Yupanqui a mirror in which he pointed out the provinces he would conquer, noting that he would be the greatest of all his ancestors, and that he should not doubt and should return to Cuzco, because he would defeat the Chancas who were advancing upon the town. Inca Yupanqui was inspired by these words and vision. Taking the mirror, which he ever after carried with him in war and in peace, he returned to the city and began to encourage those who had remained and some who were coming from afar to watch, not daring to join either side, fearing the fury of the victor if they joined the losing side. But Inca Yupanqui, although he was just a youth of twenty or twenty-two years, provided for everything as one who is planning to fight for his life.

While Inca Yupanqui was involved in this, the Chancas had advanced and reached a place very near Cuzco called Cusibamba, and between this place and Cuzco there is nothing but a lone, small hill (Figure 27.1). There the Chancas again met the Quilliscache, who said he had left to spy and was pleased to meet them. This prevaricator went from one side to the other in order to have them both favor him so as to gain the approval of whoever won. The Chancas advanced from there to enter Cuzco unexpectedly, believing they would find it defenseless. The Quilliscache, saddened by the loss of his fatherland, slipped away from them and went to Cuzco, which was close by, and sounded the alarm, shouting: "To arms! To arms, Inca Yupanqui, for the raging Chancas come!"

Inca Yupanqui, who had not dropped his guard, responded to these cries. Deploying his people, he found very few who wanted to go out with him to resist the enemy, for all were fleeing in fear to the hills to wait and see who would win. But with the few who were willing to follow him, and particularly with the seven *cinchi* brothers and captains named above, Inca Yupanqui formed a small squadron and left the town of Cuzco at a rapid pace to meet the enemy, who was advancing furiously and in disorder. Thus they started drawing closer to one another, the Chancas assaulting the city on four sides. Inca Yupanqui sent the forces that he could to all the [assailed points], while with his friends he headed straight toward the advancing statue and banner of Uscovilca, where Astoyguaraca and Tomayguaraca

FIGURE 27.1. The Chancas are said to have arrived at this small hill, just outside Cuzco.

were. There was a bloody battle between them, one side endeavoring to enter the city and the other to defend its entrance. Those who entered through a neighborhood of Cuzco called Choco and Cachona[162] were valiantly repelled by the people of that neighborhood, where they say that a woman named Chañan Curicoca fought like a man. She fought so hard in hand-to-hand combat against the Chancas who had charged there that she made them retreat. This disheartened all the Chancas who saw it.

Inca Yupanqui was so swift and skilled in his attack that those who carried the statue of Uscovilca were alarmed by his speed and prowess. The Chancas started to flee, leaving the statue of Uscovilca, and they say even that of Ancovilca, because they saw a large number of people come down from the sides of the hills, who it is said were sent by Viracocha, their Creator, to help [the Inca].[163] Charging on two other sides, Inca Roca and Apu Mayta and Vicaquirao inflicted much damage on the Chancas. Seeing that their salvation lay in their feet, the Chancas retreated at an even faster pace than the fury that had brought them to Cuzco. The Cuzcos continued the chase, killing and wounding for more than two leagues until they halted the pursuit. The Chancas returned to Ichupampa and the noblemen to Cuzco with a great victory and enriched by the spoils that the victory had given them (Figure 27.2). The Cuzcos rejoiced at this success, which they had

FIGURE 27.2. The Cuzco Valley as seen from the northwest. (Servicio Aerofoto-gráfico Nacional, Perú, 1964:negative 21366.)

obtained without expectation or hope. They honored Inca Yupanqui with many names, especially calling [him] Pachacuti, which means "returner of the land," alluding to the land and estates he had freed and secured for them, which they had thought lost with the coming of the Chancas. From then on he was called Pachacuti Inca Yupanqui.

Finding himself victorious, Pachacuti Inca Yupanqui had no desire to celebrate his triumph, although many urged him to do so. Instead, he wanted to give his father the glory of such a great victory. So he gathered the most precious spoils and sent them with a principal nobleman named Quillis-cache Urco Guaranga to his father, who was in Chita. Pachacuti sent him to beg that [his father] celebrate the triumph and tread on the spoils of their enemy. They did this as a sign of victory.[164] When Quilliscache Urco Gua-ranga arrived before Viracocha Inca, he placed the spoils [taken] from the Chancas at his feet and with great reverence said: "Viracocha Inca! Your son Pachacuti Inca Yupanqui, to whom the Sun has given such a great vic-tory over the powerful Chancas, sends his greetings through me and says that, as a good and humble son, he wishes you to celebrate his victory and to tread upon the spoils of your enemy, whom he defeated with his hands."

Viracocha Inca did not want to tread on them and said that his son Inca Urcon should do so, since he was to succeed him in the Incaship. Flustered, the messenger rose and with angry words said that he had not come so that cowards could triumph from the deeds of Pachacuti. So if he did not want to receive this service from such a valiant son of his, it would be best that he who had earned the glory should enjoy it.[165] With this he returned to Cuzco and told Pachacuti what had happened with his father.

[28]

THE SECOND VICTORY THAT PACHACUTI INCA YUPANQUI HAD OVER THE CHANCAS

*W*hile Pachacuti Inca Yupanqui sent the spoils to his father, the Chancas had time to reorganize their men and weapons in the plain of Ichupampa, from where they had departed for Cuzco the first time. The *cinchis* Tomayguaraca and Astoyguaraca began to boast that they would return to Cuzco and would leave nothing standing. News of this reached Pachacuti Inca Yupanqui. He was furious and, preparing his men, went with them to search for the Chancas. Knowing that the Cuzcos were coming, the Chancas readied themselves to meet Pachacuti. But they were not quick enough, and the army of Pachacuti Inca Yupanqui met them [while they were] still on the plain of Ichupampa.

When they came within sight of one another, Astoyguaraca, full of arrogance, sent word to Inca Yupanqui telling him to behold the power of the Chancas and that the place they now defended was not like the narrow area in Cuzco. Thus, he should not be overconfident because of the previous [battle] and should become Astoyguaraca's tributary and vassal. If not, he would soon dye his spear with the Inca's blood. But Inca Yupanqui was not frightened by Astoyguaraca's message and replied in this way to the messenger: "Go back, brother, and tell Astoyguaraca, your *cinchi*, that Inca Yupanqui is the son of the Sun and guardian of Cuzco, the city of Ticci Viracocha Pachayachachi, by whose orders I am here guarding it. For this city is not mine, but his. And if your *cinchi* wants to give his obedience to Ticci Viracocha and to me in his name, I will receive him honorably. And if Astoyguaraca sees things otherwise, lead him here where I am with my companions. If he defeats us, he can call himself lord and Inca. But he must

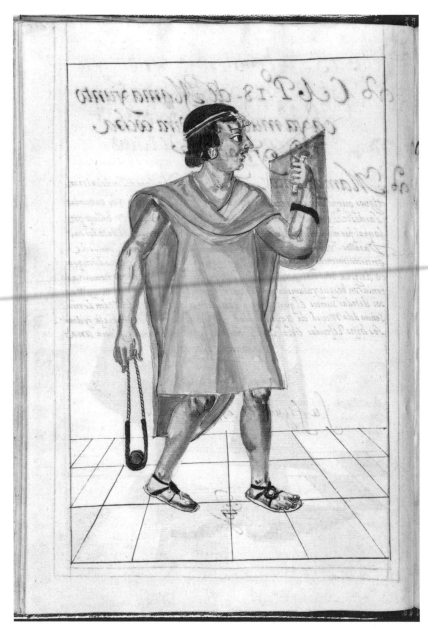

FIGURE 28.1. Inca Yupanqui as a young man, by Martín de Murúa [1590:f. 38v]. (Courtesy of The J. Getty Museum, Los Angeles, copyright © The J. Paul Getty Museum.)

understand that I did not come here to waste time in demands and replies, but to fight hand-to-hand, since Ticci Viracocha will give the victory to whomever he wishes."

With this answer the Chancas realized how little they had gained from their threats, and they readied their weapons because they saw Pachacuti, who closely followed the [messenger] bearing his reply. Thus, approaching one another in Ichupampa, they charged and fought with one another, the Chancas thrusting their long spears, the Incas [fighting] with slings, clubs, axes, and arrows, each one trying to defend himself and to attack his opponent. As the battle hung in the balance without either side gaining an advantage, Pachacuti, who had already killed Tomayguaraca, moved to where Astoyguaraca was fighting. Charging him, he hit him with the stroke of an ax, which cut off his head. He then had the heads of these two Chanca captains placed on spears and hoisted up high so their own men would see them. Once they saw the heads, the Chancas doubted they could win without leaders, and all left the field and tried to flee. But Inca Yupanqui and his men continued the chase, wounding and killing until there was no one left.[166]

Having won this great victory, so rich and plentiful in spoils, Pachacuti Inca Yupanqui proposed to go to his father to give him an account of the events and victories and to show his obedience so that Viracocha might celebrate his [son's] victory. Thus, loaded with all the spoils and Chanca prisoners, he went to visit his father. Some say that Viracocha Inca was in a town called Caquia Xaquixaguana, four leagues from Cuzco; others, that [he was] in Marco,[167] three leagues from Cuzco. There, where he found him, Pachacuti made a great obeisance and gave gifts, which they call *mochanaco*. After telling his father the story, Pachacuti Inca ordered the spoils of the enemies to be placed before his father's feet and pleaded with him to tread on them and celebrate the victory. But Viracocha Inca, still determined to leave Inca Urcon as his successor, wanted the honor that was offered to him to be enjoyed by Inca Urcon. Thus he did not want to accept the triumph for himself. But to avoid displeasing Inca Yupanqui, who had put him in such a sublime position, he said that he would tread on the spoils and prisoners and then did so. And as for going in triumph to Cuzco, he excused himself by saying that he was old and therefore wanted to excuse himself [from this task], as he desired to rest in Caquia Xaquixaguana.

With this answer Inca Yupanqui left for Cuzco with a great display of people and riches, and Inca Urcon came with him as though he was accompanying him. On the way, a quarrel broke out in the rearguard between the people of Inca Urcon and those of Inca Yupanqui. Others say that this was an ambush that Inca Urcon had laid for his brother Inca Yupanqui, and that they fought. In the end, Inca Yupanqui took no notice of it and continued his journey, reaching Cuzco amidst much applause and celebration. Then he began to distribute the spoils and give out many rewards in gifts and praise as if he thought he would assume control over the whole land and take away the esteem of the people from his father, as he later did. With the fame of these great deeds, people came to Cuzco from many places, and many of those who were in Caquia Xaquixaguana with Viracocha Inca left him and went to Cuzco to the new Inca.

[29]

INCA YUPANQUI INCA RAISES HIMSELF AS INCA AND TAKES THE TASSEL WITHOUT THE CONSENT OF HIS FATHER

*W*hen Inca Yupanqui saw that he was so strong and that many people were flocking to him, he decided not to wait until his father appointed him as successor or at least until he died; before long, he rebelled with the people of Cuzco, proposing to attack outside the city. To do this, Inca Yupanqui ordered a great sacrifice made to the Sun in Inticancha, the House of the Sun. Then they went to ask the statue of the Sun who would be Inca. The oracle of the demon that they had there, or perhaps some Indian whom they had hidden there to respond, answered that he had chosen Pachacuti Inca Yupanqui to be Inca. All who had gone to make the sacrifice returned with this answer, and they prostrated themselves before Pachacuti Inca Yupanqui, calling him *capa inca intip churin*, which means "sole lord, son of the Sun."

Then they made a very rich tassel of gold and emeralds to place on him. The next day they took Pachacuti Inca Yupanqui to the House of the Sun. When they reached the statue of the Sun, which was the size of a man and made of gold, they found it with the tassel in its hand, as if it was offering it of its own will. First carrying out his sacrifices, as they usually do, Inca Yupanqui then approached the statue of the Sun. Then the high priest of the Sun, who is called *intip apon* in their language, which means "the governor of the things of the sun," took the tassel from the hand of the statue with many ceremonies and great reverence, and with much pomp he placed it on the forehead of Pachacuti Inca Yupanqui. Then they all called him *intip churin Inca Pachacuti*, which translates as "son of the Sun, Lord, Turner of the Earth." From then on he was called Pachacuti Capac in addition to his first name, which was Inca Yupanqui. Then Pachacuti Inca Yupanqui gave many gifts and held many festivities. He ruled as the sole Inca without having been elected by his father or the people, except for those who followed him because of the gifts he gave.

[30]

PACHACUTI INCA YUPANQUI REBUILDS
THE CITY OF CUZCO

After the festivities ended, [Pachacuti Inca Yupanqui] laid out the town on a better plan than it had had before. He designed the main streets to be as they were when the Spaniards entered Cuzco. And he distributed lots for community and public and private houses, ordering them built of very fine masonry. This [masonry] is such that those of us who have seen it and know that they do not have iron or steel tools to work with, are awed upon seeing the evenness and beauty of it. And the joints and bitumen with which they join the stones are so thin that nowhere can you see if there is any mortar. Even then it is such a strong binder that lead could not join it closer. The coarse stone is an even greater sight to see because of its bonding and structure. And since only seeing it satisfies the curious, I do not want to waste time in describing it more extensively.

In addition to this, Pachacuti Inca Yupanqui, considering the limited lands that were around Cuzco for planting, supplied with skill what nature denied this place. On the slopes near the town, and on other parts as well, he made some very long steps of about two thousand paces and of more or less twenty or thirty paces wide, the fronts built of cut-stone work. He filled them with earth, much of which was brought from far away. Here we call these steps terraces and the Indians call them *sucres*. He ordered these to be sown, and with these he greatly increased the number of fields and the supplies for the companies and garrisons of the town.

So that the time for sowing and harvesting would be known precisely and would never be missed, he had four poles placed on a high mountain to the east of Cuzco, separated from one another by [a distance of] about two staffs. At the top of each pole [were] some holes through which the sun would pass like a clock or astrolabe. He made marks on the ground after observing where the sun fell through those holes at the time of plowing and sowing. He placed other poles in the area that lies to the west of Cuzco [to mark] the time to harvest the crops. When he had these poles accurately marked, he built some permanent stone columns of the same size in their place and [with the same] holes. He ordered the ground paved all around, and he engraved certain even lines in the flagstones according to the movements of the sun, which entered through the holes in the columns in such a way that it worked as an annual clock by which the sowing and harvesting were managed. Pachacuti appointed men to watch these clocks and to notify the people of the times and the differences that the clocks indicated.[168]

Then, since he was curious to know about ancient things and wanted to perpetuate his name, he personally went to the hill of Tambotoco or Pacariqtambo, which is the same thing, and entered the cave from where they claim that Manco Capac and the siblings who came with him the first time to Cuzco emerged, as has already been told.[169] After having seen and thoroughly considered all this, he made an offering to that place with festivities and sacrifices. He made gold doors for the Capactoco window and ordered that from then on that place should be greatly worshiped and revered by all. For this he established it as a shrine and *huaca*, where they would go to request oracles and to offer sacrifices.

This done, Pachacuti returned to Cuzco, where he ordered a twelve-month year, almost like ours. I say almost, because there are some differences, although few, as I will describe in their place.

Then he held a general assembly of the oldest and wisest men from Cuzco and from other places, and with much diligence inquired into and investigated the histories of the antiquities of this land, particularly that of the Incas, his ancestors. He had [the history] painted and ordered that it be preserved, as I explained when I spoke of the method used in preparing this history [chapter 9].

[31]

PACHACUTI INCA YUPANQUI REBUILDS
THE HOUSE OF THE SUN AND
ESTABLISHES NEW IDOLS IN IT

*H*aving adorned the town of Cuzco with buildings, streets, and the other mentioned things, Pachacuti Inca Yupanqui realized that none of his Inca ancestors after Manco Capac had added anything to the House of the Sun. He therefore decided to embellish it with buildings and oracles to frighten the ignorant people and fool them into blindly following him so that with them [he could] carry out the conquest of all the land that he thought of tyrannizing, which he began and accomplished to a great extent. For this he disinterred the bodies of the past seven Incas, from Manco Capac to Yahuar Huacac Inca, all of whom were in the House of the Sun. He embellished them with gold, placing masks on them, [as well as] headdresses that they call *chucos*, bangles, bracelets, scepters that they call *yauris* or *chambis*, and other gold adornments. Next he placed them on a richly worked gold bench in order of antiquity. He then ordered that great festivities and pageants of the life of each Inca be held. These festivities, which they called *purucaya*, lasted for more than four months. He offered great and sumptuous sacrifices to the body of each Inca at the completion of the pageant of his deeds and life. With this, Pachacuti endowed them with such authority that he made them be worshiped and held as gods by all the foreigners who came to see them. When these visitors saw them with such majesty, they would immediately humble themselves and place their hands on them to worship them or, as they say, *mochaban*. They were held in great respect and veneration, and so they remained until the Spaniards came to this land of Peru.

Besides these bodies, [Pachacuti] made two gold idols. One he named Viracocha Pachayachachi to represent [the deity] they call their Creator. He placed it at the right hand of the idol of the Sun. The other he named Chuquiylla to represent lightning. He placed it at the left hand of the figure of the Sun. Everyone highly venerated this idol [of lighting]. Inca Yupanqui took this idol as [his] *guauqui* idol, because he said that they had met and spoken with each other in a remote place.[170] And [he said] this idol had given him a two-headed serpent so that he could always carry it with him, saying that while he carried it nothing bad would happen in his affairs. Pachacuti

FIGURE 31.1. The church of Santo Domingo stands above the principal Inca temple to the Sun in Cuzco. (Courtesy of Library of Congress, Photograph number 2424: gift of Carroll Greenough, pre-1950.)

endowed these idols with income from lands, livestock, and servants, and especially with some women who lived like nuns in the same House of the Sun.[171] These all came in as maidens, and few remained who did not give birth [to a child] of the Inca. At the [very] least he was so depraved in this regard that they say he had intercourse with all those he liked and had access to. And because of this he had many sons, as is told of him.

In addition to this house, there were some *huacas* in the area surrounding the town. These were the *huacas* of Huanacauri, Anaguarqui, Yauira, Sinca, Picol, and another one that was called Pachatopan.[172] At many of these they would make the accursed sacrifices that they called *capac cocha*, which is to bury five- or six-year-old children alive and offer them to the devil, accompanied by many servants and gold and silver vessels.

They say that, above all, Pachacuti made a thick wool rope of many colors and plaited with gold, with two red tassels at each end. They say it was 150 fathoms long, more or less. It was used in their public festivities, of which there were four principal ones a year. The first was called *raymi* or *capac raymi*, which was when the knights had their ears pierced, which they call *guarachico*.[173] The second one was called *situay*, which was similar to our feast of St. John, in which they would all rise at midnight with torches and go to bathe, saying that in this way they would be cleansed of all illness.[174] The third was called *inti raymi*; it was the festival of the Sun, which was called *aymoray*.[175] In these festivities, they would take the rope from the House or storehouse of the Sun, and all the principal Indians, splendidly dressed, would take hold of it in [hierarchical] order. Thus they would come singing from the House of the Sun to the plaza, and they would completely encircle it with the rope, which was called *moroy urco*.[176]

[32]

PACHACUTI INCA YUPANQUI DEPOPULATES [THE AREA] TWO LEAGUES AROUND CUZCO

*A*fter Pachacuti did the above-described [things] in the city, he looked at the size of the town and the people that were in it. Seeing that there was not enough agricultural land for them to sustain themselves, he left the city

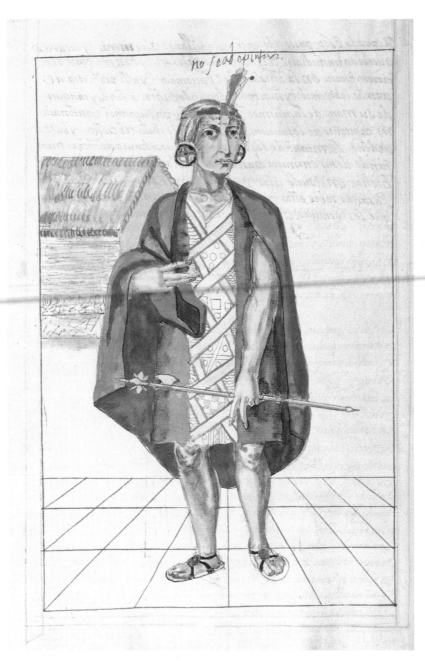

FIGURE 32.1. Inca Yupanqui, by Martín de Murúa [1590:f. 40v]. (Courtesy of The J. Getty Museum, Los Angeles, copyright © The J. Paul Getty Museum.)

and traveled through a four-league [area] surrounding Cuzco (Figure 32.1). After considering [all] the places, valleys, and settlements, he depopulated all the towns that were within two leagues of the city. He assigned the lands of the towns that he depopulated to Cuzco and its inhabitants, and he sent those that he removed to other places. With this he greatly satisfied the citizens of Cuzco, because he gave them something that cost them little. Thus he made friends by [giving them] the estates of others. He took the [Ollantay]tambo Valley, which was not his, for himself.

The news of the enlargement of the city traveled to all parts, and when it reached the ears of Viracocha Inca, who was retired in Caquia Xaquixaguana, he decided to go see Cuzco. Thus, his son Inca Yupanqui went for him and brought him to Cuzco with much rejoicing. Viracocha went to the House of the Sun and worshiped Huanacauri, and they showed him all the rest that had been enlarged and renovated in the city. Having seen the city, Viracocha returned once again to his dwelling in Caquia Xaquixaguana, where he stayed until he died. He never again returned to Cuzco or saw his son Pachacuti Inca Yupanqui.

[33]

PACHACUTI INCA YUPANQUI KILLS HIS OLDER BROTHER NAMED INCA URCON

*W*hen Pachacuti Inca Yupanqui saw that he was so powerful with all the companies that had allied themselves with him because of the largesse he showed to them, he planned to use them to subjugate all the lands that he could. For this he mustered all of his men who were in Cuzco and prepared them with the weapons and implements necessary for war. At this point, he heard that his brother Inca Urcon was four leagues away from Cuzco in the valley that they call Yucay, and that he had mustered some people. Fearing that [Inca Urcon] had done so against him, [Pachacuti] went there with his men. His brother Inca Roca, who they say was a great necromancer, went with him. When Inca Yupanqui reached the town of Paca,[177] in the Yucay Valley, his brother Inca Urcon came out against him with warriors, and they clashed in a battle during which Inca Roca hurled a stone at the throat of Inca Urcon. The blow was so strong that it knocked Inca Urcon into the river of the ravine where they fought. With great effort, Inca Urcon fled, swimming downriver with his battle-axe in his hand. In this way he arrived at a boulder called Chupellusca,[178] one league below [Ollantay]tambo, where his brothers overtook him and killed him.

From there Inca Yupanqui and Inca Roca traveled with their men to Caquia Xaquixaguana to see their father, but because [Viracocha Inca] was angry at them for the death of Inca Urcon, he never wanted to see or talk to them. But Inca Roca entered where Viracocha Inca was and told him: "Father! There is no reason for you to grieve so much for the death of Inca Urcon, for I killed him in self-defense, because Inca Urcon was going to kill me. Do not be so upset about the death of one son, since you have so many. Do not dwell on it anymore, for my brother Inca Yupanqui is to be Inca, and I have to help him and be like his father." Seeing the determination of his son Inca Roca, Viracocha Inca dared not reply or contradict him. He dismissed him, telling him that since that was what he wanted, he should do whatever he wished. With this, Inca Yupanqui and Inca Roca returned to Cuzco, and they entered the city, celebrating this victory and past ones.

The celebration was in this manner: The warriors marched in order of their squadrons, dressed in their best regalia, with many dances and songs. And the imprisoned captives, their eyes on the ground, were dressed in long robes with many tassels.[179] They paraded through the streets of the town, which were very well prepared for this. They went on, reenacting the victories and battles they had won. On arriving at the House of the Sun, they would cast the spoils and prisoners on the ground, and the Inca would walk on them, treading on them and saying: "I tread on my enemies." The prisoners were silent without raising their eyes. All their victory celebrations were performed in this way. After a while, Viracocha Inca died of anger at the death of Inca Urcon, deprived and stripped of all honor and property. They buried his body in Caquia Xaquixaguana.

[34]

THE NATIONS THAT PACHACUTI INCA DESTROYED AND THE TOWNS HE ATTACKED; FIRST, TOCAY CAPAC, THE *CINCHI* OF THE AYARMACAS, AND [THEN THE] DESTRUCTION OF THE CUYOS

*N*ear the Cuzco Valley is a nation of Indians called Ayarmacas, who had a proud and wealthy *cinchi* named Tocay Capac.[180] Neither he nor the Ayarmacas wanted to pay reverence to the Inca. Instead, they sought to ready their weapons against the Cuzcos, should they decide to turn against them. Knowing this, Inca Yupanqui called an assembly of his people and *ayllus*, and he formed the groups that they afterward called Hanan Cuzcos and Hurin Cuzcos. He combined them into one body so that once together no one could or would fight against them. This done, they discussed what they must do. They decided to join together and leave to conquer all the nations of the kingdom, and those who did not give in to them or serve them of their own free will they would utterly destroy. And [they decided] that before anything else they should go against Tocay Capac, the *cinchi* of the Ayarmacas, who was powerful and had not come to pay homage to Cuzco. And with the warriors thus gathered, they went against the Ayarmacas and their *cinchi*, and they fought each other in Guanancancha.[181] Inca Yupanqui defeated them, and he destroyed the towns and killed almost all of the Ayarmacas. He brought Tocay Capac as a captive to Cuzco and kept him in prison until his death.

After this Inca Yupanqui took as his wife Mama Anaguarqui, a native of Choco (Figure 34.1). To amuse himself and to relax somewhere away from his affairs, he went to the town of the Cuyos, capital of the province of Cuyosuyu. One day, while at a great festivity, a potter, the servant of a *cinchi*, for no apparent reason, hit and injured Inca Yupanqui on the head with a stone or, as others say, with a pot that they call *ulti*. The delinquent, who was a stranger to that nation, was imprisoned and tortured so that he would tell who had sent him. He confessed that all of the *cinchis* of Cuyosuyu, who were Cuyo Capac, Ayanquilalama, and Apu Cunaraqui, had conspired to kill Inca Yupanqui and rebel.[182] This was actually untrue, because he had confessed so out of fear of torture or, as others say, because he belonged to

FIGURE 34.1. Mama Anaguarqui, by Martín de Murúa [1590:f. 46v]. (Courtesy of The J. Getty Museum, Los Angeles, copyright © The J. Paul Getty Museum.)

an enemy nation of the Cuyos and he said this to harm them.[183] But when Inca Pachacuti heard what the potter said, he immediately ordered all the *cinchis* killed with great cruelty. After their deaths, he turned on the community and left no one alive except for some children and old women. Thus that nation was destroyed, and its towns remain ravaged even today.

[35]

THE OTHER NATIONS THAT INCA YUPANQUI CONQUERED BY HIMSELF AND WITH INCA ROCA

*W*hen Inca Yupanqui, his brother Inca Roca (who was very cruel), and their people decided to oppress and subjugate all those who wanted to be their equal and would not give them obedience, they learned that [there] were two *cinchis* in a town called Ollantaytambo (Figure 35.1), six leagues from Cuzco. The first one was named Paucar Ancho and the other, Tocori Topa. They prevented the Ollantaytambos from giving obedience [to the Inca], nor did they want to do so. The Inca went against them with many men and fought them. Inca Roca was badly wounded, but, in the end, the Ollantaytambos were defeated. Inca Yupanqui killed them all, burned the town, and destroyed it so that no memory was left of it, and he returned to Cuzco.

There was another *cinchi*, named Illacumbi, [who was the] *cinchi* of two towns four leagues away from Cuzco, one called Socma and the other Huata (Figure 35.2). Inca Yupanqui and Inca Roca sent [a message] to this *cinchi* telling him to come and pay homage. He replied that he was as noble as they were and was free, and that if they wanted something, they should decide it with their spears. Because of this answer, they took up arms against that *cinchi*. Illacumbi and two other *cinchis* [who were] his companions, named Paucar Topa and Poma Lloqui, gathered their men and left to fight with the Inca. But they were defeated and killed, along with almost all of their men. [Inca Yupanqui] destroyed all of that settlement by fire and sword with many great cruelties. From there he returned to Cuzco and celebrated this victory.

The Incas now learned that in a town called Guancara, eleven leagues

FIGURE 35.1. The town of Ollantaytambo

from Cuzco, there were two *cinchis*, one named Ascascaguana and the other Urcocona. The Inca had them summoned so that they would revere and obey him and pay him tribute. They answered that they were not women to come and serve him, that they were in their homeland, and that if anyone came looking for them, they would defend their land. Angered by this, Inca Yupanqui and Inca Roca waged war against them and killed the *cinchis* and many of the commoners. And seizing the rest, they brought them captive to Cuzco to force them to give them obedience there.

The Incas now marched against another town called Toguaro, six leagues from Guancara, and killed their *cinchi*, who was named Alcapariguana. [They killed] all the natives of the town, not sparing any except the children so that they would grow up and populate it anew. Through the cruelties that [Inca Yupanqui] committed in all the nations, he made the Cotabambas, Cotaneras, Omasuyus, and Aymaraes—the principal provinces of Chinchaysuyu—pay him tribute.

Moving toward the Soras, forty leagues from Cuzco, the natives came forth to resist them, asking [Inca Yupanqui] what he was searching for in their lands, [and telling him] that he should immediately leave them or they would expel him by force. And a battle was fought over this, and at this time, Inca Yupanqui subjugated two towns of the Soras. The first [was] called Chalco and the other one Soras. The *cinchi* of Chalco was named Puxayco, and that of Soras was Guacralla. Inca Yupanqui brought them captive to Cuzco and celebrated his victory over them.

There was another town called Acos that is ten or eleven[184] leagues from Cuzco. There were two *cinchis* in this town. The first one was named Ocaciqui and the other one Otoguasi. These [cinchis] were very openly opposed to the demands of the Inca, and they strongly resisted him. Inca Yupanqui therefore went against them with great force. But in this conquest the Inca found himself in dire straits, because the people of Acos defended themselves most bravely and wounded Pachacuti in the head with a stone.[185] As a result, the Inca did not want to end the war until, having battled them for a long time, he finally vanquished them. He killed almost all the natives of Acos. He pardoned those who survived that cruel slaughter, and he banished them to the area of Guamanga, which they now call Acos.

In all the conquests that have thus far been described, Inca Roca accompanied Inca Yupanqui in his wars, and he triumphed over all these nations. And it is to be noted that in all the provinces that Inca Yupanqui subjugated, he himself would appoint chiefs, removing the *cinchis* or killing them. Those whom he appointed functioned as guards or captains of that town, holding it in his name at his pleasure. In this manner he oppressed and tyrannized the [people], placing them under the yoke of servitude. In each province he appointed one person, superior to all the other leaders he had

FIGURE 35.2. Huata is a well-known fortified site in the Cuzco region.

appointed in the towns, to act as general or governor of that province. These are called *tucurico* in the language of this land, which means "he who sees and understands all."

Thus the first time that Pachacuti Inca Yupanqui took up arms to conquer, following the defeat of the Chancas, he conquered as far as the Soras, forty leagues west of Cuzco. Out of fear of the cruelties that he committed, the other nations mentioned and some others in Cuntisuyu came to serve him so that he would not destroy them. But they never served him of their own will.

[36]

PACHACUTI INCA YUPANQUI ENDOWS THE HOUSE OF THE SUN WITH GREAT WEALTH

After Pachacuti Inca Yupanqui conquered the above-mentioned lands and nations and triumphed over them, he entered the House of the Sun to visit it and its *mamaconas*, or nuns. He went one day to see how the *mamaconas* served food to the Sun. They offered many cooked delicacies to the statue or idol of the Sun and would then throw them into a great fire in front of it, which they had in a brazier used as an altar.[186] Beverages [were offered] in this same way. After the chief of the *mamaconas* toasted the Sun with a very small vessel, she would throw the rest into the fire. They would then pour many jugs of that brew into a basin that had a drain, dedicating all of it to the Sun.[187] This service was performed with clay vessels. Since Pachacuti believed the vessels were of poor quality, he provided the appropriate service of silver and gold that was needed. To further adorn the house, he ordered a band of fine gold made, two hands wide and as long as the courtyard. He had it nailed high up on the wall like a cornice so that it surrounded the entire courtyard. This band or cornice of gold was there until the time of the Spaniards.

[37]

PACHACUTI INCA YUPANQUI CONQUERS
THE PROVINCE OF COLLASUYU

To the south of Cuzco is a province called Collasuyu or Collao, a densely populated flat land. Here, at the same time that Pachacuti Inca Yupanqui was in Cuzco after having conquered the above-mentioned provinces, there was a *cinchi* named Chuchic Capac or Colla Capac, who is the same person. This Chuchic Capac grew so great in power and wealth with the Collasuyu nations that he was respected by all the Collas. As a result, he had himself called Inca Capac.[188]

Jealous of this, Pachacuti Inca Yupanqui decided to vanquish him and conquer all the provinces of Collao. To do this, he mustered his warriors and marched toward the Collao in search of Chuchic Capac, who awaited him in Hatuncolla—a town in the Collao where he had his home, forty leagues from Cuzco—and who was not paying attention to the movements of Inca Yupanqui or his preparations. When he was near Hatuncolla, Pachacuti Inca Yupanqui sent his messengers to Chuchic Capac, demanding that he serve and obey him, or else he should prepare himself for the next day when they would meet in battle and would try their fortunes. This message caused Chuchic Capac much grief, and he answered Pachacuti Inca Yupanqui soberly, saying that he had been rejoicing that the Inca had come to give him obedience like the other nations that he had conquered; but if this was not his intention, then let his head be prepared, for [Chuchic Capac] planned to drink from it in celebration of the victory that would be his if they met in battle.[189]

With this answer, Inca Yupanqui ordered his men [to fight] the next day, and they drew near to Chuchic Capac, who was waiting for him with his own men ready to fight. After they came within sight, they charged one another and fought the battle for a long time without either side gaining an advantage. Inca Yupanqui, as he was very skilled in fighting, was moving about everywhere, fighting and giving orders and encouraging his people. Seeing that the Collas resisted him and lasted so long in battle, he turned to face his own men and in a loud voice shamed them, saying: "Oh Incas of Cuzco! Victors of all the land! Are you not ashamed that a people so beneath you, and so unequal in weapons, proves such a match for you and resists you for so long?" And with this he returned to fight, and his own men, shamed by this reprimand, pressed upon their enemies with such skill that they broke and destroyed them. But being a great warrior, Inca Yupanqui knew that winning the battle required capturing Chuchic Capac. So although he was fighting, he was looking for him everywhere. Seeing him in the midst of his people, Inca Yupanqui charged with his guard and captured Chuchic Capac. He turned him over to [a soldier] to take him to the camp and guard him. With the rest [of his men], he finished winning the battle and continued the pursuit until he had seized all the leaders and *cinchi* captains who had been in the battle. Pachacuti went to Hatuncolla, the seat and home of Chuchic Capac, where he stayed until all the towns that obeyed Chuchic Capac came to obey him and brought him many rich gifts of gold and silver and clothes and other precious items.

Leaving a garrison and governor in his name to guard Collasuyu for him, Pachacuti returned to Cuzco, bringing Chuchic Capac captive as well as the other prisoners, with whom he entered Cuzco triumphantly. There, a most solemn victory celebration was prepared for him. During this he placed Chuchic Capac and the other Colla prisoners in front of his litter to dishonor them. They were dressed in long closed robes and covered with tassels so that they would be recognized. On arriving at the House of the Sun, he offered the captives and spoils to the Sun. The Sun—I mean his statue or the head priest—trod on all the spoils and prisoners that Pachacuti had won from the Collas, which was a great honor for the Inca. When the victory celebration was over, to properly conclude it, he had Chuchic Capac's head cut off and placed in the house called Llaxaguasi with those he had there of the other *cinchis* he had killed.[190] He had Chuchic Capac's other *cinchi* captains thrown to the beasts that he had locked up for this purpose in a house called Sancaguaci.[191]

Pachacuti was very cruel to the defeated in these victories. Because of these cruelties, he had the people so scared that those who could not resist him through force surrendered and obeyed him out of fear of being eaten by the beasts or burned or cruelly tortured. So it was with those of Cuntisuyu, who, on seeing the cruelties and power of Inca Yupanqui, humbled themselves and gave him obedience. It is to be noted that although some provinces say that they gave themselves to him and obeyed him of their own free will, it was [really] because of the above-mentioned causes and reasons and because he would threaten to destroy them if they did not come to serve and obey him.

Chuchic Capac had oppressed and subjugated [a region] more than 160 leagues from north to south. He was the *cinchi* or, as he named himself, "*capac*" or "*colla capac*" of an area from 20 leagues from Cuzco to the Chichas, including the area of Arequipa and along the coast to Atacama and the forests[192] above the Mojos. Because by this time, seeing the violence and power that the Inca of Cuzco inflicted upon all nations everywhere, without pardoning anyone, many *cinchis* would have liked to [follow this path and] do the same themselves in their own regions. So this kingdom was full of confused tyrannical tribes where no one trusted his own neighbor even in his own village. Thus, we will discuss in their places, when they present themselves, the tyrannical *cinchis*, aside from the Incas, who from the time of Inca Yupanqui began to seize some provinces, tyrannizing them.

As was mentioned above, Inca Yupanqui had endowed the House of the Sun with the things necessary for its service. Besides this, after returning from Collasuyu, he gave many of the things he had brought from there for the service and the House of the Sun and for the mummies of his ancestors that were there. And he gave them servants and estates. He ordered all the lands he conquered to recognize and venerate the above-named *huacas* of Cuzco, giving them new ceremonies for venerating them and abolishing their ancient rites. He gave Amaru Topa Inca,[193] an older legitimate son of his, the duty of inspecting the *huacas*, idols, and shrines so that he would abolish those they did not think were authentic and [see that] the others were maintained and received the sacrifices that the Inca ordered.[194] Huayna Yamqui Yupanqui, a son of Inca Yupanqui, was also in charge of this business.

[38]

PACHACUTI INCA YUPANQUI SENDS [CAPAC YUPANQUI] TO CONQUER THE PROVINCES OF CHINCHAYSUYU

When Pachacuti Inca Yupanqui returned from the conquest of Collasuyu and the neighboring provinces, as is mentioned in the preceding chapter, he was already old, though he was not yet tired of war nor had he quenched his thirst for tyrannizing the world. Because of his old age, he wanted to remain in Cuzco permanently to organize the lands he had conquered, which he knew how to do well. So as not to lose time, he ordered the warriors to assemble, and from that group they say he chose about 70,000 men. He provided them with weapons and necessary things for the

campaign and appointed his brother Capac Yupanqui as captain-general of
them all. Inca Yupanqui gave him as companions another of his brothers,
named Huayna Yupanqui, and one of his sons, named Apu Yamqui Yupanqui. Among the other individual captains who were in the army was one
from the Chanca nation named Anco Ayllu, who had been imprisoned in
Cuzco since the time when the Inca had defeated the Chancas in Cuzco and
Ichupampa. He always went about sad and, so they say, imagining how to
free himself. But he concealed this in such a way that the Cuzcos now held
him to be a brother and trusted him. This being so, the Inca appointed him
as captain of the Chanca people who were in the army, since the Inca gave
each nation a captain of their native land, because he would know how to
organize them best according to their customs and they would obey him
better. Anco Ayllu, seeing that an opportunity to attain his wish was offered
to him, expressed happiness at what the Inca entrusted him with and promised that, as a man who was familiar with the nations that they were going
to conquer, he would render the Inca great services. Once the army was
ready to march, the Inca gave the captain-general and the rest of the captains
who served him his gold weapons, with which they would enter into combat. He spoke to them, encouraging them in the task at hand and showing
them the honor they would win and the rewards that he would give them
if they served him as allies in that war. He expressly ordered Capac Yupanqui to go with those men to conquer as far as a province called Yanamayo,
bordering the nation of the Hatunguayllas, and that he should place the
Inca's boundary markers there. On no account should he press ahead. Instead, having conquered that far, Capac Yupanqui should return to Cuzco,
leaving enough garrisons to [hold] those lands. Along the roads, he should
establish runners, which they call *chasquis,* every half league; each day Capac Yupanqui was to report through them what was happening and what
he was doing.

   With this mission and order, Capac Yupanqui left Cuzco and went about
destroying all the provinces that did not surrender to him of their own will.
Upon reaching a fortress called Urcocolla, near Parcos in the area of Guamanga, he was valiantly resisted by the natives of that region. In the end
he defeated them. In the hand-to-hand battle, the Chancas distinguished
and surpassed themselves in a way that gained them more honors than the
Cuzco noblemen and the other nations.

   News of this reached the Inca, who was very distressed that the Chancas had distinguished themselves and won more honor than the Incas. He
imagined that because of this they would become prouder, and he proposed
to have them killed. Thus, he dispatched a messenger with an order for

FIGURE 38.1. Huánuco Pampa was one of the largest Inca administrative centers. This photograph shows its massive ceremonial platform in the center of its plaza. (Photograph by J. T. Zimmer, 1922; copyright © The Field Museum, negative CSA46495.)

Capac Yupanqui to prepare a plan to kill all the Chancas as best he could. He was also warned that if he did not kill them, then Pachacuti Inca Yupanqui would have him killed. The Inca's runner reached Capac Yupanqui with this order, but it could not be kept secret enough that a wife of Capac Yupanqui, who was a sister of Anco Ayllu, the captain of the Chancas, did not learn of it. This woman told her brother about it, and as he had always desired his freedom, the circumstances gave him more urgency to save his life. He thus secretly informed his Chanca soldiers of this and laid before them the anger and cruelty of the Inca and the reward of liberty should they follow him. They all agreed with him, and when they reached Guaraotambo, in the jurisdiction of the city of Huánuco, all the Chancas fled with their captain Anco Ayllu, whom other nations besides the Chancas followed as well (Figure 38.1). As they passed through the province of Huayllas, they pillaged it and, continuing their journey of flight from the Inca, they decided to search for a rugged and forested land where the Incas, even if they searched for them, would be unable to find them. Thus they entered the forests between Chachapoyas and Huánuco [195] and passed through the province of Ruparupa. According to news we now have, these are the people who are believed to have been seen near the Pacay River when Captain Gómez d'Arias took his expedition through Huánuco in the time of the Marquis of Cañete [196] in the year 1556. [They are also the people] from the information describing the land upriver from there, along the river that they call Cocama, which drains into the great river of the Marañon. So although Capac Yupanqui went after the Chancas, they were so fast in fleeing that he never caught them.

Going after them, he reached Cajamarca, crossing the borders that Inca Yupanqui had instructed him not to pass. Although he remembered the order of the Inca, he decided to conquer the province of Cajamarca, since he was already there, even though he did not have his brother's permission to do so. This province was densely populated and was rich in gold and silver, thanks to a great *cinchi* named Guzmanco Capac who lived there, and who was a great tyrant who had robbed many provinces surrounding Cajamarca.[197] As Capac Yupanqui entered the land of Cajamarca, Guzmanco Capac learned of it. He prepared his men and called another *cinchi*, his tributary named Chimo Capac, the *cinchi* of the area where the city of Trujillo is now, on the coast of Peru. Combining their forces, they came in search of Capac Yupanqui, who defeated them with an ambush and other ruses that he placed for them. He routed and captured the two *cinchis*, Guzmanco Capac and Chimo Capac, and acquired innumerable riches of gold and silver and other precious things, such as precious stones and red shells,[198] which these natives then esteemed more than silver or gold.

Capac Yupanqui gathered the treasures he had acquired into the plaza of Cajamarca. When he saw such quantity and greatness, he was filled with pride and, glorifying himself, said that he had won and acquired more than his brother Inca Yupanqui. The pride and boasting of his brother Capac Yupanqui reached the ears of the Inca, and although it greatly grieved him and he felt it heavily and wanted to seize him immediately to have him executed, he concealed it until he saw him in Cuzco. Inca Yupanqui still feared that his brother would rebel against him and therefore feigned great happiness in front of the ambassadors that his brother had sent to him. He sent back with them orders to Capac Yupanqui to return to Cuzco bringing the riches that he had won in the war and to bring the principal men of the provinces that he had conquered, as well as the sons of Guzmanco Capac and Chimo Capac. [He ordered him] to leave the two elder *cinchis* in their lands with a garrison sufficient to hold those lands for him. With this order from the Inca, Capac Yupanqui left with all the treasures he had won there and marched to Cuzco very proud and arrogant. Inca Yupanqui was jealous of Capac Yupanqui upon learning that he had won so many lands, treasures, and honor. And some even say that he was fearful and was searching for an excuse to kill him. Thus, when he knew that Capac Yupanqui was in Lima-tambo, eight leagues from Cuzco, he sent his lieutenant named Inca Capon from Cuzco to go and cut off his head, using as an excuse that Anco Ayllu had escaped him and that he had gone beyond the boundary that he had been ordered. His governor went and, as the Inca ordered, killed Capac Yu-panqui, his brother, and Huayna Yupanqui, also his brother. [The envoy] ordered the others to enter Cuzco, celebrating the Inca's victories. They did this, and the Inca trod on their spoils and honored them and granted re-wards. They say that it grieved him that his brother had won so much glory and that he wished that he had sent his son, Topa Inca Yupanqui, who was to succeed him, so that he might have enjoyed so many honors. They say that it was because of this envy that he had Capac Yupanqui killed.

[39]

PACHACUTI INCA YUPANQUI ESTABLISHES *MITIMAES* IN ALL THE LANDS HE HAD CONQUERED

*A*s all the conquests that this Inca made were done with much violence and cruelties and forces and robberies, and because the people who followed him for the booty or, that is to say, for the pillaging were numerous, he was obeyed only insofar as they felt force over them. When they found them-selves somewhat free from that fear, they would immediately rebel and seek their liberty. The Inca was therefore forced at times to conquer them again. Turning many things over in his mind, and considering solutions as to how to settle, once and for all, the many provinces he had conquered, Pachacuti came up with an idea that, although it suited his purpose, was actually the greatest tyranny that he perpetrated, even though it was tinted with gener-osity. He assigned people to go to all the provinces that he had subjugated to measure and survey them and to bring back models [of the provinces] sculpted in clay. Thus it was done (Figure 39.1). When the models and de-scriptions were placed before the Inca, he examined them and considered

FIGURE 39.1. Miniature Inca building carved in stone. (Photograph by John Weinstein, 2002; copyright © The Field Museum, negative number A114207d.)

the plains and fortresses and ordered the inspectors to carefully watch what he was doing. He then began to demolish the fortresses that he saw fit, and he moved their inhabitants to a site on the plains, and he moved those from the plains to the ridges and highlands, so far removed from one another and from their native land that they could not return to it. He then ordered the inspectors to go and do with the provinces what they had seen him do with the sculptures of them. They went and did so.

Pachacuti then ordered others to go to the same provinces and, together with the *tucuricos*, take some young men and their wives from each town. This done, they brought couples to Cuzco from all the provinces, thirty from one and one hundred from another, more or less according to the size of each town. When these chosen couples appeared before the Inca, he ordered that they be taken to settle in different regions. Those who were from Chinchaysuyu were to be settled in Antisuyu, and those from Cuntisuyu in Collasuyu, so far from their native lands that they could not communicate with their relatives or countrymen. He ordered that they be settled in valleys similar to those of their native birth, and that they take seeds from their land so that they could sustain themselves and not perish, giving them abundant lands to sow after taking them [away] from the natives of that place.

The Inca called these people *mitimaes*, which means "transposed" or "moved." He ordered them to learn the language of the natives where they were settled and not to forget the general language, which was the Quechua language that the Inca had commanded all should learn and know in all the provinces that he had conquered. They should talk and do business in it everywhere, as it was the clearest and most widespread language. The Inca gave these *mitimaes* freedom and power so that they could enter at anytime, day or night, any of the houses of the natives of the valleys where they were, and see what the natives did or said or arranged. [They were] to notify the nearest governor about everything so that in this way he would know if anything was plotted or tried against the interests of the Inca. Knowing the harm he had done, the Inca feared everyone in general and knew that none served him of their own will but only by force. Besides this, the Inca placed garrisons of Cuzco natives or its neighbors in all the fortresses that were of some importance. He called these garrisons *michocrima*.

[40]

THE COLLAS, SONS OF CHUCHIC CAPAC, RISE UP AGAINST INCA YUPANQUI, SEEKING THEIR FREEDOM

*A*fter Inca Pachacuti held the festivities celebrating the victory in Chinchaysuyu and established the *mitimaes*, he dismissed the armies and went to Yucay, where he constructed the buildings whose ruins and vestiges are now to be seen there. These finished, he continued through the same valley and down the Yucay River to a place they now call [Ollantay]tambo, eight leagues from Cuzco, where he was constructing some very sumptuous buildings (Figure 40.1). The captive sons of Chuchic Capac, the great *cinchi* of Collao who, as I mentioned before, was defeated and killed in the Collao by the Inca, provided the labor and masonry for these buildings. These sons of Chuchic Capac found themselves treated so vilely that, remembering they were the sons of such an important and wealthy man as their father, and seeing that at that time Inca Yupanqui had dismissed the warriors, they decided to risk their lives seeking their freedom. Thus, one night they fled with all the people who were there, and they left with such speed that even though the Inca sent men after them, they could not be caught or found. They started a revolt against the Inca in all the lands they passed through. This was not very difficult because, since all had been subjugated by force, they were only awaiting the first opportunity to rebel. With this favorable chance, many nations readily rebelled, even those that were very near Cuzco, but it was mainly [those of] Collasuyu and all its provinces.

Seeing this, the Inca mustered many warriors and asked Guzmanco Capac and Chimo Capac for help with men. He assembled a large number of men, made his sacrifices and *calpa*, and buried some children alive, a [rite] they call *capac cocha*,[199] so that his idols would favor him in the war. When everything was just about ready for war, he appointed two of his sons, valiant men, as captains of the army; the first was Topa Ayar Manco, and the second, Apu Paucar Usno. The Inca left Cuzco with more than 200,000 warriors and traveled in search of the sons of Chuchic Capac, who also had a large force of people and weapons and were eager to meet the Inca and fight for their lives against the Cuzcos and their followers.

Since each was looking for the other, they soon met and joined in a very long and bloody battle. There were many cruelties, because one side fought

FIGURE 40.1. The site of Ollantaytambo. (Photograph by Max. T. Vargus, ca. 1900, private collection.)

for life and liberty and the other side for honor. The Cuzcos had the upper hand, because they were more disciplined and skilled in war and greater in number than their opponents. But the Collas, who did not want to find themselves prisoners of such an inhuman and cruel man as the Inca, preferred to die fighting rather than surrender. Therefore, they would step in front of the weapons of the noblemen, who killed with great cruelty as many of the Collas as came before them. On this day, the sons of the Inca did great things in battle with their own hands.

Thus most of the Collas were defeated, killed, or imprisoned, and the Cuzcos pursued those who fled as far as a town called Lampa. There Pachacuti Inca Yupanqui treated his wounded and re-formed the squadrons and ordered his two sons Topa Ayar Manco and Apu Paucar Usno to press ahead conquering as far as the Chichas. They were to place his boundary markers there and to turn back. From there he returned to Cuzco to celebrate the victory won.

The Inca arrived in Cuzco, where he celebrated and held festivities for the victory. He found that a son had been born to him, and thus he took him before the Sun and offered him to him and gave him the name of Topa Inca Yupanqui.[200] He offered many treasures of silver and gold to the Sun and to the other oracles and *huacas* in his name, and he also held the *capac cocha* sacrifice. In addition to this, he held the most solemn and costly festivities that had ever been held throughout the land, because Inca Yupanqui wanted Topa Inca to succeed him, even though he had other older and legitimate sons by his wife and sister, Mama Anaguarqui. Because even though the custom of these tyrants was that the first and eldest legitimate son inherited the state, they seldom observed it. Instead, they would usually select the one they loved the most or the one whose mother they loved the most or the one among the brothers who was the most capable of ruling, and he received everything.

[41]

AMARU TOPA INCA AND APU PAUCAR
USNU CONTINUE THE CONQUEST
OF THE COLLAO AND DEFEAT THE
COLLAS ONCE AGAIN

After Inca Yupanqui returned to Cuzco and, as has been mentioned, left his two sons Amaru Topa and Apu Paucar Usno in the Collao, the sons of the Inca left Lampa and headed for Hatuncolla. There they found that the Collas had reorganized men and weapons to fight with the Cuzcos anew and that they had named one of the sons of Chuchic Capac as Inca.[201] The Incas arrived where the Collas were armed and waiting. They saw each other and fought valiantly against one another, and there were many deaths on both sides. Finally, the Collas were defeated in battle and the new Inca was seized. Thus the Collas were conquered by the Cuzcos for the third time. By order of the Inca, his field-general sons left the new Inca of the Collao imprisoned in Hatuncolla, guarded and well secured. The other captains continued to press the conquest onward, toward the Chichas and Charcas, as the Inca had ordered.

While they were carrying on the war, their father, Pachacuti, finished the buildings of [Ollantay]tambo and made the ponds and pleasure houses of Yucay. He built some sumptuous houses on a hill called Patallacta near the city and many others surrounding Cuzco.[202] He made many water canals for use and recreation, and he ordered all his governors to build him pleasure houses in the most suitable places in the provinces they were in charge of, for when he went to inspect them.

While Inca Yupanqui did these things, his sons continued conquering all of Collasuyu. But when they arrived near the Charcas, the natives of the provinces of Paria, Tapacari, Cotabambas, Poconas, and Charcas retreated to the Chichas and Chuyes; there they would fight together against the Incas, who arrived where those nations were assembled, waiting for them. The Incas divided their army into three parts. A squadron of 5,000 men went through the forest, another of 20,000 went through the area near the sea, and the rest took the direct road. They arrived at the strongpoint where the Charcas and their allies were, and they fought against them. The Cuzcos were the victors and seized great spoils and riches of silver that those natives extracted from the mines of Porco. (It is to be noted that nothing was ever again known of what happened to the 5,000 noblemen who entered the forest.) With this victory, Amaru Topa Inca and Apu Paucar Usno left all these provinces subdued and returned in triumph to Cuzco, where they celebrated their victories. Pachacuti gave them many rewards, and he rejoiced by holding many festivities and making sacrifices to their idols.

[42]

PACHACUTI INCA YUPANQUI APPOINTS HIS SON TOPA INCA YUPANQUI AS HIS SUCCESSOR

Seeing that he was now very old, Pachacuti Inca Yupanqui decided to appoint a successor for after his days. For this he ordered the Incas, his relatives from the Hanan Cuzco and Hurin Cuzco *ayllus*, to be summoned, and he told them: "My friends and kin! As you see, I am very old, and I want to leave you someone who will rule you and defend you from your enemies after my days. Some years have passed since I named my eldest legitimate son, Amaru Topa Inca, as my successor, [but] I do not think that he is the one who is fit to govern such a great lordship as that which I have won. I therefore want to appoint another one, who will please you more." His kin thanked him profusely for this and responded that they [would] receive great reward and benefit from whomever he appointed. He then announced

FIGURE 42.1. Inca Yupanqui passes the Incaship on to his son, Topa Inca Yupanqui, by Martín de Murúa [1590:f. 44v]. (Courtesy of The J. Getty Museum, Los Angeles, copyright © The J. Paul Getty Museum.)

FIGURE 42.2. The Field Museum has one of the few Inca seats preserved from early colonial times. (Photograph by John Weinstein, 2002; copyright © The Field Museum, negative A114206d.)

that he appointed his son Topa Inca as Inca and his successor. He ordered him to emerge from the house where for fifteen or sixteen years he had been raised without anyone seeing him except on rare occasions and as a great reward (Figure 42.1). He showed him to the people and presently ordered that they place a gold tassel in the hand of the statue of the Sun along with his headdress, which they call *pillaca llayto*. After Topa Inca offered his reverence and deference to his father, the Inca and the others rose and they went before the statue of the Sun, where they made their sacrifices and offered *capac cochas* to the Sun. They then presented the new Inca, Topa Inca Yupanqui, pleading with the Sun to protect him and raise him, and to make him so that all would hold him and judge him as the son of the Sun and as the father of the people. This said, the most elderly and principal noblemen took Topa Inca to the Sun, and the priests and stewards took the tassel, which they call *mascapaycha*, from the hands of the Sun and placed it on the head of Topa Inca Yupanqui so that it fell over his forehead. He was declared *inca capac*, and he seated himself before the Sun on a small, low gold seat, which they call *duho*, embellished with many emeralds and other precious stones (Figure 42.2). While he was seated there, they clothed him in the *capac hongo* and placed the *sunturpaucar* in his hand, giving him the other insignias of Incaship, and the priests [then] lifted him on their shoulders. When the ceremony was over, Pachacuti Inca Yupanqui ordered his son Topa Inca to remain shut in the House of the Sun as before, performing the customary fasts required to receive the order of knighthood, which was to have one's ears pierced. The Inca commanded that no announcement should be made of what transpired there until he ordered it.

[43]

PACHACUTI ARMS HIS SON TOPA INCA AS A KNIGHT

*P*achacuti Inca Yupanqui took great pleasure in leaving monuments to himself. Because of this, he did more extraordinary things in buildings and victory celebrations than his ancestors. And he did not allow himself to be seen except as a great treat to the people, for the day that he did show himself was considered as such. He then decreed that no one could see him who did not worship him and bear in his hands something to offer him, and that this custom should be kept with all of his descendants. So it was inviolably done. Thus with Pachacuti this unprecedented and inhuman tyranny was begun, reiterating the tyrannical acts of his ancestors. Since he was now old and desired to perpetuate his name, he thought that by empowering his son, Topa Inca, as his successor, he would attain what he desired. Thus he had him raised in confinement in the House of the Sun for over sixteen years, not allowing anyone to see him except his tutors and teachers until he had Topa Inca brought out to be presented to the Sun and to have him appointed, as has been described. To initiate him at his *guarachico* he established a new way in which the order of knighthood was given. In the area surrounding the city, he built for this four other houses dedicated to the Sun. [They had] large displays of gold idols, *huacas*, and retainers so that his son could walk the stations when he was armed a knight.[203]

With things in this state, Amaru Topa Inca, who was the eldest legitimate son, came to Pachacuti Inca Yupanqui. His father, Pachacuti, had named him his successor years before. He said: "Father Inca! I have learned that you have a son in the House of the Sun whom you have appointed as your successor after your days. Have him shown to me!" Inca Yupanqui, considering the boldness of Amaru Topa Inca, told him: "It is true, and I want you and your wife to be his vassals and to serve him and obey him as your lord and Inca." Amaru replied that he wished to do so and that it was for this reason that he wanted to see him and to make sacrifice to him, and he asked his father to have him taken to where his brother was. The Inca gave him permission for this, and Amaru Topa Inca took with him what was required for this act [of devotion], and he was [then] led to where Topa Inca was fasting. When Amaru Topa Inca saw him with such a majestic display of riches and lords who accompanied him, he fell with his face on the ground and adored him and offered sacrifices and obedience to him. Learning that he was his brother, Topa Inca raised him up and they kissed one another on the face.

Then Inca Yupanqui ordered the necessary preparations be made to give his son the order of knighthood. With everything arranged, Pachacuti Inca and the rest of his principal relatives and retainers went to the House of the Sun. They led Topa Inca out of there with great solemnity and display, because they also took out all the idols of the Sun, Viracocha, and the other *huacas* and the figures of the past Incas, and the great rope *moro urco*. When everything had been arranged in order and with such pomp as had never been seen before, they all went to the town plaza, in the center of which they made a very large bonfire. Many animals were killed by all his relatives and friends, who offered them as sacrifices by casting them into the fire. Then they all worshiped [Topa Inca] and offered him presents and rich gifts. And the first to offer him a gift was his father so that by his example and imitation the others would worship him, seeing that his father revered him. The Inca noblemen and all the others who were there, for they had been summoned and invited to bring their gifts to offer to the new Inca, did this.

This done, [they began] the festivity they call *capac raymi*, which means "festivity of kings" and is therefore the most solemn that was held among them. Having performed the festivity and its ceremonies, they pierced Topa Inca Yupanqui's ears, which is the sign of knighthood and nobility among them. They brought him to the stations of the Houses of the Sun, giving him the weapons and other insignias of war. This finished, his father, Inca Yupanqui, gave him one of his sisters named Mama Ocllo as wife. She was a very beautiful woman of great wisdom and ability.

[44]

PACHACUTI INCA YUPANQUI SENDS HIS SON TOPA INCA YUPANQUI TO CONQUER CHINCHAYSUYU

[With] Topa Inca Yupanqui appointed as his father's successor and armed as a knight, Inca Yupanqui wanted his son to busy himself in things [that would win him] fame. Hearing news that he could win renown and treasures among the nations of Chinchaysuyu, especially from a *cinchi* named Chuqui Sota who was in Chachapoyas, [Inca Yupanqui] ordered [his son] to prepare himself to go on a conquest of Chinchaysuyu. He gave Topa Inca two of his brothers, Anqui Yupanqui and Tilca Yupanqui, as companions and tutors and captains-general of the armies. And when the warriors had assembled and finished their preparations, they left Cuzco.

Topa Inca Yupanqui went with such majesty and pomp that wherever he passed no one dared look him in the face—such was the veneration in which he was held. The people would move away from the roads along which he passed and climb the hills, from where they would worship and pray to him. They would pull out their eyelashes and eyebrows and, blowing them, would offer them to the Inca. Others offered him handfuls of an herb very prized among them called *coca*. When he arrived in a town, he would dress in the clothes and headdress of that nation, since all were different in

FIGURE 44.1. The large Inca site of Curamba is located between Abancay and Andahuaylas.

their attire and still are. To identify the nations that he had conquered, Inca Yupanqui ordered every one to have its own dress and headdress, which they call *pillo, llayto,* or *chuco,* each one different from the other so that they could distinguish and recognize each other easily. When Topa Inca seated himself, they would make a solemn sacrifice of animals and birds to him, burning them before him in a bonfire that they made in his presence. Thus he had himself worshiped as the Sun, whom they held as a god.

In this way, Topa Inca began to renew the conquests and tyranny of all his ancestors and his father. Because, although many had been conquered by his father, all, or almost all, had taken up arms [again]. The oppressed sought their freedom, and the others defended themselves. As Topa Inca came down upon them with such power, force, and arrogance that he prided himself not only in subjugating the people but also in usurping the veneration they gave to their gods or devils—because he and his father actually made everyone worship their persons with more veneration than the Sun— these nations' armies could not withstand them.

Finally, Topa Inca departed from Cuzco and began his rampage close to the city. In the province of the Quechuas, he conquered and took the fortresses of Tohara and Cayara, and the fortress of Curamba (Figure 44.1); in the Angaraes, the fortresses of Urcocolla and Huayllapucara (and he captured its *cinchi* named Chuquis Guaman); in the province of Jauja, [the fortress of] Siciquilla Pucara; in the province of Huayllas, [the fortresses of] Chungomarca [and] Pillaguamarca; and in Chachapoyas, the fortress of Piajajalca (and he captured its wealthy *cinchi* named Chuqui Sota). He destroyed the province of the Paltas and the valleys of Pacasmayo and Chimo, which is now [part of] Trujillo, even though Chimo Capac was his subject. [He also destroyed] the province of the Cañaris. Those who resisted him were utterly destroyed. And even though the Cañaris surrendered to him, albeit out of fear, he captured their *cinchis*, named Pisar Capac, Cañar Capac, and Chica Capac, and he built an impregnable fortress in Quinchicaja.

Having obtained many treasures and prisoners, Topa Inca Yupanqui returned with all of them to Cuzco. There he was well received by his father with a most costly victory celebration and with the applause of all the Cuzco noblemen. Many festivities and sacrifices were held. To entertain the people, Pachacuti ordered the town to hold the dances and festivities called *inti raymi*, which are the "festivities of the Sun," a matter of much rejoicing.[204] He gave many rewards for the sake and love of Topa Inca so that his subjects would become fond of him, which was what he wanted. Because he was now very old and he could no longer move and felt close to death, Pachacuti sought to leave his son well liked by the warriors.

[45]

PACHACUTI INCA YUPANQUI INSPECTS THE PROVINCES CONQUERED BY HIM AND HIS CAPTAINS

*I*t has already been said how Inca Yupanqui placed a garrison of soldiers from Cuzco and a governor whom they called *tucurico* in all the provinces that he conquered and tyrannized. It should be noted that because [he] had been greatly involved in conquering other provinces, in raising warriors, and in placing his son in power and dispatching him for the conquest of Chinchaysuyu, Inca Yupanqui had been unable to put into effect his last wish and final design, which was to turn those he tyrannized into subjects and tributaries. Finding that the people felt greater fear upon seeing Topa Inca so valiant, he decided to inspect the land. For this he appointed sixteen inspectors, four for each one of the four *suyus* and provinces. These are Cuntisuyu, which is from Cuzco to the southwest up to the South Sea; Chinchaysuyu, which is from Cuzco to the west and north; Antisuyu, which is from Cuzco to the east; and Collasuyu, which is from Cuzco to the south and southwest and southeast.[205]

Each of these inspectors went to the area that he was given, and above all, they inspected the *tucuricos* who had ruled there. Then they had canals built for the fields, plowed fields where they were lacking, made new terraces where there were none, and seized pastures for the livestock of the Inca, of the Sun, and of Cuzco. Above all, they levied such a heavy tribute on all the possessions the locals had and had obtained, that it was all becoming about robbing the people and fleecing them and their estates. They passed through many settlements [while going] from one place to another. With this all completed, the inspectors returned to Cuzco after the two years they spent carrying out their inspections. They brought with them a description [painted] on some cloths of the provinces they had inspected, and gave accounts to the Inca of what they had done and what they had found.

The Inca then dispatched other noblemen as overseers to build roads and hostels with large buildings along the roads for the Inca when he traveled and for [his] warriors. Thus the overseers departed and built the roads they now call "of the Inca" in the highlands and along the coasts of the South Sea. The latter are enclosed on both sides by a high adobe wall wherever it could be built, except in the deserts where there are no building materials. These roads go from Quito to Chile and through the forests of the Andes. Although the Inca did not finish them all, it was sufficient that he made a large part of them, and his sons and grandsons finished them.

[46]

TOPA INCA YUPANQUI SETS OUT A SECOND TIME BY ORDER OF HIS FATHER TO CONQUER WHAT REMAINED OF CHINCHAYSUYU

*P*achacuti Inca Yupanqui learned from the news that Topa Inca brought him when he returned from the conquest of Chinchaysuyu that there were other large and very rich provinces and nations beyond where his son had reached. So that no place would be left unconquered, he ordered his son

FIGURE 46.1. Overview of Inca building foundations at the site of Tomebamba in the modern city of Cuenca, Ecuador. (Photograph courtesy of Tamara L. Bray.)

Topa Inca to prepare himself to return to conquer the area toward Quito. [Once] the people were ready and the captains assigned, [the Inca] gave him as companions the same brothers, Tilca Yupanqui and Anqui Yupanqui, who had accompanied Topa Inca the first time. They left Cuzco and en route they found that some of the previously conquered provinces were in a state of unrest. Topa Inca inflicted unheard-of cruelties and killings on those who defended themselves and who did not immediately come to give him obedience.

In this way he arrived at Tomebamba,[206] [in the] region of Quito, whose *cinchi*, Pisar Capac,[207] had allied himself with Pillaguaso, the *cinchi* of the provinces and region of Quito (Figure 46.1). These two *cinchis* had a large army and were determined to fight against Topa Inca to defend their land and lives. Topa Inca sent messengers to them, ordering them to come and surrender their weapons and give him obedience. They answered [that they] were in their homeland and their native place, and that they were free and did not want to serve anyone nor be tributaries.

Topa Inca and his followers rejoiced at this response, because what they really wanted was to find a pretext to fight and plunder them, which was their main intent. Thus they marshaled their people, who, they say, numbered more than 250,000 experienced warriors. They marched against the

Cañaris and Quitos, and the armies fought one another bravely and skill-
fully. Because the Quitos and Cañaris strongly resisted their enemies, for a
long time is was not clear whether the Cuzcos would prevail. Seeing this,
the Inca rose up on the litter in which he traveled, encouraging his people,
and he signaled to the 50,000 men whom he had kept as reserves to help
where most needed. As the fresh [troops] attacked on a flank, they routed
the Quitos and Cañaris and continued the pursuit, behaving and killing
cruelly, shouting: "Capac Inca Yupanqui Cuzco Cuzco!" All the *cinchis*[208]
were killed, and they captured Pillaguaso in the vanguard. No one was given
quarter so that they could plunder them and strike fear into others who
learned of it.

From here, Topa Inca went to the place where the city of San Francisco
of Quito is now, and he halted to heal the wounded and to give a much-
needed rest to the army. Thus, this very large province was conquered, and
he sent news of what he had done to his father. Pachacuti rejoiced at this
and held many sacrifices and festivities.[209]

After Topa Inca had rested in Quito and reorganized his army and healed
those who had been wounded, he went to Tomebamba, where his sister
and wife bore him a son, whom they named Tito Cusi Hualpa. Later he
was called Huayna Capac. After he had rejoiced and performed the birth
celebrations, he learned that there was a large nation of Indians called Guancabilicas in the direction of the South Sea. Although the four years that his
father had given him to complete the conquest had passed, he decided to
go down and conquer them. Above the Guancabilicas, at the head of the
highlands, Topa Inca built the fortress of Guachalla, and he [then] went
down to the Guancabilicas. He divided his army into three, and he took one
part and entered through the most rugged mountains, waging war on the
highland Guancabilicas. He penetrated so far into the mountains that for
a very long time nothing was known of what happened to him, whether he
was dead or alive. He did so much that he conquered all the Guancabilicas,
even though they were very warlike and fought by land and by sea on rafts,
from Tumbes to Guañapi and [in] Guamo, Manta, Turuca, and Quisin.

As Topa Inca Yupanqui went about conquering the coast of Manta and
the island of Puna and Tumbes, some merchants arrived who had come
by sea from the west, navigating by sail in boats. From these, he found out
about the land they came from, which were some islands, one called Avachumbi and the other Niñachumbi, where there were many people and
much gold.[210] And since Topa Inca was courageous and of high aspirations
and was not satisfied with what he had conquered on land, he decided to try
his fortune at sea. But he did not fully believe the merchant mariners, for he

said that one should not believe what merchants said straightaway, because
they are people who talk a lot. To get more information, and since it was
not something about which a lot of information could be found anywhere,
he called a man he had brought with him in the conquests named Antarqui. Everyone says that he was a great necromancer, such that he could fly
through the air. Topa Inca asked him if what the merchant mariners said
about the islands was true. After thinking about it a great deal, Antarqui
told him that what they said was true and that he would go there first. Thus
they say that through his arts he went [there] and explored the route and
saw the islands, the people, and their riches, and on returning, he confirmed
all of it to Topa Inca.

With this certainty, Topa Inca decided to go there. For this he built a
very large number of rafts, on which he embarked more than 20,000 chosen
soldiers. He took with him as captains Guaman Achachi, Conde Yupanqui,
and Quigual Topa (these were Hanan Cuzcos), as well as Yancan Mayta,
Quizo Mayta, Cachimapaca Macus Yupanqui, and Llimpita Usca Mayta
(Hurin Cuzcos). He also took his brother Tilca Yupanqui as general of all
the armada, and he left Apu Yupanqui with those who remained on land.

Topa Inca sailed and went and discovered the islands of Avachumbi and
Niñachumbi. When he returned from there, he brought back black people
and much gold and a brass chair and the skin and jawbone of a horse. These
trophies were kept in the fortress of Cuzco until the time of the Spaniards.
The skin and jawbone of the horse were kept by an important Inca who is
alive today, named Urco Guaranga, who gave this account and was present
with the others when they ratified this chronicle.[211] I make a point of this
because those who know something of the Indies will find this account
strange and difficult to believe. This journey took Topa Inca more than nine
months — others say a year — and as he took such a long time, everyone believed he was dead. But to mislead [everyone] and to pretend that he had
heard from Topa Inca, Apu Yupanqui, his captain of the land army, celebrated, although this was later misinterpreted. It was said that those were
joyous celebrations because Topa Inca Yupanqui was not returning, and this
cost Apu Yupanqui his life.

These are the islands that I discovered in the South Sea on 30 November in the year [15]67, two hundred or so leagues west of Lima. I gave news
of this great discovery to the governor and licentiate [García] de Castro.[212]
Alvaro de Mendaña, general of the armada, did not want to claim them.[213]

After Topa Inca returned from the discovery of the islands, he went to
Tomebamba to visit his wife and son and to ready himself to return to Cuzco
to see his father, who he was told was not well. On the journey, he sent men

along the coast to Trujillo, which is called Chimo, where they found great gold and silver riches worked into rods and beams in the houses of the *cinchi* Chimo Capac, all of which they gathered in Cajamarca. From there Topa Inca Yupanqui took the road to Cuzco, where he returned six years after he had left on this conquest.

Topa Inca Yupanqui entered Cuzco with the greatest, most solemn, and richest triumph with which any Inca had ever entered the House of the Sun, bringing a great variety of people, strange animals, and innumerable quantities of riches. All the people were very wealthy. But behold the evil nature of Pachacuti Inca Yupanqui and his avarice! Although Topa Inca was his son, whose prosperity he sought, Pachacuti felt such jealousy that his son had won such honor and fame in that journey and conquest that he publicly showed grief for not being the one who triumphed and for not personally having taken part in everything! He therefore decided to kill his two sons Tilca Yupanqui and Anqui Yupanqui, who had gone with Topa Inca, blaming them for having broken his command and having taken more time than he had given them for this conquest, and having taken his son Topa Inca so far away that it was believed that he would never return to Cuzco.[214] Thus they say that he killed them. Others say that he killed only Tilca Yupanqui. Topa Inca Yupanqui was greatly saddened by this, since his father had killed someone who had worked so hard with him. In the end, the murder was concealed by the many festivities that were held for the victories of Topa Inca. These festivities lasted one year.

[47]

THE DEATH OF PACHACUTI INCA YUPANQUI

*P*achacuti Inca Yupanqui derived much happiness from his grandson, the son of his son Topa Inca—so much that he always had him with him, and had him raised and pampered in his house and home. He would not allow the child to be separated from him. At the height of his reputation and power, Pachacuti fell ill with a serious malady. Feeling himself about to die, he summoned all his sons who were in the city. In their presence, he first of all divided all his jewels and personal effects among them. Then he ordered each of them to be given [foot-]ploughs so that they would know they were to be vassals of their brother and would have to eat by the sweat of their hands. He also gave them weapons to fight on behalf of their brother, and he [then] dismissed them.

Pachacuti then called the Inca noblemen of Cuzco, his kinsmen, and Topa Inca, his son, to whom he spoke a few words in this manner: "Son! You now see the many and great nations that I leave you, and you know how much toil they have cost me. Make sure that you are man enough to preserve and increase them. [Let] no one live who raises his own eyes against you, even if they be your brothers. I leave you these our kin as fathers so that they [may] counsel you. Care for them, and they shall serve you. When I am dead, you will preserve my body and place it in my homes at Patallacta (Figure 47.1).[215] You will place my gold figure in the House of the Sun, and in all the provinces subject to me you will make the solemn sacrifices. And at the end you will [perform] the *purucaya*[216] ritual so that I may go to rest with my father the Sun."

They say that having finished, he began to sing words in his language in a low and sad tone. In Spanish they mean:

> "I was born like a lily in the garden
> and thus I was raised,
> and as I grew old, I aged,
> and since I had to die,
> so I withered and died."[217]

Having said these words, Pachacuti laid his head on a pillow and passed away, giving his soul to the devil, having lived 125 years.[218] Because he succeeded, or better said, he seized the Incaship by his own hand at the age of 22, he was *capac* 103 years.

Pachacuti had four legitimate sons with his wife, Mama Anaguarqui.[219] He had one hundred sons and fifty bastard daughters, who, being so many, were called Hatun Ayllu, which means "great lineage." This lineage is [also] called by another name: Inaca Panaca Ayllu. Those who maintain this lineage who are alive today are Don Diego Cayo,[220] Don Felipe Inguil, Don Juan Quispe Cusi,[221] Don Francisco Chaco Rimache,[222] and Don Juan Illac.[223] They live in Cuzco; they are Hanan Cuzcos.

Pachacuti was a man of good stature. He was robust, fierce, lecherous, insatiably bent on tyrannizing the world, and cruel beyond measure. All the laws that he made for the people were aimed at tyranny and self-interest. He was branded as infamous because he would often take some widow as a wife, and if that widow had a daughter who pleased him, he would also

FIGURE 47.1. The archaeological complex now called Kenko, on the hill of Patallacta outside Cuzco, may have been the royal mausoleum of Pachacuti Inca Yupanqui.

have her as a wife or mistress. Moreover, if there was a gallant and handsome youth among the people who was esteemed for some reason, he would immediately order some of his retainers to befriend him and to take him to the country and kill him however they could. Furthermore, [Pachacuti Inca Yupanqui] took all his sisters as mistresses, saying they could have no better husband than their brother.

This Inca died in the year of 1191. He conquered more than three hundred leagues, about forty by himself in the company of his legitimate brothers, along with the captains Apu Mayta and Vicaquirao. The other [leagues were conquered] by Amaru Topa Inca, his eldest son; Capac Yupanqui, his brother; and Topa Inca Yupanqui, his successor son, and other captains who were also his sons and brothers. Pachacuti organized the groupings and lineages of Cuzco in the order that they are now.

Licentiate Polo [de Ondegardo] found the body of this Inca well preserved and guarded in Tococache,[224] where the parish of Lord San Blas of the city of Cuzco is now.[225] He sent it to Lima on command of the Marquis of Cañete, viceroy of this kingdom.[226] The *guauqui* idol of this Inca was called *inti illapa*. It was made of gold and was very large, and it was taken to Cajamarca in pieces. Licentiate Polo [de Ondegardo] found the house, estates, retainers, and women of this *guauqui* idol (Figure 47.2).

FIGURE 47.2. The mummy of Pachacuti Inca Yupanqui was found in the temple of Inti Illapa. The church of San Blas in Cuzco may mark this location.

[48]

THE LIFE OF TOPA INCA YUPANQUI,
THE TENTH INCA

*A*fter Pachacuti Inca Yupanqui died, they selected two noblemen to guard the body so that no one would enter or leave to pass the news of his death until the order had been given. The other Incas and noblemen went with Topa Inca to the House of the Sun, and there they summoned the twelve captains of the *ayllus* of the guard of the city and of the Inca. With these came 2,200 men whom they had under their command in the guard and who were ready for war, and they surrounded the House of the Sun. The Incas once again placed the tassel on Topa Inca Yupanqui and gave him the other insignias of Inca, as he had now inherited and succeeded his father. Placing him in the middle of [the Incas] and of warriors of the guard, they took him to the plaza, where he sat on a magnificent throne with great majesty. They issued an edict that on pain of death everyone in the city should come to give obedience to Topa Inca Yupanqui.

Those who had come with him went to their houses to bring presents to show reverence and to give their obedience to the new Inca. Topa Inca Yupanqui remained with only the guard, and then [the others] returned and gave him obedience, offering him their gifts and worshiping him. The remaining common people of the town did the same. They then offered him sacrifices. But it is to be noted that only those of Cuzco did this, and if any [of the] others who were present there did so, they must have been forced or frightened by the weapons and the proclamation.

This over, [the noblemen] came to Topa Inca and told him: "Capac Inca, your father now rests!" At these words, Topa Inca showed great grief and covered his head with the cloth that they call *llacolla*, which is a square cloak or blanket. Then he went with all his retinue to where the body of his father was, where he dressed for mourning. When all the things for the obsequies were prepared, Topa Inca Yupanqui did everything that his father had ordered on his deathbed regarding the cult of his body and other matters.

[49]

TOPA INCA YUPANQUI CONQUERS
THE PROVINCE OF THE ANDES

With Pachacuti Inca Yupanqui dead, Topa Inca saw that he was the sole Inca, and he issued a summons to the *cinchis* and headmen of the provinces that he had conquered. Fearing the fury of the Inca, they came, and with them came the Indians of the province of Antisuyu, who live in the forests to the east of Cuzco, and who had been conquered in the time of Pachacuti, his father.

Topa Inca ordered them all to give him obedience, and he made himself be sacrificed to and worshiped. He ordered the Andes Indians to bring some palm-wood spears from their land for the service of the House of the Sun. The Andes, who did not serve of their own will, considered this a method of servitude imposed upon them. For this reason they fled Cuzco and went to their lands, and they raised the land of the Andes [in revolt], proclaiming freedom.

Topa Inca Yupanqui became indignant about this, and he formed a powerful army, which he divided into three parts. He took one part and with it entered the Andes through Aguatona. Another section he gave to a captain called Otorongo Achachi, who entered the Andes by a town or valley that they call Amaru; and the third he gave to Chalco Yupanqui, another captain, who entered by a town called Pilcopata. All these entrances were close to one another, and thus they began to enter and they assembled three leagues inside the forest at a place called Opatari, which is where the settlements of the Andes then began. The inhabitants of these regions were Andes called Opataries; they were the first to be conquered. Chalco Yupanqui carried the image of the Sun.

But as the forest was thick with trees and full of undergrowth, they could not cut it, nor did they know in what direction they should go to reach the settlements that were well hidden in the forest. To find them, the scouts would climb the highest trees and would point toward the area where they saw smoke. Thus they forged a path until they lost that sign and would then look for another one. In this way the Inca made a road where it seemed impossible to make one.

The *cinchi* of most of these provinces of the Andes was an individual called Condin Cabana, who they say was a great sorcerer and enchanter.

And they believed, and even now claim, that he could transform himself into different shapes.

Topa Inca and his captains thus entered the Andes, which are very terrible and frightening forests with many rivers. There he and the people that he took from Peru suffered great hardships with the changing climate, because Peru is a cold and dry land and the forests of the Andes are hot and humid. The warriors of Topa Inca fell sick and many died. Topa Inca himself, with a third of the people that he took with him to conquer, wandered about for a long time lost in the forests, without knowing whether to go in one direction or another, until Otorongo Achachi met up with him and guided him.

At this time Topa Inca and his captains conquered four great nations. The first was that of the Opataries Indians, and the second was called Mano-suyu. The third is said to be the Mañaries or Yanaximes, which means "those of the black mouths," and there was the province of Río and the province of the Chunchos. Topa Inca covered much land going down the River Tono and reached the Chiponauas. He sent another great captain of his named Apu Curimache by the road that they now call Camata. He went toward the rising sun and traveled as far as the river called the Paytite,[227] which has now been reported on again.[228] There he put the boundary markers of Inca Topa. In the conquests of these above-mentioned nations, Topa Inca and his captains captured the following *cinchis:* Vinchincayna, Cantaguancuru, and Nutanguari.

An Indian from the Collao called Coaquiri, who was part of this conquest, fled with his company and returned to his land. He reported that Topa Inca Yupanqui was dead and told them all to rebel, since there was no longer an Inca, and that he would be their captain. He then named himself Pachacuti Inca, and the Collas rebelled and took him as their captain. News of this reached Topa Inca in the Andes where he was fighting, and he decided to leave to put down the Collas and punish them. Thus Topa Inca left, and Otorongo Achachi stayed in the Andes to finish their conquest. Topa Inca left him an order that, upon finishing the conquest, he should leave for Peru, but he was not to enter Cuzco celebrating their victories until Topa Inca arrived.[229]

[50]

TOPA INCA YUPANQUI GOES TO CONQUER AND PUT DOWN THE RISEN COLLAS

*A*s the Collas were some of those who most sought their freedom, they would try whenever they found a chance, as can be inferred from what has already been said. Thus Topa Inca Yupanqui decided to defeat them once and for all. After he left the Andes, he expanded his army and appointed as captains Larico, the son of his cousin Capac Yupanqui; Chachi, his brother; Conde Yupanqui; and Quigual Topa. With this army Topa Inca marched toward the Collao. The Collas had become strong with four well-known [towns], which were Llallaua, Asilli, Arapa, and Pucara. He captured their greatest leaders, who were Chucachuca and Pachacuti Coaquiri, the one that we said had fled the Andes. These [men] were afterward made into drums for Inca Topa. Finally, with the great diligence of Topa Inca, even though some years were spent in this war, he defeated and subdued them all, committing great cruelties on them.

Continuing his pursuit of the vanquished, Topa Inca went so far from Cuzco that he found himself in the Charcas and decided to press ahead, conquering all that he received news of. Thus he continued his conquest toward Chile, where he defeated the great *cinchi* Michimalongo, and Tangalongo, the *cinchi* of the Chileans from this side of the Maule River northward. He reached Coquimbo in Chile and the Maule River, where he placed his columns or, as others say, a wall as a border and boundary marker of his conquest. He brought great riches in gold from there. Having discovered many gold and silver mines in different places, he returned to Cuzco (Figure 50.1).

Topa Inca combined these spoils with those of Otorongo Achachi—who had already returned from the Andes, where he had been for three years, and was waiting for his brother in Paucartambo—and entered Cuzco with a very great victory celebration. Great festivities were held for the victories won, and Topa Inca gave many gifts and rewards to all the soldiers who had gone to war with him. Seeing the strength and greatness of Topa Inca Yupanqui, the provinces of Chumbivilicas came together with those of Cuntisuyu to give him service.

Topa Inca then went to the Chachapoyas and squashed what was suspicious there, and he visited many provinces along the way.

FIGURE 50.1. Topa Inca Yupanqui discovered many mines and conquered as far as Chile. By Martín de Murúa [1590:f. 49v]. (Courtesy of The J. Getty Museum, Los Angeles, copyright © The J. Paul Getty Museum.)

On his return to Cuzco, he passed certain laws, for both peace and war, and he increased the *mitimaes* that his father had created, as is told in the account of his life, giving them greater privileges and liberties. He then ordered a general inspection from Quito to Chile and made a census of all the people in an area of more than one thousand leagues. Topa Inca placed such heavy tributes on them that no one was the lord of a single ear of maize, which is the bread they eat, nor of a single *ojota*, which are their shoes, nor of [their own] marriages, nor of anything without the express permission of Topa Inca. Such was the tyranny and oppression that Topa Inca subjugated them with and placed on them. Topa Inca placed other [officials] called *micho* over the remaining *tucuricos* to collect the taxes and tributes.

Topa Inca saw that in the towns and provinces the *cinchis* were trying to inherit one from another and descend by succession. He thought to abolish even this practice and above all to squash the spirits of the greater and lesser [*cinchis*]. Thus he removed the existing *cinchis* and introduced a type of steward to his own liking, which he appointed in this way: He placed one steward in charge of ten thousand men and called him *huno*, which is "[ten] thousand." He created another steward of one thousand [people] and called him *guaranga*, which is "one thousand." He made another steward to whom he entrusted the care of five hundred inhabitants and called him *piscapachaca*, which means "five hundred." To another he entrusted one hundred and called him *pachac*, which is "one hundred," and he placed another one in charge of fifty and called him *piscapachac*,[230] which is "fifty." He placed another one in charge of ten men and called him *chunga curaca*.[231] Besides these titles, he called them *curacas*, which means "headman" or "chief"; [according to] the number of men they had under their charge. These [appointments] were by the will of the Inca, who would appoint them and remove them as he saw fit, so that they had no pretensions of inheritance or succession, nor was there [any]. They were henceforth called *curacas*—which is the proper name for the headmen of this land—and not *caciques*, as the vulgar Spaniards indiscreetly call them. The name *cacique* is from the islands of Santo Domingo and Cuba.[232] From here on we will drop the name of *cinchi* and use that of *curacas*.

[51]

TOPA INCA MAKES THE *YANAYACOS*

*A*mong the brothers that Topa Inca had was one called Topa Capac, an important man to whom Topa Inca had given many servants to work his fields and to serve on his estates. It should be known that Topa Inca Yupanqui made his brother Topa Capac inspector general of all the land that he had conquered until then. As Topa Capac conducted the inspection, he reached the area where his brother had given him those servants. Using these servants as an excuse, he attached many others [of that area] to himself, saying that they were all his *yanaconas*, which is what they call their servants. He did not include these people in his inspection, telling them that he wanted to increase their number and rebel against his brother and that if they helped him, he would greatly reward them. With this, he returned to Cuzco a very wealthy and powerful [man], and there he showed hints of his intentions.

Despite his secrecy, [the rebellion] was discovered and Topa Inca was warned of it. He returned to Cuzco, having been away arming one of his sons, Ayar Manco, as a knight. An investigation revealed the rumors to be true, and he executed his brother Topa Capac and all his counselors and allies (Figure 51.1). Learning how Topa Capac had left many people out of the census for this reason, Topa Inca left Cuzco, inspecting and inquiring about them in person.

While doing this, he arrived at a place that they call Yanayaco, which means "black water," because a river of very black water passes through that valley. Thus, they call the river and the valley Yanayaco.[233] Heretofore, Topa Inca had been carrying out a very cruel punishment without pardoning anyone that he found guilty, either in word or deed. In the Yanayaco Valley, his sister and legitimate wife, Mama Ocllo, pleaded with him not to continue with such cruelty, as it was more a barbaric butchery than a punishment, and to kill no more but to pardon them, assigning them as servants to her household. At her request, Topa Inca stopped the executions and said that he pardoned them all. And because the pardon took place at Yanayaco, he ordered that all the people reprieved should be called *yanayacos*. He counted them so that they were known and were not included among the servants of the Sun, nor within the inspection. Thus the *curacas* stayed with the *yanayacos*. This done, Topa Inca declared null and void the inspection that his

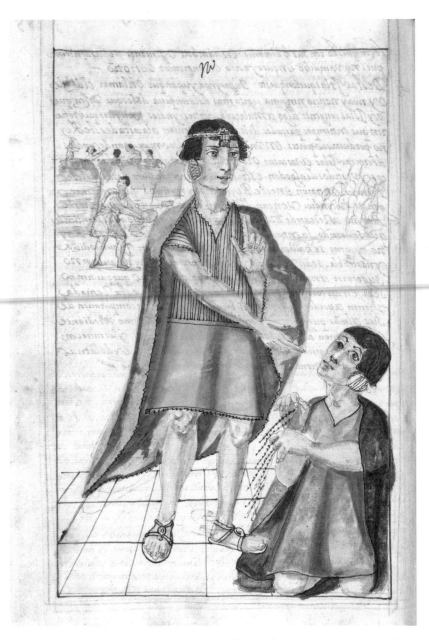

FIGURE 51.1. Topa Inca Yupanqui ordered the death of Topa Capac, by Martín de Murúa [1590:f. 51v]. Note that Topa Capac holds a *quipu* in his hands, presumably with the results of his fraudulent inspection. (Courtesy of The J. Getty Museum, Los Angeles, copyright © The J. Paul Getty Museum.)

brother Topa Inca had made, and he returned to Cuzco with the purpose of ordering the inspection redone.

[52]

TOPA INCA YUPANQUI ORDERS A SECOND INSPECTION OF THE LAND AND DOES OTHER THINGS

*S*ince the inspection that he entrusted to his brother Topa Capac was not to his liking, Topa Inca annulled it and appointed another of his brothers named Apu Achachi as inspector general. The Inca ordered him not to include the *yanayacos* in the inspection that he would carry out, because what they had done made them unworthy of being counted with the others. Thus, Apu Achachi left and carried out his general inspection. And he relocated many of the Indians into towns and houses (because before they lived in caves and hills and on the banks of the rivers, each by himself). He moved those who were in fortified places to the plains so that they would not have a place that would make them feel strong enough to rebel. He relocated them to provinces, giving them their *curacas* in the way that is told above. But he did not select the son of a deceased *curaca* as a *curaca;* instead, [he appointed] whoever had more knowledge and ability to command and rule according to the will of the Inca. If during his *curaca*ship he did not please Topa Inca, he had him removed without further ado and appointed another one so that no *curaca*, greater or lesser, felt secure in his position. And from his own hand he would give these *curacas* servants, women, and farms, because although they were *curacas*, they did not have permission to take anything by their authority without the Inca's express permission, on pain of death.

In each of these provinces, everyone would cultivate for the Inca a very large field full of all types of food, which the Inca's stewards would collect during the harvest. Above everyone was a *tucurico apu*, who was the deputy governor of the Inca in that province. The truth is that Inca Yupanqui was the first Inca who forced the Indians of this land to render tribute in particular items and in a specified amount. But Topa Inca assessed them and made a record of the tributes that they were to give, and he levied the taxes according to what was to be given in each province, both for the general tax as well as for the *huacas* and the Houses of the Sun. Thus, he had them so burdened with taxes and tributes that they needed to work continuously, day and night, to pay them. Yet they could not fulfill [the quotas] even if they had left no time for the work and labor that was needed for their own sustenance.

Topa Inca divided the estates of the whole land using the [unit of] measure that they call *topo*. He divided the months of the year for the work and labors of the field in the following way: He gave the Indians only three months a year to work their fields; during the rest [of the year] they had to occupy themselves in working for the Sun, the *huacas*, and the Inca. Of the three months that he left [for them], one month was for sowing and plowing, one for harvesting, and the other was for their summer festivities and so that they could spin and weave for themselves, because he ordered that they spend the remaining [nine months] in his service and in that of the Sun and the *huacas*.

This Inca ordered that there should be merchants so that he might profit from their trade in the following way. He ordered that whenever any merchant brought any gold or silver or precious stones and other exquisite things to sell, he should be seized and asked where he had obtained or extracted it. In this way, they would tell of the mines and places where they had extracted it; thus [Topa Inca Yupanqui] discovered a great number of mines of gold and silver and [other] very fine colors.

This Inca had two governors-general in all the land called *suyuyoc apu*; one lived in Jauja and the other in Tiahuanaco, a town of Collasuyu.

Topa Inca [also] ordered the seclusion of certain women in the manner of our cloistered nuns, maidens twelve years and older whom they call *acllas*. They took them out of [their seclusion] to be given in marriage by the *tucurico apu* or by order of the Inca. Whenever any captain was leaving to conquer or returned victorious, the Inca would distribute these women as a gift and reward that was much appreciated to the captains and soldiers and to other retainers who served or somehow pleased him. As some women were removed, others were put in [their place] so that they would always remain according to the designs of Inca Topa. And should any man remove one, or be caught inside with her, they were both hanged alive, tied up together.

And this Inca made many laws in his tyrannical style that will be written in a separate volume.[234]

[53]

TOPA INCA BUILDS THE FORTRESS OF CUZCO

*A*fter Topa Inca inspected his realm, he went to Cuzco, where he was served and adored. Finding himself idle, he remembered that his father, Pachacuti, had called the city of Cuzco the lion [i.e., puma] city. He said the tail was where the two rivers that pass through the city join.[235] The body was the plaza and the surrounding houses. [He also said] that the head was lacking, but that one of his sons would build it. Having consulted about this matter with the noblemen, [Topa Inca] said that the best head that he could build would be to make a fortress on a high hill that is on the north side of the city (Figure 53.1).

FIGURE 53.1. The fortress of Sacsayhuaman is on a high plateau to the north of the city. (Courtesy Servicio Aerofotográfico Nacional, Peru.)

FIGURE 53.2. The city of Cuzco. The fortress Sacsayhuaman is to the upper left, and the area of the puma's tail is marked by the two intersecting roads, formerly rivers, to the lower right. (Courtesy Servicio Aerofotográfico Nacional, Peru.)

This decided, he sent orders to all the provinces for the *tucuricos* to send him great quantities of men to work on the fortress. Once they arrived, he divided them into groups, giving each one its task and its leader. Thus, some quarried stone, others worked it, moved it, or set it. Their diligence was such that in just a few years they had built the great fortress of Cuzco, sumptuous, very strong, and of coarse stone — a most remarkable thing to behold (Figure 53.2). The separated interior rooms were made of small and polished stones so beautiful that their beauty and strength are not to be believed unless they are seen. And what is even more amazing is that they had no tools with which to carve them, save for other stones. This fortress stood until the [time of the] clashes between Pizarro and Almagro, after which the Spaniards began to dismantle it to build their houses in Cuzco — which is at the foot of the fortress — with its masonry.[236] Those who now see its ruins are filled with great sadness. Once it was ready, the Inca built many warehouses around Cuzco for supplies and clothes [to be used] in times of need and of war, which was a very great thing (Figure 53.3).

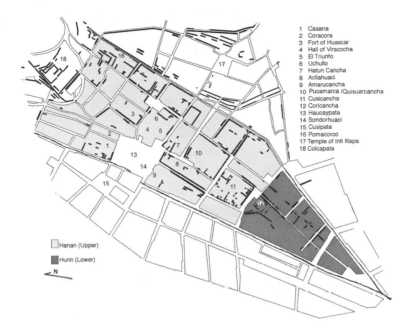

1 Casana
2 Coracora
3 Fort of Huascar
4 Hall of Viracocha
5 El Triunfo
6 Uchullo
7 Hatun Cancha
8 Acllahuaci
9 Amarucancha
10 Pucamarca /Quisuarcancha
11 Cusicancha
12 Coricancha
13 Haucaypata
14 Sondorhuaci
15 Cusipata
16 Pomacorco
17 Temple of Inti Illapa
18 Colcapata

Hanan (Upper)

Hurin (Lower)

N

FIGURE 53.3. Map of Inca Cuzco.

[54]

THE DEATH OF TOPA INCA YUPANQUI

*H*aving inspected and distributed the lands and built the fortress of
Cuzco and many others, as well as innumerable houses and buildings, Topa
Inca Yupanqui then went to Chinchero, a town near Cuzco where he had
some very elaborate houses for his leisure. There he ordered great estates
made for his household. When [they] were finished, Topa Inca fell sick with
a serious illness and did not wish to be visited by anyone. Since his illness
worsened and he felt he was dying, Topa Inca called for the Cuzco noblemen, his relatives, and the retainers who were present. When he had them
before him, he said: "My relatives and friends! I will have you know that the
Sun, my father, wants to take me with him, and I wish to go to rest with
him. I have called you so that you will know who I will leave as your lord,
my heir and successor, who will govern and rule you." To this they replied

FIGURE 54.1. Mama Ocllo, by Martín de Murúa [1590:f. 54v]. (Courtesy of The J. Getty Museum, Los Angeles, copyright © The J. Paul Getty Museum.)

that his illness grieved them much, but if the Sun, his father, wished it so, then his will must be done, and that he should do them the favor of naming who was to remain as *capac* in his stead. Topa Inca replied: "I appoint my son Tito Cusi Hualpa, the son of my sister and wife, Mama Ocllo, as my successor" (Figure 54.1). For this they gave him many thanks. After this he let himself fall back on the pillow and died, having lived for eighty-five years.

Topa Inca Yupanqui succeeded his father when he was eighteen. He was *capac* for sixty-seven years. He had two legitimate sons and sixty bastard [ones] and thirty daughters. Others say that at the time of his death, or sometime before, he had appointed as his successor a bastard son of his named Capac Guari, the son of a mistress named Chuqui Ocllo.

Topa Inca Yupanqui left an *ayllu* or lineage called Capac Ayllu; the leaders who maintain this *ayllu* who [are] now alive are Don Andrés Topa Yupanqui,[237] Don Cristóbal Pisac Topa,[238] Don García Vilcas,[239] Don Felipe Topa Yupanqui, Don García Ayache, and Don García Pilco.[240] They are Hanan Cuzcos.

Topa Inca was frank, merciful in peace and cruel in war and in punishments, a friend of the poor, brave, a man of much industry, a builder. He was the greatest tyrant of all the Incas. He died in the year 1258. His body was burned by Chalco Chima [in the] year [15]33 when he captured Huascar, as will be said in its place.[241] His ashes and *guauqui* idol, called *cusichuri*, were found in Calispuquio[242] where they had been hidden and had been offered many sacrifices.[243]

[55]

THE LIFE OF HUAYNA CAPAC, THE ELEVENTH INCA

*A*fter Topa Inca died, the noblemen who had been with him at the time of his death went to Cuzco to carry out the customary ceremony, which was to proclaim his successor as ruler before the death of the Inca was known, as had been done at the death of Pachacuti Inca Yupanqui. But as the wives and children of Topa Inca also went to Cuzco, it could not be kept secret, because a woman, a mistress to the dead Inca named Curi Ocllo, and a relative of Capac Guari, spoke to her kin and to Capac Guari's kin as soon as she arrived at Cuzco. She told them: "Lords and kin! Know that Topa Inca is dead and that when in [good] health he had named Capac Guari as his son and heir. But at the end, being near death, he said that Tito Cusi Hualpa, the son of Mama Ocllo, should succeed him. You must not allow this or [let] it pass. You should instead call all your relatives and friends together and appoint and raise Capac Guari, your elder brother, the son of Chuqui Ocllo, as Inca." All the relatives of Capac Guari agreed, and so they had all their other relatives summoned.

While the kin of Capac Guari organized what has been described, the noblemen of Cuzco, unaware of what was going on, were arranging how to give the tassel to Tito Cusi Hualpa. But the people of Capac Guari were overheard and their plans discovered by Guaman Achachi, Topa Inca's brother. He assembled some of his friends, with whom he went armed to where Tito Cusi Hualpa was resting and hid him. He then went with his men to where the faction of Capac Guari was gathering and killed many who were there, including Capac Guari. However, some say that he did not kill Capac Guari then, but seized him instead. His mother, Chuqui Ocllo, was charged with being a rebel and having killed Topa Inca, her lord, with spells, and [thus] they killed her. They banished Capac Guari to Chinchero, where they fed him, and he never again entered Cuzco until he died. They also killed the woman Curi Ocllo, who had advised that they should raise Capac Guari as Inca.

[56]

THEY GIVE THE TASSEL OF INCA TO HUAYNA CAPAC, THE ELEVENTH INCA

Once the city of Cuzco was pacified, Guaman Achachi went to Quispicancha[244] — [which is] three leagues from Cuzco — where Tito Cusi Hualpa, his nephew, was hidden, and he brought him to Cuzco and took him to the House of the Sun. After the accustomed sacrifices and ceremonies, the figure of the Sun placed the tassel on Tito Cusi Hualpa.

When this was over and the new Inca had been invested with all the insignias of *capac* and placed in a rich litter, they took him to the *huaca* of Huanacauri, where he offered his sacrifice. The noblemen returned him to Cuzco by the route along which Manco Capac had come.[245]

On arriving at the first plaza of Cuzco, which is called Rimapampa,[246] the succession was announced to the people, and they were ordered to come there to offer obedience to the new Inca. And when all the people had come to do so and they beheld their Inca so youthful, never having seen him before, they all raised their voices as one and called him Huayna Capac, which means "the rich youth" or "the youthful prince." From this time on and for this reason, they called him Huayna Capac and no longer called him Tito Cusi Hualpa. They held his festivities and armed him as a knight and worshiped him and presented him with many gifts, as was the custom among them.

[57]

THE FIRST THINGS THAT HUAYNA CAPAC DID AFTER BEING INVESTED AS INCA

Since Huayna Capac was very young when he was named Inca, they gave him Gualpaya, a son of Capac Yupanqui, the brother of Inca Yupanqui, as coadjutor and tutor. Gualpaya sought to take over the Incaship himself, but this was discovered by Guaman Achachi, who was governor of Chinchaysuyu and was in Cuzco at the time. They killed Gualpaya and the others who were found guilty.

Huayna Capac began ruling and soon afterward began to govern by himself, although he always had Auqui Topa Inca, his brother by both his father and mother, with him as a counselor. Then Huayna Capac went to the House of the Sun and inspected it; he took account of its stewards and provided what was lacking, and gave the *mamaconas* the necessary things. He removed the custody of the Sun from the one who held it and took it for himself, and he called himself the Shepherd of the Sun. He inspected the other *huacas* and oracles and their estates. He also inspected the buildings in the city of Cuzco and the houses of the noblemen.

Huayna Capac then had his father, Topa Inca, embalmed. After he performed his sacrifices and ceremonies and mourning, he placed his father in the houses that Huayna Capac had already prepared for this, and he gave Topa Inca's retainers everything that was needed for the maintenance and service [of his father]. Huayna Capac himself cried for his father, as well as [for his] mother, who also died shortly thereafter.[247]

FIGURE 58.1. The remains of Inca buildings in Yucay

[58]

HUAYNA CAPAC CONQUERS THE CHACHAPOYAS

*A*fter Huayna Capac had given orders in the above-mentioned matters, he learned that there were certain lands near the Chachapoyas that he could conquer, and on the way he could also put down the Chachapoyas, who had rebelled. Having given notice to his noblemen, he gathered a large number of warriors. Huayna Capac left Cuzco, having first performed his sacrifices and observed the *calpa*, and while en route he reformed many things to his liking. He reached the Chachapoyas and the other surrounding nations, which went on the defensive with their weapons in hand. But in the end, Huayna Capac defeated them, perpetrating great cruelties on them, and he returned to Cuzco, where he celebrated the victory that he had won over the Chachapoyas and other lands.

While he was on this expedition, Huayna Capac left one of his bastard brothers named Cinchi Roca, an ingenious architect, as governor of Cuzco. Thus, Cinchi Roca made all the buildings in Yucay and the houses of the

Inca in the Casana, in the city of Cuzco.[248] Huayna Capac himself then built other edifices around Cuzco in the areas that he thought most suitable (Figure 58.1).

[59]

HUAYNA CAPAC INSPECTS ALL THE LAND FROM QUITO TO CHILE

*H*uayna Capac rested long in Cuzco. Desiring to do something, he [realized] that it had been a long time since the land had last been inspected. Huayna Capac decided to do so and appointed his uncle, Guaman Achachi, to inspect the area of Chinchaysuyu as far as Quito, and he took charge of inspecting the area of Collasuyu.

Thus each one departed for what they had to inspect, and Huayna Capac took the road to the Collao. Along the way, he was occupying the residences of his *tucurico* governors, and placing and removing governors and *curacas*, and clearing lands, and making bridges and canals. And having done these things, he reached the Charcas. From there he went to Chile, which his father had conquered. Huayna Capac removed the governor he had placed there and entrusted the rule of these provinces to the two native *curacas* of Chile, Michimalongo and Tangalongo, whom his father had defeated. Having reorganized the garrison there, he continued inspecting as far as Coquimbo and Copiapo, and from there up to Atacama and Arequipa. Huayna Capac continued inspecting along Antisuyu and Alayda, entering the Collao and Charcas. He arrived at the Cochabamba Valley, and there he established a settlement of *mitimaes* from all parts [of his realm], because the natives were few and all that fertile land abounded in resources.[249] From there he went to Pocona to organize the frontier against the Chiriguanas and to rebuild a fortress that his father had constructed.[250]

While engaged in these matters, Huayna Capac received news that the provinces of Quito, Cayambes, Carangues, Pastos, and Guancabilicas had rebelled. He therefore prepared to return and arrived at Tiahuanaco, where he announced the war against the Quitos and Cayambes. He laid out the ways in which the Uros were to live, and he gave them places where each Uro town was to fish in the lake. Huayna Capac also visited the Temple of the Sun and the *huaca* of Ticci Viracocha on the island of Titicaca. And he

sent orders that all the provinces should send men to partake in the war he had announced (Figure 59.1).

[60]

HUAYNA CAPAC WAGES WAR ON THE QUITOS, PASTOS, CARANGUES, CAYAMBES, AND GUANCABILICAS

[When] Huayna Capac learned that the Pastos Indians and the Quitos, Cayambes, Carangues, and Guancabilicas Indians had rebelled, killed the *tucuricos*, and strengthened their people and forces, he swiftly gathered many men from all the divisions of the four *suyus*. He appointed Michi of the Hurin Cuzcos and Auqui Topa of the Hanan Cuzcos as captains and left his uncle Guaman Achachi as governor in Cuzco. Others say that he left Apu Hilaquita and Auqui Topa Inca in Cuzco, together with his son who was to succeed him, named Topa Cusi Hualpa Inti Illapa. And [they say] that he left with him another of his sons named Tito Atauchi, who remained fasting as was prescribed by the rites.[251] And it should be noted that Huayna Capac was married, according to their customs, to Cusi Rimay, with whom he had no male son. He therefore took his sister Araua Ocllo as his wife (Figure 60.1), with whom he had the aforementioned Topa Cusi Hualpa, who is usually called Huascar.[252] When he was ready for the expedition, Huayna Capac ordered Atahualpa and Ninan Cuyoche,[253] his two bastard sons[254] who were now young men, to prepare to leave with him. He ordered Manco Inca and Paullu Topa,[255] who were also his bastard sons, to remain with Huascar in Cuzco. When Huayna Capac was thus organized, he left for Quito. Progressing through his expedition, he reached Tomebamba, where he had been born. And there he constructed many great buildings, in which he placed with much solemnity the placenta in which he was born (Figure 60.2). Huayna Capac pressed ahead, and reaching the frontier where the Quitos had rebelled, he marshaled his squadrons and immediately decided to send his army to conquer the Pastos. For this he appointed two captains from the Collao, the first of whom was named Mollo Cabana and the second Mollo Pucara. Two more were from Cuntisuyu, the first one named Apu Cautar Cabana and the other one Conti Mollo. To

FIGURE 60.1. Araua Ocllo, found in Martín de Murúa's [1590:f. 79] manuscript. The figure was drawn by Guaman Poma de Ayala. (Courtesy of The J. Getty Museum, Los Angeles, copyright © The J. Paul Getty Museum.)

FIGURE 60.2. Huayna Capac at Tomebamba, by Martín de Murúa [1590:f. 62]. (Courtesy of The J. Getty Museum, Los Angeles, copyright © The J. Paul Getty Museum.)

these he gave many men of their [own] nations and two thousand noblemen to strengthen and to guard them. Auqui Topa Inca, the brother of Huayna Capac, and Acollo Topa, of the lineage of Viracocha, went as their captains. They went to the land of the Pastos, who retreated to their main town, leaving the women, children, and the elderly and a few men behind so that the Inca would think there was no one else. The Inca's forces easily defeated them and, believing that there were no more, became careless, giving themselves up to idleness and pleasures. And one night in the midst of a great celebration, while [they were] eating and drinking freely without a guard, the Pastos attacked them and committed a great slaughter and ruin on them, mostly on the Collas.[256] Those who remained retreated until they encountered the rest of the Inca's army, which was following them. They even say that Atahualpa and Ninan led this reinforcement, and that with the anger that Huayna Capac felt at this, he ordered the war [to] be waged very cruelly. Thus, for a second time, they entered [that region], destroying and burning the settlements and killing all sorts of people, young and old, men and women, children and the elderly. Having destroyed that province, Huayna Capac placed his governor in it.

Inca Huayna Capac returned to Tomebamba, where he rested for a few days; then he moved his camp in order to conquer the Carangues, a very warlike nation. In this [campaign], Huayna Capac conquered the Macas Indians and the area of the Cañaris, as well as the Quisna, and the Ancasmarca, and the province of Puruvay, and the Indians of Nolitria and other neighboring nations.

Huayna Capac then went down to Tumbes, a seaport, and he reached the fortresses of Carangui and Cochisque. When he began to conquer Cochisque, he found it well defended by valiant men, and many died on both sides. In the end, he took it by force, and the people who escaped withdrew to the fortress of Carangui. The Inca's men decided to conquer the area surrounding this fortress first. Thus, they began destroying as far as Angasmayo and Otabalo. The people of these provinces who escaped the hands and fury of the Inca withdrew to the fortress. When Huayna Capac later attacked [the fortress] with all his men, he was repelled by those who were inside; hence many of his men were killed and the noblemen were forced to flee. They were routed by the Cayambes, and Inca Huayna Capac was thrown from his litter. He would have died had the members of his guard, who numbered one thousand men, not arrived or if his captains Cusi Topa Yupanqui and Huayna Achachi had not rescued him and raised him.[257] Beholding this sight, the noblemen took heart and returned to aid their Inca. This time they attacked the Cayambes in such a way that they trapped them in their fortress. But in the first and in the second encounters, the Inca lost many men.

Huayna Capac therefore returned to Tomebamba, where he reorganized his army to return against the Cayambes.[258] Meanwhile, the noblemen were angry with the Inca and decided to desert him and return to Cuzco. But the Inca stopped them by generously giving them many items of clothing, food, and other riches, and he formed a good army.

At this time Huayna Capac learned that the Cayambes had left the fortress and had assailed a company of the Inca's men that he had left there as a garrison. The Cayambes had routed them and killed many, and the rest had run away. This caused Huayna Capac great grief, and he dispatched his brother Auqui Toma, with the army that he had mustered from all the nations, to go against the Cayambes in the fortress. Auqui Toma left, attacked the fortress, captured four lines of defense, and on entering the last wall — for there were five — the Cayambes killed Auqui Toma, the captain of the Cuzcos, who had fought most bravely. This attack and resistance was so bitter and [was fought] with such courage on both sides that a very large number of men died, so many that those who fought did not have anywhere to walk except upon the piles of the dead. They all desired so to win or die, that when they had used all of their spears and arrows, they charged with their fists. But when the Inca's men saw that their captain was dead, they began to retreat until [they reached] a river, into which they threw themselves recklessly, to save their lives. But as the river's waters were high, many of them died by drowning, and so this was a great loss of men for Huayna Capac. Those who escaped from the river and from the hands of the enemies stopped on the other side of the river, from whence they sent a messenger to Huayna Capac telling what had happened. The Inca received this news [with] the greatest sorrow that he had ever felt, because he dearly loved his brother Auqui Toma, who had fallen there and, with him, many men and the finest of his armies.

But as Huayna Capac was valiant, he did not lose heart because of this. Instead his spirits were raised and he proposed to take revenge. He immediately prepared his people for this, and he set out in person for the Cayambes' fortress.[259] He divided the army into three parts. He sent Captain Michi with a third of the army, together with the Cuzco noblemen, to pass by one side of the fortress without being seen. The people of Chinchaysuyu were sent to another side, to advance five marches beyond the fortress and then at a certain time they were to return, ravaging and destroying. The Inca, with the rest of the army, personally stormed the fortress and began to attack it with a great and unstoppable fury.

This lasted for some days, during which time Huayna Capac lost many men. During this attack, Michi and the Chinchaysuyus returned, burning, razing, and destroying all the land of the Cayambes with such rage that they made the earth tremble and left nothing standing. When Huayna Capac learned that his men were near the fortress, he pretended to retreat. And as the Cayambes were not aware of what was coming upon them from behind, they left the fortress in pursuit of Huayna Capac. When the Cayambes were some distance away from the fortress, the armies of Michi and the Chinchaysuyu came within sight. As the Cayambes were occupied fighting Huayna Capac, Michi and the Chinchaysuyus met no resistance in the fortress and easily entered it and set fire to it in many places, killing and capturing those they found within.

When the Cayambes who were fighting against Huayna Capac saw their fortress and houses burning, they lost hope in their defense. Leaving the battle, they fled toward a nearby lake, thinking that they would be able to save themselves in the marshes and reeds that were there. But Huayna Capac swiftly followed them and had the lake surrounded so that none would escape him. The men of Huayna Capac, who himself fought bravely, did such damage and killing that the entire lake was tinted with the blood of the dead Cayambes. For this reason, from then on they called that lake Yahuar Cocha, which means "lake" or "sea of blood," because of the amount that was spilled there.

It is to be noted that in the middle of this lake there were two willows that some Cayambes climbed. Among them were their two leaders, named Pinto and Canto, both very valiant Indians. Huayna Capac's men pelted them with stones and there they captured Canto, but Pinto escaped with one thousand valiant Cañaris.[260]

With the Cayambes defeated, the Cuzcos began to choose among the vanquished those they thought were the best with whom to enter Cuzco in triumph. But the Cayambes, believing that they were being chosen to be killed, preferred to die fighting rather than tied up like women. Thus they re-formed and began to fight anew. Seeing this, Huayna Capac had them all killed.

Huayna Capac placed a garrison in the fortress, and he dispatched a captain with men in pursuit of Pinto, who was fleeing and doing much harm. He pursued him until Pinto and his companions entered a forest, where he escaped for some time. Later, after Huayna Capac had rested a few days in Tomebamba, he learned that [Pinto] was in the forests. He surrounded and blocked all the entrances and exits of those forests, and thus, fatigued from hunger, [Pinto] and his people surrendered. Pinto was very valiant, and he had such hatred of Huayna Capac that, even after being captured, when the Inca gave him many gifts and good treatment, he never showed his face. Thus, he died stubborn, and because of this Huayna Capac ordered him flayed and his skin made into a drum so that they could perform a *taqui*[261] with it in Cuzco, which is to dance to the Sun. When this was finished, he sent it to Cuzco, and with this the war came to an end.[262]

[61]

THE CHIRIGUANAS LEAVE TO WAGE WAR IN PERU AGAINST THOSE CONQUERED BY THE INCAS

*W*hile Huayna Capac was occupied in this war with the Cayambes, the Chiriguanas gathered. This is a nation of the forests who [are] naked and eat human flesh and have public butchery for this. Leaving the wilderness, they entered the land of the Charcas, which had been conquered by the Incas of Peru. They attacked the fortress of Cuzcotuyo, where the Inca had a great frontier garrison [to defend] against the Chiriguanas. Since their attack was a surprise, they entered the fortress and killed everyone there and caused great disruptions, robberies, and deaths among the people of that land.

This news reached Huayna Capac in Quito, and he received it with great sadness. He immediately dispatched a captain of his named Yasca so that he would go to Cuzco to gather men, and with them go to wage war on the Chiriguanas. This captain departed for Cuzco, taking with him the *huacas* Catiquilla of Cajamarca and Guamachuco[263] and Curichaculla of the Chachapoyas, and the *huacas* Tomayrica and Chinchaycocha, along with many servants of these *huacas*. He arrived in Cuzco, where he was very well received by the governors named Apu Hilaquita and Auqui Topa Inca. Having mustered the men, he left Cuzco for the Charcas. Along the way, he took many men from the Collao, with whom he attacked and waged a cruel war on the Chiriguanas. He captured some of them, whom he sent as examples to Huayna Capac in Quito so that he could see the strangeness of these people. Captain Yasca rebuilt the fortresses that were around there, and placing the necessary garrison in them, he returned to Cuzco, where he dismissed his men, and each returned to his own land.

[62]

WHAT HUAYNA CAPAC DID
AFTER THOSE WARS

*A*s soon as Huayna Capac dispatched the captain who went to the Chiriguanas, he left Tomebamba to organize the nations that he had conquered as far as Quito, Pasto, and Guancabilicas. Thus, he reached [as far as] the river called Angasmayo, between Pasto and Quito, where he placed boundary markers as the limit and borders of the land that he had conquered. He placed certain gold staves on the boundary markers in memory of this and as symbols of his greatness. He followed the same river down in search of the sea, looking for people to conquer, since he had heard that in the lower region there was a great number of people.

On this journey, Huayna Capac's army suffered great dangers and hardships due to the lack of water in some large deserts that they traveled through.[264] One day, at dawn, the Inca's men found themselves surrounded by an infinite [number of] people whom they were not familiar with. In fear, [Huayna Capac's army] began to retreat toward their Inca. And as the Inca's soldiers were determined to flee, a young man who looked like an Inca came to Huayna Capac and said to him: "Lord! Fear not, for these are the people for whom we are searching! Let us attack them!" The Inca thought this was good advice, and he ordered that they attack them quickly, promising that what each man seized would be his. With this they attacked the men surrounding them with such skill that in a short time they broke through their lines. They broke them and chased them to their settlements, which were on the seacoast near Coaques. There they seized great quantities of rich spoils and very rich emeralds, turquoises, and large stores of very fine *mullu*,[265] which is a kind of powder made from seashells that is more prized among them than gold or silver.

Here Huayna Capac received messengers from the *cinchi* or *curaca* of the island of Puna.[266] He sent a great gift and beseeched [the Inca] to come to his island of Puna to receive his service. Huayna Capac did so.

From there, he went to Guancabilica, where he joined the rest of the army that he had left [behind]. There he learned that there was a great pestilence in Cuzco and that his governors Apu Hilaquita, his uncle; Auqui Topa Inca, his brother; and his sister Mama Coca were dead [as well as] many of his other relatives.[267] And to establish order in the lands that he had conquered in the area, he departed for Quito so that from there he could leave for Cuzco to rest.

However, upon arriving in Quito, he became ill with a fever, although others say it was smallpox or measles. As he felt [the disease] to be deadly, he summoned his noblemen relatives, who asked him whom he was naming as his successor. He answered that his son Ninan Cuyoche [should succeed him] if the augury of the *calpa* gave positive indications that he would succeed him well. If not, then his son Huascar [should succeed].

He therefore ordered that the ceremony of the *calpa* be held, which was conducted by Cusi Topa Yupanqui, whom Huayna Capac had already appointed as the steward of the Sun. When the first *calpa* was done, he found that Ninan Cuyoche would not succeed him well. He then [cut] open another lamb and took out the lungs, and upon inspecting certain veins, he saw that Huascar would not succeed him well either.[268] Returning to Huayna Capac with this message so that he might name another [successor], they found him already dead. As the noblemen [were left] in suspense about the succession, Cusi Topa Yupanqui said: "You tend to the body while I go to Tomebamba to give the tassel to Ninan Cuyoche!" But when he reached Tomebamba, he found that Ninan Cuyoche was [also] dead from the smallpox pestilence.[269]

Seeing this, Cusi Topa Inca said to Araua Ocllo: "Do not be sad, *coya*, ready yourself and go to Cuzco to tell your son Huascar how his father appointed him as Inca to follow his days!" He gave her two principal noblemen for company. He ordered these men to tell the Incas of Cuzco that they should immediately give the tassel to Huascar. He remained behind, preparing to depart soon after with Huayna Capac's body so as to enter Cuzco in triumph with it, following the orders Huayna Capac had noted on a staff on his deathbed.

Huayna Capac died in Quito at the age of eighty. He left more than fifty sons. He succeeded at twenty, [and] was *capac* for sixty years. He was valiant but cruel.

He left his lineage or *ayllu* called Tomebamba Ayllu. The heads of it who are alive now are Don Diego Viracocha Inca,[270] Don García Inguil Topa,[271] and Don Gonzalo Sayre. The sons of Paullu Topa, son of Huayna Capac, ally themselves with this *ayllu*.[272] They are Hanan Cuzcos.

Huayna Capac died in the year of 1524[273] of the birth of our Lord Jesus Christ. The most invincible Emperor Charles V of glorious memory, father of Your Majesty, was the king of Spain, and the pope [was] Paul III.

The lawyer Polo [de Ondegardo] found the body of Huayna Capac in the city of Cuzco in a house where they had hidden it.[274] Two of his servants guarded it; the first [was] named Hualpa Tito and the other Suma Yupanqui.[275] His *guauqui* idol was called *guaraqui inca,* and it was a large gold idol that has not yet been found.

[63]

THE LIFE OF HUASCAR INCA, THE LAST INCA, AND THAT OF ATAHUALPA

*W*ith Huayna Capac dead and the news of this known in Cuzco, they raised Topa Cusi Hualpa Inti Illapa as Inca. [He was also] called Huascar, because he was born in the town [of] Huascarquiguar,[276] four and a half leagues from Cuzco. Those who remained in Tomebamba embalmed Huayna Capac's body and gathered all the spoils and captives he had won in the wars so as to enter Cuzco in triumph with them.

It is to be noted that when the time came to leave [for Cuzco], Atahualpa [did not appear among those departing]. Huayna Capac had taken Atahualpa, the bastard son of Huayna Capac and Tocto Coca—his cousin from the lineage of Inca Yupanqui—with him to war to see how he proved himself. This was during the first campaign against the Pastos, and Atahualpa turned in flight, and because of this, his father insulted him with strong words. For this reason, Atahualpa did not appear among the people, and therefore he said this to the Inca noblemen of Cuzco: "Lords! You already know how I am a son of Huayna Capac and how my father brought me with him to see how I did in war; and because we lost the campaign in the Pastos, my father insulted me. Thus, I dare not appear among people, and much less among my relatives in Cuzco, who believed that my father would leave me in good standing. Instead, I have been left poor and disfavored. As a result, I have decided to stay here and die where my father died and not live among those who will rejoice at seeing me alone, poor, and disfavored. Thus, you do not have to wait for me." Atahualpa stayed in Tomebamba after embracing them and saying farewell to them. They left with great sadness and tears.

The noblemen brought Huayna Capac's body to Cuzco. They entered with it in great celebration, as he had ordered, and they performed the funeral rites, just as with the other [Incas]. Huascar then gave out some rewards of gold and silver and women, as there were many secluded in the house of the *acllas* from the time of his father. He constructed the buildings in Huascarquiguar, where he had been born. In Cuzco he built the houses of Amarucancha, where the monastery of the Nombre de Jesús is (Figure 63.1). He also [built] Colcampata, where Don Carlos, an Indian son of Paullu, [now] lives (Figure 63.2).

After this, Huascar summoned Cusi Topa Yupanqui and the other principal noblemen who had traveled with his father's body. They were of the lineage of Inca Yupanqui and relatives of Atahualpa's mother. He asked them why they had not brought Atahualpa with them, since undoubtedly they had left him there so that he could rebel in Quito, and then when he had rebelled, [the noblemen] would then kill him [Huascar] in Cuzco. The noblemen, finding themselves new at this business, replied that they knew nothing about this other than that Atahualpa had remained in Quito so as to avoid finding himself dishonored and impoverished among his relatives in Cuzco, as he had told them publicly. Since Huascar did not believe them, he tortured them, though they never confessed to more than this. Seeing the harm that he had done to such principal noblemen and [understanding] that he would never have them as good friends nor be able to trust them, Huascar had them killed.²⁷⁷ This caused great sadness in Cuzco and great hatred against Huascar among the Hanan Cuzcos, the lineage to which the dead [men] belonged. Seeing this, Huascar publicly said that he disowned them and would separate himself from the kin and lineage of the Hanan Cuzcos, because Atahualpa, who was a traitor because he had not come to Cuzco to give him obedience, belonged to them.²⁷⁸ He then publicly declared war against Atahualpa and mustered men to send against him. In the meantime, Atahualpa sent his messengers to Huascar with gifts to tell him that he was his vassal and that, as such, he should say how he could serve him [in Quito]. Huascar ridiculed Atahualpa's gifts and messengers, and they even say he killed them. Others [say] that he cut their noses off, [cut] their clothing down to the waist, and thus sent them [back] dishonored.

While this was happening in Cuzco, the Guancabilicas rebelled. Atahualpa assembled a large army, and he appointed Chalco Chima, Quizquiz, Incura Hualpa, Ruminaqui Yupanqui, Urco Guaranga,²⁷⁹ and Uña Chullo as captains. He marched against the Guancabilicas, defeated them, and inflicted great punishment on them. He then returned to Quito, from where he sent an account to his brother of what he had done. At this time, Atahualpa received news of what Huascar had done to his messengers, that he had killed the noblemen, that he was assembling men against him, that he had separated himself from the Hanan Cuzcos, and that he [had] publicly denounced Atahualpa as a traitor, which they call *auca*. Seeing the bad

FIGURE 63.1. The Jesuit church in Cuzco was built on top of the Amarucancha.

FIGURE 63.2. The remains of Colcampata can still be seen in Cuzco. (Anonymous photograph, ca. 1940, private collection.)

intentions that his brother had against him, and that it behooved him to defend himself, Atahualpa took counsel with his captains. They all agreed that he should not dismiss the army, [but] should instead gather more men and enlarge it as much as he could, because those events would lead to war.

At this point, a nobleman named Hango and another named Atoc came to Tomebamba to offer a sacrifice to the figure of Huayna Capac on Huascar's orders. They took the women of Huayna Capac and the insignias of the Inca without talking to Atahualpa. Because of this, Atahualpa captured them, and under torture, they confessed to what Huascar had ordered and how warriors [were] already moving against Atahualpa. Atahualpa ordered these [men] killed and drums made of them. Then he dispatched runners along the road to Cuzco to see if they could learn of the army that Huascar, his brother, was sending against him. While en route, the scouts found Huascar's army, and they returned to tell Atahualpa about it.

Atahualpa organized his people and left Quito in search of his enemies. Both armies clashed in a very drawn out and bloody battle in Río Pampa, but Atahualpa [was] victorious. There were so many dead that Atahualpa ordered heaps made of them and their bones [left] as a memorial. And even today you can see the fields full of the bones of those who died in that battle.[280]

At this time Huascar had sent his captains Tambo Usca Mayta and Tito Atauchi, Huascar's brother, to conquer the nations of Pomacocha, who are a people to the east of the Pacamoros. When the news came of the defeat of his men, Huascar created a larger army and named Atoc, Guaychao, Hango, and Guanca Auqui as his captains. Now, as this Guanca Auqui[281] was unfortunate, he lost many men in the Pacamoros, so his brother, the Inca Huascar, sent him women's gifts to insult him, accusing [him] of acting like one. Because of this slight, Guanca Auqui decided to do something that seemed manly, and he went to Tomebamba, where the army of Atahualpa was camped, resting. And as he found them unprepared, he attacked and routed them, killing many.[282]

This news reached Atahualpa in Quito, and he felt much sorrow that his brother Guanca Auqui had mocked him in that way, for at other times when he could have killed him, he had let him go, overlooking [their enmity] because he was his brother. Atahualpa prepared himself and he ordered Quizquiz and Chalco Chima to march with his army in search of Guanca Auqui. They left and caught up with him at Cusibamba, where they fought. Guanca Auqui was defeated, with many losses on both sides. But Guanca Auqui fled, and Atahualpa's forces followed him to Cajamarca, where Guanca Auqui found a large force of people that Huascar had sent to help him. Guanca Auqui ordered them to meet up with Chalco Chima and Quizquiz while he remained in Cajamarca. The ten thousand [troops] sent by Guanca Auqui were Chachapoyas accompanied by many other [nations]. They then marched and encountered Atahualpa's forces in Cochaguayla, near Cajamarca, where they clashed. But the Chachapoyas were defeated by Chalco Chima and Quizquiz, and no more than three thousand Chachapoyas escaped. Guanca Auqui retreated toward Cuzco, followed by Atahualpa's forces.

In the province of Bombon, Guanca Auqui found a large army [made up] of all the nations that Huascar was sending him.[283] Guanca Auqui waited with them for his enemies, who came in pursuit. When they arrived, they fought a battle that lasted for two days without either side gaining an advantage. However, on the third day, Guanca Auqui was defeated by Chalco Chima and Quizquiz.

Guanca Auqui escaped from this defeat and arrived at Jauja, where he found more reinforcements of many Soras, Chancas, Aymaraes, and Yauyos Indians that his brother had sent to him. He left Jauja with them and in a place or valley called Yanamarca he came across his pursuing enemies. A battle no less bitter than the past ones was fought there between both armies. Finally, as fortune was against Guanca Auqui, he was defeated by Chalco Chima, the most fortunate captain of Atahualpa.

Most of Guanca Auqui's men died there. He fled and did not stop until [he reached] Paucaray, where he found a large company of noblemen from Cuzco, who had come with a captain named Mayta Yupanqui. [This captain] reprimanded Guanca Auqui on behalf of Huascar, asking how it was possible to lose as many men and battles as he had lost without secretly being in collusion with Chalco Chima. To this Guanca Auqui replied that what Mayta Yupanqui was saying was not true, that he had been unable to do anything more, and that Mayta Yupanqui should fight against Chalco Chima, and he would [then] see the strength that Chalco Chima had. Guanca Auqui would have gone over to Atahualpa's side then, but his captains did not let him do so. Mayta Yupanqui went on to fight Chalco Chima, whom he met on the bridge of Angoyaco, where they had many skirmishes. But in the end, the noblemen were destroyed.

[64]

HUASCAR INCA LEAVES IN PERSON TO FIGHT AGAINST CHALCO CHIMA AND QUIZQUIZ, ATAHUALPA'S CAPTAINS

*A*s the fortune of Huascar and his captains, especially that of Guanca Auqui, was so inferior to that of Atahualpa and his fortunate and skillful captains Chalco Chima and Quizquiz, there was nothing that did not favor the latter nor handicap the former. It should be noted that with the defeat that Chalco Chima and Quizquiz inflicted on the brave and very confident noblemen on the Angoyaco bridge, as was told [above], Guanca Auqui and the other captains who came with him became so fearful that they fled without stopping until they reached Vilcas[huaman], twenty or so leagues from Angoyaco in the direction of Cuzco (Figure 64.1).

In addition to the delight that Atahualpa's captains felt at the glory of attaining as many victories as they had won, another, greater [pleasure] came with the news that Atahualpa sent. He told them how he had arrived in person at Cajamarca and Guamachuco and had made himself be received and obeyed as Inca by all the nations through which he had passed. He had taken the tassel of Inca and the *capac hongo* and now called himself the paramount Inca of all the land. He said that there was no other Inca but him. He ordered them to press ahead, conquering until they encountered Huascar. They were to fight him and defeat him like the others and seize him if they could.

Atahualpa became so conceited with his victories and saw himself in such majesty that he did not want to hear of negotiations, nor could anyone raise their eyes to look at him. For those who had some business with him, he had appointed a lieutenant, whom they called *inca apu*, which means the "lord of the Inca," who was seated beside the Inca. [The *inca apu*] negotiated with those who had something to transact. They would enter with a load on their back, and, looking at the ground, they would discuss their business with the *apu*. He would then rise and go inform the Inca Atahualpa, who would order what was to be done. The *apu* would [then] tell the messenger or negotiator, and in this way the order would be dispatched.[284]

Atahualpa was extremely cruel. He would kill right and left, destroy, burn, and raze whatever [was] before him. Thus, from Quito to Guama-

FIGURE 64.1. Vilcashuaman was an important center for the Inca.

chuco he committed the greatest cruelties, robberies, insults, and tyrannies that had ever been done in this land.

When Atahualpa reached Guamachuco, two principal lords of his house [went to] make a sacrifice to the idol or *huaca* of Guamachuco and to ask it if they would be successful in their affairs.[285] The noblemen went, made the sacrifice, and consulted the oracle. It told them that Atahualpa would come to a bad end, because he was so cruel and a tyrant and spiller of so much human blood. The noblemen delivered this devil's message to Inca Atahualpa, and because of this he became angry at the oracle. He prepared his warriors and went to where the *huaca* was. Surrounding this place, he grabbed a gold halberd in his hand and took with him the two [noblemen] from his house who had gone to make the sacrifice. When he arrived where the idol was, an old man came out who was more than one hundred years old. He was the priest of the oracle who had given the answer. [He was] dressed in very woolly clothing [that was] covered with seashells [and that] reached down to his feet. When Atahualpa learned who he was, he raised the halberd and gave him a blow that cut off his head. He then entered the idol's house and demolished its head with blows as well, even though it was made of stone. He then ordered that the old man, the idol, and its house be burned, reduced to ashes, and scattered to the wind.[286] And even though it was very large, he leveled the hill where that oracle and idol or *huaca* of the devil stood.

After Chalco Chima and Quizquiz learned of all of this, they held great celebrations and festivities and began to march toward Cuzco. Huascar Inca, who was in Cuzco [and was] distressed by the many men he had lost, received news of this. He clearly saw that his only recourse was to go out and fight in person to test his fortune, which had been so adverse for him. He fasted for this—for these heathens also have a certain type of fasting—and made many sacrifices to the idols and oracles of Cuzco, asking them for a reply. They all answered that it would [go] badly for him. Having heard this answer, he consulted his fortunetellers and sorcerers (whom they call *omo*), who, to please him, gave him hope of a fortunate ending. Thus, he gathered a powerful army and dispatched runners to find their enemies, who were found at a place called Curaguasi, fourteen leagues from Cuzco. There they found Chalco Chima and Quizquiz and learned that they had left the main Cuzco road and were taking the Cotabamba [road]. This is to the right of the main route coming from Cajamarca or Lima to Cuzco. They did this to avoid the poor road and dangerous pass that is near the Apurimac Bridge.[287]

Huascar divided his army into three parts. One third consisted of the Indians of Cuntisuyu, Charcas, Collasuyu, Chuyes, and Chile, and he gave them Arampa Yupanqui as [their] captain. He ordered that they march above Cotabamba, toward another neighboring province of the Omasuyus, so that they would push the enemy toward the Cotabamba River and the Apurimac Bridge. He ordered Guanca Auqui, Agua Panti, and Paca Mayta, his captains, to take the remaining men from the past battles. They were to move toward Cotabamba and take the enemy from one side. Huascar himself went with another group of men. And all of the armies of Huascar and Atahualpa marched toward Cotabamba.

When Arampa Yupanqui learned that Atahualpa's forces were traveling via a small valley or ravine that leads to Huánuco Pampa,[288] he came out to meet them and fought against one of Chalco Chima's squadrons. This was a very bitter encounter in which many of Atahualpa's men died, including one of his captains named Tomay Rima. Huascar received great pleasure from this and laughingly told the noblemen of Cuzco: "The Collas have won this victory; look at the duty we have to imitate our ancestors!" Afterward, the captains-general of his army, who were Tito Atauchi and Topa Atao, his brothers, and Nano and Urco Guarga, ordered the army to fight Atahualpa's forces with all their strength. Facing each other, the armies attacked with skill and order. The battle lasted from morning until almost sunset, and many men on both sides died in it, although Huascar's men were not hurt as much as those of Chalco Chima and Quizquiz. Seeing what danger they were in, many of [the latter] retreated to a great scrubland that was near Huánuco Pampa.[289] Huascar thought about this and had the scrubland set on fire, and a large portion of Atahualpa's force was burned in it.

However, Chalco Chima and Quizquiz retreated to the other side of the Cotabamba River. Huascar, pleased with the results, did not continue the chase, enjoying the victory that fortune had placed in his hands. Because of this he halted. Chalco Chima and Quizquiz, who were experienced men in such situations, saw that they were not followed and wanted to raise the morale of their troops so that the next day [they could] counterattack those who believed themselves to be victors. They sent spies to Huascar's camp and learned from them how Huascar had divided his men in such a way as to trap Chalco Chima and Quizquiz and not allow them to escape.

[65]

THE BATTLE BETWEEN THE FORCES OF
ATAHUALPA AND HUASCAR AND THE
IMPRISONMENT OF HUASCAR

*W*ith the next day's dawn, Huascar decided to finish off his brother's forces in one stroke. He ordered Topa Atao to take a squadron of men through the ravine to look for the enemy and to notify him of what he discovered. Topa Atao departed with this order and entered the ravine in great silence and looked everywhere. But the spies of Chalco Chima saw everything without being seen and warned him and Quizquiz about this. Having heard this, Chalco Chima divided his men into two parts and placed them on both sides of the road by which he knew that the men would pass. When Topa Atao arrived, they attacked him as one so that almost everyone was captured or killed. They captured a gravely wounded Topa Atao, and from him Chalco Chima learned that Huascar was coming behind Topa Atao and would soon be there with a squadron of only five thousand men, leaving the rest of his men in Huánuco Pampa.

Chalco Chima sent this information to Quizquiz, who was not there, so that he would come join him. [He told him that] he had destroyed Topa Atao and was waiting for Huascar, who was coming unaccompanied, and that he wanted to attack him and trap him between them. Thus it was done. They divided their men on both sides of the road like the first time. Huascar, who was confident that his brother Topa Atao was ahead, traveled rapidly and without caution or suspicion. Chalco Chima's spies told him how Huascar was very carelessly coming in his litter. Shortly after they entered the ravine, Huascar and his men came across the dead bodies of Topa Atao's men. Recognizing them, Huascar wanted to turn back, realizing that they were all dead and that it must be an ambush, but he could not because he was surrounded by his enemies. Then Chalco Chima's men appeared and attacked Huascar. When he tried to flee ahead of those who were attacking his rear, he fell into the hands of Quizquiz, who was waiting for him farther down. Chalco Chima's forces came upon Huascar and his people on one side and Quizquiz's men [came] on the other in such a way that they spared no one, killing everyone with great ferocity. Chalco Chima, who was looking for Huascar, saw him in his litter and chased him and seized him and pulled him down from the litter.[290] Thus, the unlucky Huascar Inca, twelfth and last of the tyrant Inca Capacs of Peru, was easily captured and placed in the power of another greater and more cruel tyrant than he, with his army dead, defeated, and destroyed.

Placing Huascar under good protection with sufficient guard, Chalco Chima left in Huascar's litter. He detached five thousand men and he traveled ahead toward the rest [of the men], who remained on the plains of Huánuco Pampa. He ordered that all the rest should follow with Quizquiz, and that when he let the sun shade [of the litter] fall, they should attack. This was a ruse so that Huascar's forces would think that he was Huascar returning victorious and [would] wait [to attack]. Thus, he marched and arrived where Huascar's forces were waiting for their lord. When they saw him, they believed that he was Huascar returning victorious and that he brought the enemy captured. When Chalco Chima found himself near, he released one of Huascar's gravely wounded, captured men. [The man] told Huascar's forces about what was happening and how it was Chalco Chima, who was coming to kill them all with this ruse. When this was known, and because Chalco Chima immediately ordered all his own [men] to attack by letting the sun shade fall, which was the signal, Huascar's forces gave up and fled. This is what Chalco Chima had wanted. Atahualpa's forces attacked, wounding and killing with great fury and cruelty, and [they] continued the pursuit until the Cotabamba Bridge, causing unheard-of havoc. As the bridge was narrow and all could not cross, out of fear of the enemy who fiercely wounded them, many threw themselves into the river and drowned. Atahualpa's forces crossed the river, continuing the pursuit and enjoying the victory. They captured Huascar's brother Tito Atauchi during this pursuit. When Chalco Chima and Quizquiz reached some houses that they call Quiuipay,[291] about half a league from Cuzco, they imprisoned Huascar there under a strong guard and established their encampment and halted.[292]

Chalco Chima's soldiers pressed ahead to look down on Cuzco from the top of [the hill of] Yauira[293] that overlooks the city. From there they heard the screams and wailing in the city, and they returned to tell Chalco Chima and Quizquiz about it. [The latter] sent [a messenger] to Cuzco to tell the crying inhabitants not to be afraid, since they understood that the war had been between brothers, caused by their particular passions. And if any of them had helped Huascar, they were not to be blamed, as they were obliged to serve their Inca and were not at fault. And if any of them [were at fault], [the captains] would excuse it and pardon them in the name of the great lord Atahualpa. They then ordered them all to come to offer reverence to the statue of Atahualpa called *ticci capac*, which means "lord of the world."

The people of Cuzco then held a meeting and decided that they would go and obey the command of Chalco Chima and Quizquiz.[294] They came according to their *ayllus*, and upon arriving at Quiuipay, seated themselves in order. Then the men of Atahualpa's captains, who were warned to have their weapons ready, surrounded everyone who had come from Cuzco. They imprisoned Guanca Auqui, Agua Panti, and Paucar Usno, against whom they held a grudge because of the battle they had fought against Atahualpa's forces in Tomebamba. They imprisoned Apu Chalco Yupanqui and Rupaca and priests of the Sun, because they had given the tassel to Huascar Inca. [Once they were] imprisoned, Quizquiz stood up and told them: "You know about the battles that you fought against me along the way, the trouble that you have caused us, and that you also made Huascar the Inca without him being the heir. You badly treated Inca Atahualpa, whom the Sun protects, and for this you deserve painful deaths. However, behaving toward you with benevolence, I pardon you in the name of my lord Atahualpa, whom the Sun makes prosper."

But so that they would not be left completely unpunished, he had some of them beaten on their backs with a large stone and he executed some of the most guilty. He then ordered all to fall to their knees, face turned toward Cajamarca or Guamachuco, where Atahualpa was, and, plucking their eyebrows and eyelashes, they should blow them and offer them up and worship Atahualpa. All the noble inhabitants of the town did this out of fear and in one loud voice shouted: "Hurrah! Long live Atahualpa our Inca, [may] his father the Sun increase his life!"

Huascar's mother, named Araua Ocllo, and his wife, Chucuy Huypa, were there at that time. Quizquiz verbally dishonored and greatly insulted them. Huascar's mother said in a loud voice to her son who was imprisoned: "You unfortunate man! Your cruelties and wickedness have brought this upon you! Did I not tell you not to be so cruel and not to kill or dishonor the messengers of your brother Atahualpa?" They say that having said these words, she attacked him and hit him in the face.

After this was done, Chalco Chima and Quizquiz dispatched messengers to Atahualpa, telling him all that had happened and how they had imprisoned Huascar and many others, and asking for orders for what they should do.

[66]

WHAT CHALCO CHIMA AND QUIZQUIZ
SAID TO HUASCAR INCA AND THE
OTHERS OF HIS GROUP

*A*fter Chalco Chima and Quizquiz dispatched the messengers to Atahualpa, they ordered that the captives be brought before them. In the presence of all, as well as the mother and wife of Huascar, they directed their words to Huascar's mother, saying that she was a mistress and not the wife of Huayna Capac, and that while she was his mistress she had given birth to Huascar and that she was a lowly woman and was not a *coya*. Pointing their fingers at Huascar, Atahualpa's forces mockingly shouted at the noblemen: "See there your lord, the one who said that in the battle against his enemies he would turn into fire and water." Huascar was then tied hand and foot on a bed of straw ropes. Ashamed, the noblemen lowered their heads. Quizquiz then asked Huascar: "Who of these made you lord, when there were others more worthy and more valiant than you who could have been [chosen]?" Araua Ocllo, speaking to her son, told him: "Son, you deserve all this that is said to you. It is all due to the cruelties that you inflicted on your own kin!" To this Huascar replied: "Mother, that can no longer be changed! Leave us!" He then spoke to the priest Chalco Yupanqui and said to him: "You talk and reply to what Quizquiz asks me!" The priest said to Quizquiz: "I invested him as Inca and lord by order of his father, Huayna Capac, and because he was the son of a *coya* (which is like saying '*infanta*'[295] among us)." Chalco Chima became indignant and called the priest a deceiver and a liar in a loud voice. Huascar replied to Quizquiz: "Let us stop arguing! This matter is between my brother and me, and not between the Hanan Cuzcos and the Hurin Cuzcos. We will discuss it, and you do not have to meddle between us on this point."

Chalco Chima was angered by this and ordered Huascar returned to prison. He told the Incas, to reassure them, that they could now go [back] to town, since they were pardoned. The noblemen returned to Cuzco speaking loudly, invoking Ticci Viracocha with [these] words: "Oh Creator, who gave life and favor to the Incas, where are you now? How did you permit such persecution to come upon them? Why did you raise them up if they were to have such an end?" While saying these words, they shook their robes as a sign of execration, desiring that [this curse] descend upon them all.

[67]

THE CRUELTIES THAT ATAHUALPA ORDERED BE COMMITTED AGAINST THE DEFEATED AND CAPTURED MEN OF HUASCAR

*W*hen Atahualpa heard from Chalco Chima and Quizquiz's messengers about what had happened, he ordered one of his relatives named Cusi Yupanqui to go to Cuzco and not leave any relative or supporter of Huascar alive. Cusi Yupanqui arrived in Cuzco, and Chalco Chima and Quizquiz then delivered the captives to him. He made an inquiry into everything that Atahualpa had ordered. Cusi Yupanqui [then] commanded that many poles be driven into the ground on both sides of the road along no more than a quarter of a league of the Xaquixaguana road.[296] They then took Huascar's pregnant and recently delivered wives out of prison. He ordered them hung on the poles with their children, and he had the children cut out of the pregnant women's wombs and hung from their arms.[297] Then they brought out the sons of Huayna Capac who were there [in Cuzco] and hung them from the same poles.

Among the imprisoned sons of Huayna Capac was a son called Paullu Topa, who, while they were trying to kill him, argued, saying that there was no reason for them to kill him, because he had previously been imprisoned by Huascar for being a friend and partisan of his brother Atahualpa, and that Chalco Chima had taken him out of Huascar's jail. Chalco Chima told Cusi Yupanqui that Paullu Topa spoke the truth, that he had taken him out of Huascar's prison. Because of this they released him, and he escaped alive.[298] But the reason Huascar had him imprisoned was that he had been found with one of Huascar's wives, and Huascar only allowed him to be fed very little, deciding that he should die in the prison, giving him [only] a cup of food. Huascar had the wife with whom Paullu Topa was caught buried alive.[299] When the wars started, he escaped following what has been said.

After this the lords and ladies of Cuzco who were discovered to be Huascar's friends were imprisoned, and they were also hung on those poles. [Atahualpa's men] then went through all the houses of the dead Incas, inquiring about anyone who had been on Huascar's side and enemies of Atahualpa. They found that Topa Inca Yupanqui's house had sided with Huascar. Cusi Yupanqui entrusted the punishment of this house to Chalco Chima and Quizquiz, who then seized the steward of the house and the mummy of Topa Inca and [the members] of his house and hung them all. They had the body of Topa Inca burned outside the town and reduced to ashes. After burning it, they killed many *mamaconas* and servants, leaving almost no one of this house [alive] except some people of no importance. After this they ordered all the Chachapoyas and Cañaris killed, as well as their *curaca* named Ulco Colla, who they said had stirred up trouble between the two brothers.[300]

These deaths and cruelties were performed in front of Huascar to further torment him. They killed more than eighty of Huascar's sons and daughters. But what hurt him the most was seeing one of his sisters and mistresses named Coya Miro killed before his eyes. She had one of Huascar's sons in her arms and another on her back. And [they killed] another very beautiful sister of his named Chimbo Cisa. His heart broke to see such sad sights and the cruelties that he could not prevent. With a loud sigh he said: "Oh Pachayachachi Viracocha, you who so briefly favored and honored me and gave me life, make whoever treats me this [way] find himself in this same situation [one day], so that he himself may witness what I in my [life] have seen and see!"

Some of Huascar's mistresses escaped from this calamity and cruelty because they were neither pregnant nor had they had children by Huascar and because they were beautiful. They say that they kept them to take to Atahualpa. Among those who escaped were Doña Elvira Chonay, daughter of Cañar Capac; Doña Beatriz Caruamaruay, daughter of the *curaca* [of] Chinchaycocha; Doña Juana Tocto; and Doña Catalina Usica, who was the wife of Don Paullu Topa and mother of Don Carlos,[301] who are alive today.[302] In this way the line and lineage of the unfortunate tyrant Huascar, the last of the Incas, was completely destroyed.

[68]

NEWS OF THE SPANIARDS REACHED ATAHUALPA

*A*tahualpa was in Guamachuco holding great celebrations for his victories and wanted to go to Cuzco to receive the tassel in the House of the Sun, where all the past Incas had received it. As he was about to leave, two Tallane Indians arrived. They were sent by the *curacas* of Payta and Tumbes to tell Atahualpa how [*como*] men had arrived by sea, which they call *cocha*. They were people with different clothing than their own, with beards, and who brought with them some animals that were like large sheep. They thought that the leader of them was Viracocha, which means "their god," and that he brought with him many Viracochas, as if to say "many gods."[303] They said this about the governor Don Francisco Pizarro, who had arrived there with 180 men, and they brought horses, which they called sheep. Because the details of what happened will be described in the history of the Spaniards, which will be the third part that follows this one,[304] only a summary of what occurred between the Spaniards and Atahualpa will be presented [here].

When Atahualpa learned this, he greatly rejoiced and believed [it] was Viracocha who had returned, as he had promised them when he departed, according to the [legend] we recounted at the beginning of this history.[305] He gave thanks to Viracocha because he had returned during his lifetime, and he sent back the Tallane messengers, thanking their *curacas* for the news and ordering them to notify him about any new developments. He chose not to go to Cuzco until he knew what all of this was about and what the Viracochas decided to do. He sent an order to Chalco Chima and Quizquiz to take Huascar to Cajamarca under close guard. He would wait for them there because news had reached him that some Viracochas had arrived by sea and he wanted to be there to see what this was all about.

Since no additional news followed—because the Spanish Viracochas had settled in Tangarara—Atahualpa let down his guard, believing they had left. [This was] because once before, when he had been with his father during the Quito wars, news had reached Huayna Capac that Viracocha had arrived on the coast of Tumbes but had [then] left. This was when Don Francisco Pizarro had arrived during the first discovery [in 1526–1527] and then returned to Spain [to ask] for the governorship, as will be recounted in its place. So [Atahualpa] believed that this would happen [again].

[69]

THE SPANIARDS REACH CAJAMARCA AND CAPTURE ATAHUALPA, WHO ORDERS THAT HUASCAR BE KILLED, AND HE ALSO DIES

*B*ecause the details of what this chapter touches on belong in the third part of the history of the Spaniards, only a summary will be provided here of what occurred between them and Atahualpa.[306] So it was that, although Atahualpa forgot about the Viracochas, they lost no time, and when they received news of where Inca Atahualpa was, they departed from Tangarara and went to Cajamarca. When Atahualpa learned that the Viracochas were near, he left Cajamarca and went to some baths that were half a league away so that from there [he could] decide the best course [of action]. When Atahualpa understood that they were not gods, as they had earlier led him to believe, he prepared his soldiers [to fight] against the Spaniards. However, in the end, he was captured by Don Francisco Pizarro after Fray Vicente Valverde, the first bishop of Peru, had first performed a certain requirement in the plaza of Cajamarca.[307]

When Don Francisco Pizarro learned of the dispute that existed between Atahualpa and Huascar, and that Huascar was imprisoned by the captains of Atahualpa, he strongly urged Atahualpa to have his brother Huascar quickly brought [to him]. He was already being brought on orders of Atahualpa by the road that leads to Cajamarca, as was said earlier. Atahualpa sent the order to bring him. Chalco Chima followed this order, and they departed with Huascar and the other captives, Huascar's captains and relatives who had escaped the butchery of Cusi Yupanqui. Atahualpa was suspicious of what Don Francisco Pizarro said and asked him why he wanted to see [Huascar]. Don Francisco Pizarro said that he had been told that Huascar was the eldest and most important lord of that land and that was why he wanted to see him, and so he should have him come or be brought. Atahualpa feared that if Huascar arrived alive and the governor Don Francisco Pizarro found out what had happened [in the succession], he would make Huascar lord and remove him from the position he now had. As he was astute, [Atahualpa] therefore decided to prevent this so that he could benefit from it later. He sent a swift messenger to tell the captain who was bringing the captive Huascar that, wherever he found him, he should kill Huascar and all the prisoners.[308] The messenger left and he found the captive Huascar in Antamarca, near the Yanamayo, and he gave the message that he brought from Atahualpa to the captain of the guard that held him captive.

The captain carried out Atahualpa's order as soon as he heard it. Thus, he killed Huascar and cut him into pieces and threw him into the Yanamayo. He also killed all the other brothers, relatives, and captains who were held captive with him in the same way.

[This happened] in the year 1533, Huascar having lived forty years. He succeeded his father at thirty-one and was *capac* for nine years, six in peace and three in war. His wife was Chucuy Huypa, with whom he had no male son. He did not leave a lineage or *ayllu*, although of those who are alive now only one, named Don Alonso Tito Atauchi,[309] the nephew of Huascar, son of Tito Atauchi, whom they killed along with Huascar, maintains the name of the *ayllu* of Huascar, called Huascar Ayllu.

Atahualpa had placed his boundary markers at the Yanamayo River when he first rebelled, saying that [the area] from the Yanamayo to Chile belonged to his brother Huascar, and from the Yanamayo below [was] his. Thus, with the death of Huascar, all the Incas of this kingdom of Peru were completely destroyed. They and their entire line and the descendants from the line that they claimed was legitimate [were eliminated], without a man or woman remaining who could have rightfully laid claim to this land, even if they had been the native and legitimate lords of it, according to their tyrannical customs and laws.[310]

Don Francisco Pizarro later killed Atahualpa [in punishment] for this death and for other severe and sufficient reasons. Atahualpa tyrannized the natives of this land and his brother Huascar. He lived thirty-six years. He was not an Inca lord of Peru, but a tyrant. He was prudent and astute and valiant, as will be described in the third part, since it involves things that pertain to the deeds of the Spaniards. This suffices to end this second part, finishing the history of the deeds of the twelve tyrant Incas who ruled this kingdom of Peru, from Manco Capac, the first, until Huascar, the twelfth Inca and last tyrant.

[70]

NOTING HOW THESE INCAS WERE OATH-BREAKERS AND TYRANTS AGAINST THEIR OWN, IN ADDITION TO BEING AGAINST THE NATIVES OF THE LAND

*I*t is important to note for our purposes here that the general tyranny of these tyrannical and cruel Incas of Peru against the natives of the land is a true and evident thing that easily follows from this history. Those who will carefully read it and consider the order and manner of their actions [will understand] the fact that their violent Incaships [took place] against the will or choice of the natives. These [natives] always had their weapons in their hands, [prepared] for each time that an opportunity arose to rebel and gain their freedom from the tyrannical Incas who oppressed them. Thus, each of the Incas not only continued the tyranny of his father, but also began the same tyranny anew through force and killings, robberies and plunder. None of them could therefore claim to have begun [their rule] in good faith, nor did any of them ever possess the land in peaceful ownership. On the contrary, there was always someone who would oppose them and take up arms against them and their tyranny. Moreover, what must be noted above all, in order to fully understand the terrible inclinations of these tyrants and their horrible avarice and tyranny, is [that] they were not satisfied with being evil tyrants over the natives. They also proceeded like this against their own sons, brothers, relatives, and own blood and against their own laws and statutes. They were the most terrible and persistent oath-breaking tyrants [possessed by] a kind of unheard-of inhumanity. Because even though they established among themselves through their tyrannical customs and laws that the eldest legitimate son would succeed to the Incaship, they almost never did this, as is the case for the Incas that I will present here.

First of all, Manco Capac, the first tyrant, who came from Tambotoco, was inhumane toward his brother Ayar Cache, knowingly sending him to Tambotoco, where he ordered Tambo Chacay to kill him. [He did this] out of jealousy from seeing that Ayar Cache was more courageous than he, believing that for this reason Ayar Cache would be more respected [than he]. And after Manco Capac reached the Cuzco Valley, not only did he tyrannize the natives of that place, but also Copalimayta and Culunchima, who, although they were already considered natives of that valley, were his relatives and of his class, as they were noblemen. Moreover, Cinchi Roca, the second Inca, had an older legitimate son named Manco Sapaca, to whom the succession to the Incaship should have passed according to the law that Cinchi Roca and his father had made. Cinchi Roca deprived him of [the succession] and appointed Lloqui Yupanqui, [his] second son, as his heir. In this same way, Mayta Capac, the fourth Inca, appointed Capac Yupanqui as his successor, [although he] had another older legitimate son named Conde Mayta, whom he disinherited. And Viracocha, the eighth Inca, had an older legitimate son named Inca Roca whom he did not appoint as his successor. Nor [did he appoint] any of his legitimate sons, but rather a bastard named Inca Urcon. Because of this, Inca Roca did not succeed, but neither did Inca Urcon nor [did] the eldest legitimate son enjoy it. Instead, Inca Yupanqui intervened through new tyranny. He deprived both of them and stripped his father of honor and state. And Inca Yupanqui himself, having an older legitimate son named Amaru Topa Inca, did not appoint him. Instead, [he appointed] Topa Inca Yupanqui. The same Topa Inca, being just like his father, had an elder legitimate son [named] Huayna Capac, but appointed Capac Guari as [his] successor. However, the relatives of Huayna Capac did not permit this, and they elevated Huayna Capac as Inca. And if Capac Guari was legitimate, as the relatives of Capac Guari state, we will ascribe this wickedness to Huayna Capac, who took the Incaship from his brother Capac Guari and banished him. And [he] killed Capac Guari's mother and all his relatives and discredited them as traitors, even though he was the actual [traitor], according to what is said. And although Huayna Capac appointed Ninan Cuyoche, he was not the eldest. Because of this, the succession remained unclear, which caused the disputes between Huascar and Atahualpa, from which the greatest [and most] unnatural tyrannies of all came. Turning their weapons against their own relatives, robbing each other, and fighting [among] themselves inhumanly with internal wars that were more than civil [wars], they totally destroyed one another. And just as they began by their own authority,[311] they thus all destroyed themselves by their own hands.

It may be that God Almighty permitted some to be tormentors of others for their wickedness so that this would give way to His most holy gospel, which was brought to these blind, barbarous, heathen Indians by the hands of the Spaniards and by order of the most happy, Catholic, and undefeated emperor and king of Spain Charles V of glorious memory, father of Your Majesty. Had the strength and power of the Incas been [at its] peak and [had they been] unified, it would seem humanly impossible for so few Spaniards, who numbered 180 and first entered with the governor Don Francisco Pizarro, to do what they did.

It is thus established that it is false and without reason or right to claim that there is now in these kingdoms any person from the lineage of the Incas who can claim a right to the succession of the Incaship of this kingdom of Peru, either by being native or legitimate lords. [This is] because [the Inca] were [neither]. Nor does anyone remain who could say that he is heir to all or part of this land, even according to their laws, because only two of Huayna Capac's sons escaped from Atahualpa's cruelty. These were Paullu Topa, later named Don Cristóbal Paullu, and Manco Inca, who were [both] bastards, which is publicly known among them. Any honor or estate that these or their descendants have was given to them by Your Majesty and was much more than what they would have had if their brothers [had] remained in control and with power. They would have been their tributaries and servants. These were the lowest of all [the descendants], because their lineage was based on the side of the mothers, which is what they value in [innuoo] of birth

And Manco Inca was a traitor against Your Majesty, having rebelled in the Andes, where he died or was killed.[312] Your Majesty brought his son Don Diego Sayre Topa out of those forests of savages in peace and made him a Christian and supported him, particularly feeding him and his sons and descendants.[313] He died as a Christian.[314] And the [Inca] named Tito Cusi Yupanqui[315] who is now rebelling in the Andes, he is not a legitimate son of Manco Inca;[316] rather, [he is] a bastard and apostate. Instead, they consider legitimate another named Amaru Topa, who is with Tito himself.[317] He is incompetent, which the Indians refer to as *uti*. But neither one nor the other is heir of the land because their father was not [an heir].

Your Majesty honored Don Cristóbal Paullu with titles and gave him a very large land grant of Indians, from which he lived very well. Now his son Don Carlos possesses it.[318] Only two legitimate sons of Paullu remain alive today; the first is the said Don Carlos and [the second is named] Don Felipe.[319] In addition to these, he had many bastard and natural sons. Therefore, the known grandsons of Huayna Capac, who are now alive and are held as such and as leaders, are those mentioned [above]. Besides these, [there is] Don Alonso Tito Atauchi,[320] the son of Tito Atauchi, and other bastards, but none have the right to be called a native lord of this land.

For the reasons given, the right to say that Your Majesty and Your successors have the most just and legitimate title to these parts of the Indies will be for those who have the duty to determine such an evident truth, based on what is written and proved here. And the title that the Crown of Castile has to these kingdoms of Peru is especially without question. Accordingly, Don Francisco de Toledo, Your viceroy in these kingdoms, has been a beacon and a careful inquisitor, as zealous in the unburdening of Your Royal conscience as in the salvation of Your soul, as he has shown and now [shows] in this general inspection. He is personally conducting this [inspection] by order of Your Majesty, with no care to the many great difficulties and dangers that he suffers in these journeys. A very great service to God and Your Majesty is resulting from this.

[71]

SUMMARY ACCOUNT OF THE TIME THAT THE INCAS OF PERU LASTED

*T*he ancient and terrible tyranny of the Capac Incas of Peru, who had their seat in the city of Cuzco, began in the year 565 of our Christian era. Justinian II was emperor;[321] and Loyba, son of Athanagild the Goth, was king of Spain; and John III was the supreme pontiff.[322] It ended in the year 1533, when the most Christian Charles V was the most meritorious emperor and king of Spain and its annexes, patron of the Church and the hand of Christianity. [He was] truly worthy of such a son as Your Majesty, whom [may] God our Lord take by the hand, as the Holy Christian Church has provided. Paul III was then pope.[323] The whole period, beginning with Manco Capac until the end of Huascar, [lasted] 968 years.

It is not surprising that these Incas lived so long, since in that age [people were] naturally stronger and more robust than [they are] now. Moreover, at that time the men did not marry until [they were] over thirty years [old], and thus they reached old age with whole and undiminished substance. Because of this, they lived many more years than now. And the land where they lived required little maintenance and had uncorrupted air. The land is cleared, dry, without lakes, marshes, or forests of thick trees, all [of] which bring [good] health and therefore long life for its inhabitants. May God our Lord guide them in his holy faith for the salvation of their souls. Amen.

STATEMENT OF THE PROOFS AND
VERIFICATION OF THIS HISTORY

The very great glory of Viceroy Toledo has grown,
While his brilliant care puts to flight the shadows of the kingdom.
Depart far away, ill-informed complainers,
There is no place for such as you here!
For our king holds the Indians innocently.[324]

In the city of Cuzco on the twenty-ninth day of the month of February of 1572, before the very excellent lord Don Francisco de Toledo, steward of Your Majesty and Your viceroy, governor and captain-general of these kingdoms and provinces of Peru, and president of the Royal Audiencia[325] and Chancellery, who resides in the city of Los Reyes,[326] and before me, Alvaro Ruiz de Navamuel, his secretary and of the government and general inspection of these kingdoms, the captain Pedro Sarmiento de Gamboa presented a petition of the following tenor:

Most Excellent Lord,
[I], Captain Pedro Sarmiento, cosmographer-general of these kingdoms of Peru, say that by order of Your Excellency I have collected and written into a history the general account of the origin and succession of the Incas and of the particular deeds that each one did in his time and place. [This includes] how each one of them was obeyed and the tyranny with which, since [the time of] Topa Inca Yupanqui, the tenth Inca, they oppressed and conquered these kingdoms of Peru until, by order of the emperor [Charles V] of glorious memory, Don Francisco Pizarro came to conquer them. I have collected this history from the inquests and other investigations that, by order of Your Excellency, have been carried out in the Jauja Valley and in the city of Guamanga[327] and in other areas through which Your Excellency has come inspecting. But [the history was] principally [collected] in this city of Cuzco, where the Incas had their permanent residence, and [where] there is more information about their deeds, and where the *mitimaes* of all the provinces, whom the Incas brought here, were assembled, and [where] their true memory remains with their *ayllus*. For this history to have greater authority, I present it before Your Excellency and implore that you order it to be inspected and corrected and interpose

on it your authority, so that, wherever it is seen, it is given full faith and credit.

Pedro Sarmiento de Gamboa

This petition [having been] received by His Excellency, he said that in order to know if this history conforms with the reports and inquests that have been conducted with the Indians and other persons of this city and [in] other parts, he ordered that the doctor Loarte, mayor of Your Majesty's court, summon before him the most important and most knowledgeable Indians of the twelve *ayllus* and descendants of the twelve Incas and [any] other persons he wishes. And once before me, the present secretary, this history is to be read and explained to all of them by [an] interpreter in the language of these Indians so that they may all see and discuss among themselves whether it conforms to the truth that they know. And should there be anything to correct and amend, or that may appear to be contrary to what they know, it [is to] be amended and corrected. And thus he decreed it and signed it.

Don Francisco de Toledo

Before me, Alvaro Ruiz de Navamuel

After [this], on the same above-mentioned day, month, and year, the illustrious lord Doctor Gabriel de Loarte, in fulfillment of what His Excellency decided and ordered, and before me, the said secretary, did order to appear before him the Indians who claimed to be of the following names and ages and *ayllus*:

Ayllu of Manco Capac:
Sebastian Ylluc, thirty years old
Francisco Paucar Chima, thirty years old

Ayllu of Cinchi Roca:
Diego Cayo Hualpa, seventy years old [328]
Don Alonso Puscón, forty years old [329]

Ayllu of Lloqui Yupanqui:
Hernando Hualpa, sixty years old
Don García Ancuy, forty-five years old
Miguel Rimache Mayta, thirty years old

Ayllu of Mayta Capac:
Don Juan Tambo Usca Mayta, sixty years old[330]
Don Felipe Usca Mayta, seventy years old
Francisco Usca Mayta, thirty years old

Ayllu of Capac Yupanqui:
Don Francisco Copca Mayta, seventy-one years old
Don Juan Quispe Mayta, thirty years old
Don Juan Apu Mayta, thirty years old

Ayllu of Inca Roca:
Don Pedro Hachacona, fifty-three years old
Don Diego Mayta, forty years old

Ayllu of Yahuar Huacac:
Juan Yupanqui, sixty years old
Martín Rimache, twenty-six years old

Ayllu of Viracocha:
Don Francisco Anti Huallpa, eighty-nine years old[331]
Martín Quechgua Sucsu, sixty-four years old
Don Francisco Challco Yupanqui, forty-five years old

Ayllu of Pachacuti:
Don Diego Cayo, sixty-eight years old
Don Juan Hualpa Yupanqui, sixty-five years old
Don Domingo Pascac, ninety years old[332]
Don Juan Quispe Cusi, forty-five years old
Don Francisco Chauca Rimache, forty years old
Don Francisco Cota Yupanqui, forty years old
Don Gonzalo Guacanqui, seventy years old
Don Francisco Quicgua, sixty-eight years old

Ayllu of Topa Inca:
Don Cristóbal Pisac Topa, fifty years old
Don Andrés Topa Yupanqui, forty years old
Don García Pillco Topa, forty years old
Don Juan Cuzco, forty years old[333]

Ayllu of Huayna Capac:
Don Francisco Sayre, twenty-eight years old[334]
Don Francisco Ninan Coro, twenty-four years old[335]
Don García Rimac Topa, thirty-four years old

Ayllu of Huascar:
Don Alonso Tito Atauchi, forty years old

And besides these ayllus:
Don García Paucar Sucsu, thirty-four years old
Don Carlos Ayallilla, fifty years old
Don Juan Apanca, eighty years old [336]
Don García Apu Rinti, seventy years old
Don Diego Viracocha Inca, thirty-four years old [337]
Don Gonzalo Topa, thirty years old

Once all gathered in the presence of His Excellency, the Lord Mayor of the Court addressed the Indians through Gonzalo Gómez [338] Jiménez, His Excellency's interpreter, in the general language of the Indians: "His Excellency wished to investigate and put in writing and chronicle the origin of the Incas, their ancestors and their descendants and the deeds that each one of them did in his time, and which areas obeyed each [Inca], and which of them was the first to leave Cuzco to rule other lands, and how Topa Inca Yupanqui and after him Huayna Capac and Huascar, his son and grandson, became lords of all Peru by force of arms. And to be able to do this with more authenticity, he ordered that information be collected and other interviews [be conducted] in this city and in other areas, and from this information and interviews the captain Pedro Sarmiento, to whom he entrusted it, should extract the true history and chronicle. Pedro Sarmiento has now completed it and [has] presented it to His Excellency to find out whether it is truthfully written and conforms to the statements and declarations that various Indians of the above-mentioned *ayllus* gave in the interviews. And because His Excellency is informed that the *ayllus* and descendants of each one of the twelve Incas have preserved among themselves the memory of the deeds of their ancestors and are those who could know best if this chronicle is true or defective, he has ordered them to be assembled here so that it can be read and understood in their presence. [This is] so that they can discuss among themselves what is read and said to them in their language, to see if it conforms to the truth as they know it. And so that they [would have] a greater obligation to tell what they know, he ordered that they take an oath."

The Indians said that they understood why they had been summoned and what was asked of them; and they swore by God our Lord in that language, making the sign of the cross, that they would tell the truth about what they knew concerning this history. With the oath done, the sum and substance [of the account] was read to them. They were read [to] and the reading was finished and discussed that same day and the next, from the fable that the Indians tell of their creation [339] until the end of this history of the Incas. As each chapter was read, one by one, it was translated into that language; the Indians [then] talked and conferred among themselves about each of the chapters. Together they all agreed and said through the interpreter that this history was good and true and conformed to what they knew and had heard told by their fathers and ancestors, who had heard it told by theirs. Since they did not have writing like the Spaniards, they did not have a way to preserve these antiquities among themselves except by transmitting them from mouth to mouth and from age to age and from one to another. They had heard their fathers and ancestors say that Pachacuti Inca Yupanqui, the ninth Inca, had investigated the history of the other Incas that had come before him and [had] painted it on some boards. Their fathers and ancestors had also learned it from these and had told it to them. They only amended some names of some people and places and other slight things that the Lord Mayor of the Court ordered inserted as these Indians spoke, and thus they were inserted. With these amendments, all those Indians together stated that this history was good and true, conforming to what they know and [what they had] heard their ancestors say about it, because they have conferred and discussed it among themselves from the beginning to the end. They believe that no other history that has ever been written will be as accurate and true as this one, since such a diligent examination has never been done, nor have they been asked anything, and they are the ones who know the truth. The Lord Mayor of the Court signed it and so did the translator.

The doctor Loarte
Gonzalo Gómez Jiménez
Before me, Alvaro Ruiz de Navamuel

After the above-mentioned [took place] in the city of Cuzco on the second day of the month of March of the same year, His Excellency, having seen the declaration of the Indians and the oaths that were made by them, said he was ordering and ordered that this history should be sent to Your Majesty with the amendments that those Indians said should be made. [Then it was] signed and authorized by me the secretary. And the doctor Gabriel de Loarte, who was present, wrote and signed the verification that was conducted with the Indians, and it was signed by

Don Francisco de Toledo

Before me, Alvaro Ruiz de Navamuel

I, Alvaro Ruiz de Navamuel, secretary to His Excellency and of the government and general inspection of these kingdoms and Your Majesty's scribe, do swear that the contents of this testimony and verification took place before me, that it was taken from the original, which remains in my possession, and the Lord Mayor of the Court, who signed—the doctor Loarte—said that he placed and interposed on it his authority and judicial decree so that it is valid and accepted in court and elsewhere. I affix here my signature in testimony of the truth.

Alvaro Ruiz de Navamuel

Appendix 1
SAMPLE TRANSLATION

To illustrate the final form of our translation, we provide below both the original Spanish* and the English translation for Chapter 1. Paragraphs have been changed for ease of reading and comparison between the two columns.

DIVISIÓN DE LA HISTORIA

Esta general historia, que por mandado del muy excelente Don Francisco de Toledo virrey destos reinos del Pirú yo tomé a mi cargo, será divisa en tres partes.

La primera será historia natural destas tierras, porque será particular descripción dellas, que contendrá maravillosos hechos de naturaleza, y otras cosas de mucho provecho y gusto, la cual quedo acabando, para que tras esta se embíe a Vuestra Magestad, puesto que debiera ir antes.

La segunda y tercera informarán de los pobladores destos reinos [y] de las hazañas dellos, en esta manera. En la segunda parte, que es la presente, se escribirán los antiquísimos y primeros pobladores desta tierra en génere, y descendiendo a particularidades, escribiré la terrible y envejecida tiranía de los ingas capacs destos reinos hasta la fin y muerte de Guascar, último de los ingas.

DIVISION OF THE HISTORY

This general history that I undertook by order of the most excellent Don Francisco de Toledo, viceroy of these kingdoms of Peru, will be divided into three parts.

The first will be a natural history of these lands, because it will be a detailed description of them that will include the wondrous works of nature and other things of much benefit and pleasure. (I am now finishing it so that it can be sent to Your Majesty after this [second part], since it should go before.)

The second and third parts will tell of the inhabitants of these kingdoms and their deeds, in this manner. In the second part, which is the present one, the first and most ancient settlers of this land will be described in general. Then, moving into particulars, I will write of the terrible and ancient tyranny of the Capac Incas of these kingdoms until the end and death of Huascar, the last of the Incas.

La tercera y última parte será de
los tiempos de los Españoles y sus
notables hechos en los descubrimien-
tos y poblaciones deste reino y otros
contingentes á él, por las edades de
capitanes, gobernadores, y virreyes, que
en ellos han sido, hasta el año presente
de mil y quinientos y setenta y dos.

The third and last part will be about
the times of the Spaniards and their
noteworthy deeds during the discoveries and settlements of this kingdom
and others adjoining it, divided by the
terms of the captains, governors, and
viceroys who have served in them until
the present year of 1572.

* Sarmiento (1906:10 [1572:Ch. 1]).

Appendix 2
EDITIONS OF PEDRO SARMIENTO DE GAMBOA'S *THE HISTORY OF THE INCAS*

1906   *Segunda parte de la historia general llamada Índica . . .* [1572]. In *Geschichte des Inkareiches von Pedro Sarmiento de Gamboa,* edited by Richard Pietschmann. Abhandlungen der Königlichen Gesellschaft der Wissenschaften zu Göttingen, Philologisch-Historische Klasse, Neue Folge, vol. 6, no. 4. Berlin: Weidmannsche Buchhandlung.

1907   *History of the Incas.* Translated and edited by Sir Clements Markham. London: The Hakluyt Society. Series 2, Volume 22. (Reprinted various times, including 1967 and 1999.)

1942   *Historia de los incas.* Buenos Aires: Emecé.

1942   *La historia índica de Sarmiento de Gamboa.* Edited by Roberto Levillier. In *Don Francisco de Toledo, supremo organizador del Peru: Su vida, su obra (1515–1582).* Vol. 3. Buenos Aires: Espasa-Calpe.

1960   *Historia Índica.* In *Obras completas del Inca Garcilaso de la Vega,* vol. 4, edited and introduction by Carmelo Sáenz de Santa María. Biblioteca de Autores Españoles, vol. 135. Madrid: Ediciones Atlas.

1964   *La "Historia Índica" de Pedro Sarmiento de Gamboa* [1906]. Nota preliminar de Alberto Tauro. Colección Comentarios del Perú 2. Lima: Universidad Nacional Mayor de San Marcos.

1988   *Historia de los incas.* Madrid: Miraguano Ediciones and Ediciones Polifermo.

Appendix 3
THE RULE OF THE INCAS, FOLLOWING DATES PROVIDED BY SARMIENTO DE GAMBOA

Inca	Lifespan	Age at Accession	Years of Rule	Year of Death	Corrected Year of Death*
1. Manco Capac	144	44	100	665	
2. Cinchi Roca	127	108	19	675	
3. Lloqui Yupanqui	132	21	111	786	
4. Mayta Capac	112	[not provided]	[not provided]	896	
5. Capac Yupanqui	104	15	89	985	1008
6. Inca Roca	123	20	103	1088	1097
7. Yahuar Huacac	115	19	96	[not provided]	1200
8. Viracocha Inca	119	18	101	[left blank]	1296
9. Pachacuti Inca Yupanqui	125	22	103	1191	1397
10. Topa Inca Yupanqui	85	18	67	1258	1464
11. Huayna Capac	80	20	60	1524	1524

* Sarmiento errs in his date calculations. Working back from 1524, the death of Huayna Capac, the following corrections can be suggested.

Appendix 4
THE INCAS OF CUZCO, FOLLOWING INFORMATION PROVIDED BY SARMIENTO DE GAMBOA

Inca	Coya	Ayllu	Guauqui Idol	Mummy
1. Manco Capac	Mama Ocllo	Chima	A bird called *inti*	Found in Wimpillay
2. Cinchi Roca	Mama Coca	Raura	A fish-shaped stone called *guanachiri amaru*	Found in Wimpillay with copper bars
3. Lloqui Yupanqui	Mama Cava	Avayni	Called *apu mayta*	Found with the rest
4. Mayta Capac	Mama Taucaray	Usca Mayta	An idol	Found with the rest
5. Capac Yupanqui	Curihilpay	Apu Mayta	Called *apu mayta*	Found with the rest in a town near Cuzco
6. Inca Roca	Mama Micay	Vicaquirao	A stone idol called *vicaquirao*	Found in Larapa
7. Yahuar Huacac	Mama Chicya	Aucaylli		Margin note: Found in Paullu
8. Viracocha Inca	Mama Rondocaya	Socso	*inca amaru*	Burned by Gonzalo Pizarro
9. Pachacuti Inca Yupanqui	Mama Anaguarqui	Inaca	Gold image called *inti illapa*	Housed in Patallacta but found in Tococache
10. Topa Inca Yupanqui	Mama Ocllo	Capac	Called *cusichuri*	Kept in Calispuquio; burned during civil war
11. Huayna Capac	Cusi Rimay	Tomebamba	*guaraqui inca*	Found in Cuzco

Notes

PREFACE

1. It is worth noting, however, that these chapters are not without a political agenda. At the beginning of Chapter 5, Sarmiento de Gamboa argues that the first inhabitants of Atlantis were early Spaniards, and it was the Atlanteans who eventually peopled the New World. Thus with the conquest of the Indies, these native populations were reunited, as it were, with their distant Spanish cousins (Sabine Hyland, pers. comm., 2004).

INTRODUCTION

1. The formal title of the manuscript is *Second Part of the General History Called Indica . . . [Segunda parte de la historia general llamada Índica . . .]*. It is, however, generally known among researchers as *The History of the Incas*.

2. It is difficult to judge whether this method was an initiative of Sarmiento or of the viceroy himself, since Alvaro Ruiz de Navamuel and the other authors of Toledo's *Informaciones* relied on discussions with groups of witnesses to confirm their data.

3. For a discussion of the other items taken from Peru to Spain by Jerónimo Pacheco, see Julien (1999).

4. Many now see Toledo as one of the most influential Spaniards to serve the Crown during the Colonial Period.

5. Richard Pietschmann (1906) was the first to suggest that Sarmiento's manuscript was relegated to obscurity because of the execution of Tupac Amaru.

6. A new transcription of Sarmiento de Gamboa's *History of the Incas* is currently under preparation by Jean-Jacques Decoster and Brian S. Bauer.

7. Although widely cited, Markham's translation has been criticized for its many errors and omissions.

8. *Encomiendas* were grants of native labor that were initially given to Spaniards to encourage them to settle permanently in Peru.

9. In 1542 a series of ordinances, generally referred to as the "New Laws," were issued that contained sweeping reforms of the *encomienda* system. King Charles I sent Viceroy Blasco Núñez Vela to Peru to enforce these new ordinances; however, the viceroy was killed by Gonzalo Pizarro in 1546.

10. Much of the information obtained during this inspection of the Peruvian land has been preserved (AGI, Lima 28B; AGI, Patronato 294; Levillier 1940).

11. Polo de Ondegardo served two terms as the corregidor (chief magistrate) of Cuzco (Rowe 1980:5). The first was from December 1558 to December 1560. It was during this period that he conducted his well-known search for the Inca mummies and compiled a detailed history of the Incas (now lost). His second term was from August 1571 until October 1572.

12. Collasuyu comprised the part of Peru southeast of Cuzco, all of highland Bolivia (including the Lake Titicaca region) and the adjacent piedmont, northwest Argentina, and the northern half of Chile.

13. For additional biographic information on Pedro Sarmiento de Gamboa, see the various editions of his writings as well as Means (1928) and Arciniega (1956).

14. Landín Carrasco (1945:11) mentions Bartolomé Sarmiento, from Pontevedra, and María de Gamboa, a native of Bilbao in Vizcaya, as the parents of Pedro Sarmiento de Gamboa. Doubt exists, however, about his place of birth, since in his testimony in front of the Holy Office of the Inquisition, he declared that he was born in Alcala de Henares (Medina 1952 [1890]:214), whereas in other documents, he identifies himself as a native of Pontevedra.

15. For a discussion of Sarmiento's role in this expedition, see Mendaña (1901 [1568]).

16. For accounts of this voyage, see Sarmiento de Gamboa (1895, 1988, 2000).

17. A similar outline is provided by Sarmiento as a closing statement in his cover letter to King Philip II.

18. Despite what Sarmiento states in a letter to the king, the illustrations ordered by Toledo were not limited solely to genealogy or to narratives of the Incas (Letter from Sarmiento to the king, 31 March 1573, AGI, Lima 270, cited in Zimmerman 1938:105.)

19. "Segunda parte de la Historia general llamada Índica, la cual por mandado del excelentísimo señor Don Francisco de Toledo, virrey, gobernador y capitán general de los reinos del Pirú y mayordomo de la casa real de Castilla, compuso el capitán Pedro Sarmiento de Gamboa."

20. Formerly attributed to Tristán Sánchez (Porras Barrenechea 1986:724–725). Unfortunately, Salazar's own work on the life of Pizarro has also been lost.

21. "De las averiguaciones que el visrey mandó hacer sobre el origen y descendencia de los ingas."

22. Por ser en aquesta cibdad la córte y antiguo asiento de los ingas, señores que llamaban destos reinos, y ser de los antiguos indios muchos vivos, y de los conquistadores primeros algunos; antes que de todo punto se acabasen los unos y los otros, mandó hacer informaciones y averiguaciones de la genealogía, principio y descendencia de los ingas, por escrito y por pintura, y verificó ser tiranos y no verdaderos señores como hasta allí se había entendido. Y porque lo que en dos libros impresos estaba escrito, uno del origen deste nuevo descubrimiento, otro del discurso de las guerras civiles que entre españoles habían sucedido, hizo hacer con los conquistadores antiguos la información de todo, para que ambas historias pudiesen salir á luz nuevamente corregidas y llenas de verdades que faltaba en muchas cosas á las demás. Cometiólo á Pedro Sarmiento de Gamboa, cosmógrafo y de entendimiento muy capaz para ello, con escribano ante quien los dichos y deposiciones pasasen, y que dellos diese fé. No sé en el estado que este negocio quedó, ni lo que de los papeles se ha hecho, que eran de harta importancia y consideración. (Salazar 1867:262–263 [1596])

23. This was the son of Quispe Curi (also called Inés), the daughter of Huayna Capac, and Francisco de Ampuero, a servant of Francisco Pizarro (see Hemming 1970).

24. Markham indicates this report was written on 15 April 1581 and was preserved in the private papers of the Comte de Valencia de Don Juan.

25. "En quanto al memorial de Pedro Sarmiento en lo que dize del Inga, el Consejo no sabe qe en esto aya cosa alguna que pueda dar cuidado antes se entiende que no ay de tener reçelo porque los indios estan con mas menos cabo y sin fuerças que nunca y los españoles mas presençia con todo eso siendo V. M. sauido se escriuira al virrey queste muy aduertido en esto y auisedelo que entendiese" (AGI, Indiferente 739; transcription by Jean-Jacques Decoster).

26. It seems that Bernabé Cobo saw a copy of one of these cloths while he was in Cuzco, since he writes: "This history, in my opinion, must have been taken from one that I saw in that city [i.e., Cuzco] outlined on a tapestry of *cumbe* [fine cloth], no less detailed and carefully represented than if it were on fine royal fabric" (Cobo 1979:99 [1653:Bk. 12, Ch. 2]).

27. In a later case against him, Gómez Jiménez stated that at times he had distorted the testimonies of the natives to please Toledo (Hemming 1970:452).

28. Wind roses, similar to compass roses, are placed on maps to help position the reader. However, rather than marking magnetic north, they indicate the speed and directionality of wind at that location on a specific date.

29. The tradition of painted genealogical cloths would continue for some time in Peru. For example, in 1603 the remaining Inca nobility (totaling some 569 individuals) sent Garcilaso de la Vega a cloth showing their relations to the kings of Cuzco, hoping that he would present their request for tribute exemptions to the king of Spain. Garcilaso describes what these cloths looked like: "They include a genealogical tree showing the royal line from Manco Capac to Huayna Capac painted on a vara and a half of white China silk. The Incas were depicted in their ancient dress, wearing the scarlet fringe on their heads and their ear ornaments in their ears; only their busts were shown. . . ." (Garcilaso de la Vega 1966:625 [1609:Pt. 1, Bk. 9, Ch. 40]). It is also worth noting that, centuries later, explorer Paul Marcoy (1875:209–217; 2001) was shown a copy of a large cloth in Cuzco that contained an extensive genealogy of the Incas.

30. Later, in a possible act of revenge, María Cusi Huarcay would accuse Don Carlos and several other prominent members of Cuzco's indigenous elite of being in contact with her brothers in Vilcabamba. This accusation would aid Toledo in temporarily banishing these leaders from Cuzco.

31. Mancio Sierra de Leguizamo was the last of Pizarro's men to die. In his will, written in 1589, he bemoaned the state of the indigenous people of Peru and the role that he played in their downfall (Stirling 1999).

32. She was the daughter of Huayna Capac and was also called Curicuillor.

33. Copies of the cloths may, however, have been made before the fire (Barnes 1996).

34. Chapters 2 through 5 discuss the possible peopling of the New World through various means. The next three chapters deal largely with the myth of Viracocha, the Andean creator god who walked across the highlands calling for the founding ancestors of different ethnic groups to emerge from their separate origin places.

35. Molina (1989:49–50 [ca. 1575]) writes: "Y para entender donde tuvieron origen sus ydolatrías, porque es así que éstos no usaron de escritura, y tenían en una casa de el Sol llamada *Poquen Cancha*, que es junto al Cuzco, la vida de cada uno de los yngas y de las

tierras que conquistó, pintado por sus figuras en unas tablas y qué origen tuvieron" [And to understand where their idolatries originated, because it is true that these people did not use writing, and they had in a House of the Sun called Poquen Cancha, that is next to Cuzco, the life of each one of the Incas and of the lands that he conquered, and what their origin was, painted with figures on some boards].

Since Sarmiento and Molina both refer to the history boards in the past tense, they may have already been destroyed. Nevertheless, the boards may have served as a source of inspiration for the painted cloths that were sent to Spain by Toledo.

36. Chapters 6-70.

37. Ruiz de Navamuel's margin notes are included within our English translation.

38. In the 18 July 1571 interview, he is listed as being eighty-one years old.

39. The interview with Toledo indicates that he was a member of Raura Panaca and confirms that he was a descendant of Cinchi Roca. In contrast, his name is found among those of Lloqui Yupanqui's kin group at the verification of the cloths in Cuzco on 14 January 1572.

40. Cayo Topa was later baptized as Diego Cayo.

41. A "Panaca" was a royal kin group.

42. Not surprisingly, the ages for many of the individuals are simply estimates. For example, at the verification of the cloths Diego Cayo is reported to be sixty-five years old. In Sarmiento's work his age is written as sixty-eight, and during the interviews with Toledo, he is listed as being seventy years old.

43. He also signed a 1562 testimonial of Mancio Sierra de Leguizamo's past services to the king, in which he is listed as being fifty-eight years old (Stirling 1999:178).

44. In other words, second in command behind Huayna Capac.

45. Sarmiento reports that the bodies of both Huascar and Alonso Tito Atauchi's father were thrown into the Yanamayo River.

46. For additional information on Diego Topa and Alonso Tito Atauchi, see Hemming (1970) and Decoster (2002).

47. After the collapse of the Inca Empire (1532-1536), a series of Inca nobles, including Manco Inca and his sons Sayre Topa, Tito Cusi Yupanqui, and Tupac Amaru, maintained a forty-year rebellion against Spanish rule of the Andes.

48. The Incas appealed this sentence, and after spending a year in prison in Lima and having their possessions and *yanaconas* (servants) confiscated, they were able to return to Cuzco (AGI, Justicia Leg. 465; Decoster 2002:262-263).

49. His wife, Cusirimay Ocllo (called Doña Angelina by the Spaniards), had formerly been married to Atahualpa. After his death, she lived for a time with Francisco Pizarro.

50. Betanzos' work was not published until modern times. A partial text was published in the nineteenth century, but it was not until 1987 that a full text became available to scholars.

51. It is possible that Cobo had access to an earlier draft, or the notes of the interviews, and thus did not feel a need to mention Sarmiento.

52. For additional information on the similarities and differences between Sarmiento, Cabello Balboa, Cobo, and Murúa, see Rowe (1986) and Julien (2000).

53. Many of the illustrations found in what is frequently called the Wellington Manuscript, currently owned by the Getty Museum in Los Angeles, have been used in this new English translation of Sarmiento's *History of the Incas*.

54. It is difficult to summarize Murúa's works because his three manuscripts overlap, yet each also contains unique information not found in the others (see Murúa 1946, 1987, 2004).

55. Murúa (1987:61 [1590:Ch. 7]) provides very little information on this marriage, writing only that "others say that one day his bastard brother Manco Capaca took him in his arms and carried him to where the Coya, his wife, Mama Cura, was" [otros dicen que su hermano bastardo Mancocapaca, un día le tomó en los brazos y llevó adonde estaba la coya su mujer Mamacura].

56. "... a quien tan buena esperanza hauia puesto en su pecho su hermano Mango Sacapa, (que mas sentia la falta de Sobrino eredero que otro ninguno) se dispuso muy de proposito, a buscar muger ligitima para el Ynga su hermano, y auiendo comunicado el negocio con el sagaz Pachachulla viracocho, tomo el la mano, en el negocio y bien acompañado, se fue á los pueblos de Oma, y a su Cacique le pidio su hija para darla por muger á el Ynga y el se la otorgo, esta se llamaua Mama Caua..." (Cabello Balboa (1951:283 [1586:Pt. 3, Ch. 12]).

57. "Vivió en gran sosiego y prosperidad, porque de diversas partes le vinieron a ver muchas naciones, así como guaro llamado Huamac Samo Pachachulla Viracocha y los ayarmacas y los quiles caches" (Murúa 1987:60–61 [1590:Bk. 1, Ch. 7]).

58. "... los primeros y mas señalados que vinieron fueron Guaman Samo (Cacique y Señor de Guaro) Pachachulla viracochá (hombre de gran discrecion y prudencia) y las naciones Ayarmacas con sus Señores y regentes: Tambo vincais: y Quiliscochas y otros linages circunvecinos..." (Cabello Balboa 1951:283 [1586:Pt. 3, Ch. 12]).

59. "... aunque siempre lo yvan sus vasallos notando de cruel, y sanguinolento, porque siendo niño (jugando con otros de su edad y naturales de el Cuzco) los maltrataba, quebrandoles las piernas y brazos, y aun matando algunos, especial maltrato y ofendio gravemente un dia a unos hijos de ciertos Caciques de Allcay villas, y Culluim Chima por cuia ocasión..." (Cabello Balboa 1951:284 [1586:Pt. 3, Ch. 12]).

60. "En vida de su padre hizo algunas travesuras, de donde procedió ser odiado, aunque temido, tanto que estando jugando con otros mozos de su edad y con los naturales del Cuzco, llamados Alcyvisas y Cullumchima, mataba a los mozos y les quebrada las piernas y los perseguía y seguía hasta sus casas" (Murúa 1987:63 [1590:Ch. 9]).

61. "Porque la relación que a vuestra Señoría Ilustríssima di de el trato, del origen, vida y costumbres de los Ingas, señores que fueron de esta tierra y quántos fueron y quién fueron sus mugeres y las leyes que dieron y guerras que tuvieron y gentes y naciones que conquistaron y en algunos lugares de la relación trato de las ceremonias y cultos que ynventaron aunque no muy especificadamente..." (Molina 1989:49 [ca. 1575]).

62. For additional information on the 1559 report of Polo de Ondegardo, see Bauer (1998).

63. The most numerous documents available from the Conquest and Colonial Periods in Peru are the various records produced by the Crown and regional authorities (e.g., reports, letters, censuses, inspections, lawsuits, wills, sales records) as well as by Church officials (e.g., reports, letters, confessions, as well as baptismal, marriage, and death records).

64. For extensive discussions of the written sources on the Incas, see Porras Barrenechea (1986) and Pease (1995), among many others.

65. Among the most famous indigenous writers are Titu Cusi Yupanqui (2005

[1570]), Juan de Santa Cruz Pachacuti Yamqui Salcamayhua (1950 [1613]), and Felipe Guaman Poma de Ayala (1980 [1615]).

66. These include the famous works of Blas Valera (1950 [ca. 1585]) and that of Garcilaso de la Vega (1966 [1609]).

67. The Quechua documents, of which the most well known is the Huarochirí Manuscript (1991 [1608]), tend to be late, written one or two generations after the collapse of the empire.

68. Examples of these conquest accounts include Sancho de la Hoz (1917 [1534]), Mena (1929 [1534]), Xérez (1985 [1534]), and Pizarro (1921 [1571]).

SECOND PART OF THE GENERAL HISTORY CALLED THE INDICA

1. Philip II, king of Spain (1556–1598).

2. *Cicero pro rege Deyotaro* is written in the margin of the document.

3. *Oldradus ca. 94* is written in the margin of the document.

4. *Bartolomeus Marlianus yn tipographia et Antoninus Florentinus theologus* is written in the margin of the document.

5. *Homerus lib. 17 Odissea and Timquellus* de *nthl. c. 3 y c. 76* are written in the margins of the document.

6. *Suetonius et Eusebius chronographus et Eutropius* is written in the margin of the document.

7. *Vergilius* is written in the margin of the document.

8.

Nocte pluit tota, redeunt spectacula mane;
Divisum imperium cum Jove Caesar habet
(Translation from Latin by Bill Hyland)

9. *Im proemio Catilinarij* is written in the margin of the document.

10. "Inscription on the ancient pillars of Hercules" is written in the margin of the document.

11. "Discovery of the Indies" is written in the margin of the document.

12. *Plus ultra* is written in the margin of the document.

13. The words *plus ultra* can be seen on twin Herculean pillars on the coat of arms of Castilla and León and of Philip II (see Figures I.1 and I.2 of the introduction).

14. *Optima cibus invidiae* is written in the margin of the document.

15. *Verg quid non mortalia pectora cogis auri sacra fames* is written in the margin of the document.

16. Pope Alexander VI (1492–1503) granted Spain possession of all lands to the south and west of the Azores and Cape Verde Islands that were not held by other European princes on Christmas Day 1492. The drawing of this line of demarcation was hardly done on the sole initiative of the pope.

17. Local lords.

18. King of Spain as Charles I (1516–1556) and Holy Roman emperor as Charles V (1519–1558).

19. "Bishop of Chiapa" is written in the margin of the document.

20. Fray Bartolomé de Las Casas (1474–1566), the bishop of Chiapas, fought against the exploitative practices of the Spaniards in the New World and often successfully lobbied the Crown to institute measures meant to protect the indigenous peoples.

21. "Don Francisco de Toledo, viceroy of Peru" is written in the margin of the document.

22. From Cuzco, Toledo was to continue with his general inspection and travel to the Lake Titicaca region and areas farther south.

23. Here Sarmiento speaks of the creation of *reducciones*. Beginning in 1571, Viceroy Toledo implemented a systematic reorganization of the Andean demographic landscape. In an effort to more efficiently extract tribute, land, and labor, as well as to provide religious teaching, the Spaniards forced the local inhabitants of the Andes to abandon their traditional settlements and live in a series of newly created towns.

24. See Chapters 50 and 52 of Sarmiento's *History of the Incas*.

25. Francisco de Victoria wrote several works legitimating the conquest of the Americas by the Spanish.

26. *Parte 3 Titu. 22 c. 5 c. 8* and *Titulo 6* are written in the margin of the document.

27. "Nombre de Jesús Islands" is written in the margin of the document.

28. Alvaro de Mendaña departed from the port of Callao in 1567 and, early in 1568, landed in the Solomon Archipelago. He returned to colonize the islands in 1595 but died soon after reaching them. For additional information on the discovery of the Solomon Islands, see Chapter 46.

29. It appears that Philip II never followed up on Sarmiento's request to colonize the Solomon Islands. However, much later, in 1581, Sarmiento was granted permission to establish a colony in the Strait of Magellan.

30. There is evidence to suggest that Sarmiento continued to work on the first part of his history after he departed from Cuzco. The fate of the third part is unknown.

31. From this statement, it appears that the first part of Sarmiento's general history had been started but was unfinished in 1572.

32. As a result of Inca colonization policies, numerous Cañaris were living in the Cuzco region at the time of the Spanish Conquest. Sarmiento unquestionably relied on some of these individuals for this origin myth.

33. Cobo (1979:13–15 [1653:Bk. 13, Ch. 2]) and Molina (1943 [ca. 1575]) tell similar, albeit not identical, versions of the Cañari origin myth.

34. Sarmiento dedicates Chapters 2 through 5 to discussions of Atlantis and various theories concerning the peopling of the Americas.

35. This unusual translation appears to have been provided by Diego Lucana in Jauja on 22 November 1570 (Levillier 1940:25).

36. Here Sarmiento refers to the unfinished first part of his account that described the natural history of Peru.

37. Modern Rachi. For additional information on Rachi, see Sillar and Dean (2002).

38. Here Sarmiento describes an ancient lava flow near the town of Rachi.

39. Betanzos (1996:7–10 [1557:Pt. 1, Chs. 1–2]) provides a similar description of Viracocha at Tiahuanaco, Rachi, and Urcos. See also Cieza de León's description of Viracocha at Rachi (1976:27–29 [1554:Pt. 2, Ch. 5]).

40. The shrine to Viracocha was built on top of the mountain now called Viraco-

chan, just outside of Urcos. The summit of the mountain is now destroyed by looters; however, fragments of cut-stone blocks and a large number of human remains can be seen in the looters' pits.

41. Similar descriptions of the role of *cinchis* can be found throughout Toledo's inspection report (Levillier 1940).

42. We have selected to translate *behetrías* (existing in a state of equality) as "tribes."

43. According to Sarmiento, Manco Capac began his rule in AD 565, so this would put the flood around 3046 BC.

44. See Chapters 49 to 59.

45. This may be a reference to Sarmiento's unfinished first volume.

46. At this point in the manuscript, the words "the second Antasayas" are crossed out and a footnote has been added by Ruiz de Navamuel stating, "The Indians with whom this was verified attested that this was not so."

47. See Chapter 11.

48. An accountant in the house of Aragon.

49. Molina (1943 [ca. 1575]) mentions these painted boards, and they are also mentioned in other Cuzco interviews (Levillier 1940:140, 173).

50. Unfortunately, none of these testimonies have been preserved.

51. This section appears to have been added after the public reading of the document in Cuzco on 29 February 1572.

52. That is to say "caves."

53. Cobo provides a very truncated but similar version of this origin myth (Cobo 1979:103–104 [1653:Bk. 12, Ch. 3]. Also see Cabello Balboa (1951:256–264 [1586:Pt. 3, Ch. 9]). For other versions of this myth, see Bauer (1991).

54. The first five groups were members of Hurin Cuzco, and the second five were members of Hanan Cuzco.

55. Juan Pizarro Yupanqui was interviewed by the Spanish authorities on numerous occasions: 28 June and 28 July 1571 and 26 January 1572 (Levillier 1940:143, 175, 186). He is listed as being seventy-eight years old, a native of Cuzco, a descendant of Ayar Uchu, and a member of Aray Uchu Ayllu. He was also present in Cuzco for the viewing of the painted cloths (14 January 1572).

56. Francisco Quispe was interviewed on 26 January 1572 and is listed as a member of Aray Uchu Ayllu (Levillier 1940:186).

57. On 28 June 1571, twenty-two natives of the Cuzco region were interviewed by Spanish authorities about the customs of the Incas. Among those present at the meeting were Gonzalo Ampura Llama Oca (eighty years old) and his son Alonso Llama Oca, both of Maras Ayllu (Levillier 1940:142). They were interviewed again on 28 July 1571 (Levillier 1940:175).

58. Cayocache was a large settlement just south of Cuzco. Numerous other early colonial writers mention Cayocache (Bauer 1998).

59. For a retracing of the mythical journey of Manco Capac and his siblings from Tambotoco to Cuzco, see Bauer (1991).

60. Near the modern ruins of Maukallacta (province of Paruro).

61. Most likely modern Yaurisque (province of Paruro).

62. In other retellings of this myth, Betanzos (1996 [1557]) and Cobo (1979:104 [1653:Bk. 12, Ch. 3)] indicate that these were maize seeds. Also see Cabello Balboa (1951:256–264 [1586:Pt. 3, Ch. 9]).

63. A llama.

64. *Huaca* = shrine.

65. It is worth noting that this statement echoes that of Noah after the biblical flood.

66. Modern Matoro (Rowe 1944; Bauer 1998).

67. The *guarachico* ritual involved giving young men weapons and a loincloth and piercing their ears. The Incas held this male-initiation rite each December as part of the *capac raymi* celebrations.

68. The festival of *capac raymi* was held on the days surrounding the December solstice (Bauer and Dearborn 1995).

69. The first hair cutting is still widely celebrated in the Andes.

70. Cabello Balboa also describes the actions of Mama Huaco and the conquest of the Cuzco Valley by the first Incas (1951:264–273 [1586:Pt. 3, Ch. 10]). Also see information collected by Toledo during his 26 January 1572 meeting with native leaders in Cuzco (Levillier 1940:182–194).

71. Colcabamba was located where the plaza of San Sebastián is now (Bauer 1998).

72. Huanaypata was a large terraced area on the outskirts of Cuzco (Bauer 1998).

73. At this point in the manuscript a footnote has been added by Ruiz de Navamuel stating, "Of the two stories told on this page about the testing of the fertility of the land (by Mama Huaco and Manco Capac with the golden staff or rod), the witnesses swore to the one about Manco Capac."

74. The area of Saño is located between modern San Sebastián and San Jerónimo in the Cuzco Valley (Bauer 1998).

75. Also called Manco Sapaca.

76. For information on the *capac cocha* ritual of the Incas, see McEwan and Van de Guchte (1992).

77. At this point in the manuscript the word "where" is inserted and the word "was" is highlighted. There is a footnote by Ruiz de Navamuel stating, " 'Where' is written between the lines, and 'was' is highlighted."

78. The Arco de la Plata was located just east of the plaza of Limacpampa Grande, on the edge of Spanish Cuzco (Bauer 1998).

79. For additional information on the deeds of Mama Huaco, see Bauer (1996).

80. See Chapter 9.

81. Otherwise known as Coricancha.

82. Cabello Balboa also describes the division of Cuzco into these same four partitions (1951:270 [1586:Pt. 3, Ch. 10]). They are also mentioned in an interview with Cuzco natives on 26 January 1572 (Levillier 1940:182–194).

83. The convent of Santa Clara in Cuzco was founded in 1551. In 1572 it was located on the Plaza de Nazarenas; it was later moved to its current location (Burns 1999).

84. That is to say, "the lordless."

85. The area of Bimbilla is now called Wimpillay (Bauer 1998). It is mentioned by numerous early colonial writers.

86. In 1558 Juan Polo de Ondegardo was asked by the archbishop of Lima (Jerónimo de Loayza) and the viceroy (Andrés Hurtado de Mendoza) to conduct a large-scale investigation concerning the history and ritual practices of the Incas. In the course of this investigation, Polo de Ondegardo discovered the remains of the previous kings of Cuzco, several of which were then sent to Lima (Hampe Martínez 1982; Bauer 2004).

87. Cobo provides very similar information, writing:

From this first king came the *ayllo* and family called Chima Panaca, which adored no human body other than that of Manco Capac, while the other families and lineages adored this one and the bodies of their founders. When Licentiate Polo Ondegardo, with unusual diligence and cunning, found the bodies of the Inca kings and their idols and took them out of the hands of their families in the year 1559 (which was a major factor in eliminating many idolatries and superstitions), he was unable to discover the body of Manco Capac because (or so it seems) his descendants never had it, rather they believed that it turned into stone, and they said that it was a stone that Licentiate Polo himself found, all dressed and properly adorned, in a town near Cuzco that was called Membilla. (Cobo 1979:111–112 [1653:Bk. 12, Ch. 4])

88. Emperor of the Byzantine Empire (668–685).

89. The town of Saño was located within the Cuzco Valley (Bauer 1998).

90. Alonso Puscón was present in Cuzco for the public hearing of Sarmiento's *History of the Incas* (29 February–1 March 1572).

91. Diego Quispe was present in Cuzco for the viewing of the painted cloths (14 January 1572).

92. Emperor of the Byzantine Empire (775–780). Sarmiento appears to be a hundred years off in his calculation of emperors.

93. Pope Donus (676–678).

94. Cobo (1979:114 [1653:Bk. 12, Ch. 5]), who had access to Polo de Ondegardo's report, provides similar, albeit more detailed, information on the mummy of Cinchi Roca. He writes:

From this Inca came the *ayllo* and family called Rauraua Panaca. He left a stone idol in the form of a fish that was named Huanachiri Amaro, and he was adored through it the same as the other Incas from the first one on, and these stone idols were kept and venerated as gods. Cinchi Roca's body was found in the town of Membilla when the bodies of the rest of the Incas were discovered. It was between some copper bars and sewed with *cabuya*, but it was already consumed. His idol was next to the body, and this idol was much venerated and had servants and a *chacara*. (Cobo 1979:114 [1653:Bk. 12, Ch. 5])

Elsewhere, again using information from Polo de Ondegardo, Cobo (1990:71 [1653:Bk. 12, Ch. 15]) notes that the building in which the mummy of Cinchi Roca was kept was called Acoywasi (House of the Dead).

95. Modern Huaro (department of Cuzco).

96. Following information provided by Cabello Balboa (1951:283 [1586:Pt. 3, Ch. 12]), it is clear that this passage should read, ". . . communicating with some leaders called Guamay Samo (*cacique* and Lord of Guaro), Pachachulla Viracocha (a man of great distinction and prudence), as well as with . . ."

97. Location unknown.

98. Cobo provides a similar passage about the communications between the Incas and other nearby groups during the life of Lloqui Yupanqui:

The first ones to do this were from the Valley of Guaro, six leagues from Cuzco; it had many people, and the lords of the valley were very powerful at that time. The most important ones were called Guama Samo and Pachachulla Viracocha. These were followed by the Ayarmacas of Tambocunca and the Quilliscaches with their caciques . . . (Cobo 1979:115 [1653:Bk. 12, Ch. 6])

99. Located near modern San Jerónimo (department of Cuzco).

100. See both Cabello Balboa (1951:283 [1586:Pt. 3, Ch. 12]) and Cobo (1979:115 [1653:Bk. 12, Ch. 6]) for similar, although not identical, accounts of this marriage. It is worth noting that Cabello Balboa's account is more complete than — and reconciles differences found in — the accounts provided by Sarmiento and Cobo.

101. Pope Leo IV (847–855).

102. Agustín Conde Mayta was among the first individuals expelled from Cuzco during Toledo's 1572 purge of Inca nobility.

103. At this point in the manuscript the words "the body and idol of this Inca" are crossed out and the words "figure of this Inca" are inserted. Ruiz de Navamuel adds a note indicating that these changes were made because "the witnesses said that the figure and not the body had been found."

104. Cobo writes:

Lloque Yupanqui founded the lineage called Ahuani Ayllu, which was spread out in the towns of Cayucache, Membilla, and the area surrounding Cacra. He had an idol that was discovered with his body in the same manner as the rest, and it was much venerated by those of this *ayllo*, and they had the same fiestas and sacrifices for it as for the others. (Cobo 1979:117 [1653:Bk. 12, Ch. 6])

Elsewhere Cobo notes that the mummy was found in a town near Cuzco (Cobo 1979:123 [1653:Bk. 12, Ch. 8]).

105. See Cabello Balboa (1951:280–289 [1586:Pt. 3, Ch. 12]) for additional information concerning the early life of Mayta Capac.

106. Acosta (2002:368 [1590:Bk. 6, Ch. 23]), in a short and unusual listing of the Inca kings, states that Tarco Guaman and his unnamed son became Incas. Polo de Ondegardo (1965:12 [1585]) also lists Tarco Guaman within his list of Inca kings.

107. A Juan Tambo of Mayta Panaca is mentioned by Acosta (2002:368 [1590:Bk. 6, Ch. 23]).

108. Juan Tambo Usca Mayta was present in Cuzco for the public hearing of Sarmiento's *History of the Incas* (29 February–1 March 1572).

109. Cobo's description of this mummy suggests that it may have been housed in Cayocache with members of his family.

He lived many years, and he left the *ayllo* and tribal groups called Usca Mayta, of which the greater part lived in Cayucache. The body of this Inca was taken from his family and the idol that he left of himself was also taken; the same veneration and sacrifices were performed for this body as for the rest. (Cobo 1979:120 [1653:Bk. 12, Ch. 7])

110. The site of Cuyumarca is located north of Pisaq (Covey 2003).

111. The site of Ancasmarca is located north of Calca.

112. It is well documented that the Mohina and the Pinahua were located in what is now called the Lucre Basin (Espinoza Soriano 1974; Bauer and Covey 2002; Bauer 2004).

113. The site of Caytomarca is located in the Vilcanota River Valley, between Calca and Pisaq (Covey 2003).

114. Cabello Balboa (1951:294 [1586:Pt. 3, Ch. 13]) also mentions the division of the waters of Cuzco.

115. The Huayllacan were located on the south side of the Vilcanota River Valley (Bauer and Covey 2002).

116. Sarmiento fails to record the name of the fourth son.

117. Cabello Balboa (1951:294 [1586:Pt. 3, Ch. 13]) also mentions the division of Cuzco.

118. Francisco Guaman Rimache Hachacoma was present in Cuzco for the viewing of the painted cloths (14 January 1572).

119. Now called Larapa.

120. Cobo provides similar information:

> His body was found well adorned and with much authority in a small town of the Cuzco region called Rarapa, along with a stone idol that represented him, of the same name as his *ayllo*, Vicaquirao, and this body was much honored by those of the aforesaid *ayllo* and family; in addition to the ordinary adoration and sacrifices made for it, when there was a need for water for the cultivated fields, they usually brought out his body . . .(1979:125 [1653:Bk. 12, Ch. 9])

121. Location unknown.

122. Location unknown.

123. Location unknown.

124. This suggests that there was an exchange of royal daughters between the leaders of the Incas and the Ayarmacas.

125. Modern Mullaca, near Moray (R. Alan Covey, pers. comm., 2003).

126. Modern Vichu.

127. Modern Pillawara (Covey 2003).

128. Modern Chueca (Covey 2003).

129. Location unknown.

130. Location unknown.

131. Modern Taucamarca.

132. Location unknown.

133. No date is provided in the document.

134. Juan Concha Yupanqui was present in Cuzco for the viewing of the painted cloths (14 January 1572) and the reading of Sarmiento's *History of the Incas* (29 February–1 March 1572).

135. Martín Tito Yupanqui was present in Cuzco for the viewing of the painted cloths (14 January 1572) and the reading of Sarmiento's *History of the Incas* (29 February–1 March 1572).

136. Gonzalo Paucar Aucaylli was present in Cuzco for the viewing of the painted cloths (14 January 1572).

137. At this point in the manuscript Ruiz de Navamuel adds a footnote stating, "The

witnesses said they believe that the licentiate Polo [de Ondegardo] brought it." Other writers confirm that Yahuar Huacac's mummy was found by Polo de Ondegardo in Paullu (Cobo 1979:129 [1653:Bk. 12, Ch. 10]); Acosta (1986:421 [1590:Bk. 6, Ch. 20]).

138. See Chapter 7.

139. Modern Santa Ana.

140. Garcilaso de la Vega (1966:307 [1609:Pt. 1, Bk. 5, Ch. 28]) reports seeing the mummy of Mama Rondocaya in the house of Polo de Ondegardo in 1560.

141. Located near the modern town of Cayra, at the eastern end of the Cuzco Basin (Bauer 1998).

142. Location unknown.

143. Location unknown.

144. Modern Rondocan.

145. Location unknown.

146. Perhaps Caytomarca.

147. Most likely near Huarocondo (Villanueva 1982:185; R. Alan Covey, pers. comm., 2003).

148. Location unknown.

149. Caquia Xaquixaguana is now called Huchuy Cuzco.

150. Location unknown

151. Location unknown.

152. The year is missing from the manuscript.

153. Amaru Tito was present in Cuzco for the viewing of the painted cloths (14 January 1572).

154. Francisco Chalco Yupanqui was present in Cuzco for the viewing of the painted cloths (14 January 1572) as well as for the reading of Sarmiento's *History of the Incas* (29 February–1 March 1572).

155. Francisco Anti Hualpa was present in Cuzco for the viewing of the painted cloths (14 January 1572) as well as for the reading of Sarmiento's *History of the Incas* (29 February–1 March 1572).

156. Polo de Ondegardo later sent this ceramic jar to Lima (Hampe Martínez 1982; Bauer 2004).

157. Modern Ayacucho.

158. Modern Chitapampa.

159. Betanzos (1996:21–22, 71 [1557:Pt. 1, Ch. 6]) also mentions that Apu Mayta, Vicaquirao, and Quilliscache Urco Guaranga remained in Cuzco to help their brother during the Chanca-Inca war. These three appear to have been leaders of Lower Cuzco.

160. The Incas inflated the lungs of sacrificed animals as a form of divination.

161. Modern Susurmarca (Bauer 1998:87).

162. Choco and Cachona are two villages to the south of Cuzco. They are mentioned in a number of local land documents (Bauer 1998).

163. The Incas believed that Viracocha converted the stones surrounding Cuzco into warriors to help the young prince win this critical battle. The largest of these were called Pururaucas and were considered *huacas* (Bauer 1998).

164. Betanzos (1996 [1557]) also describes the Inca treading on captured warriors and the spoils of war as a sign of triumph.

165. See Betanzos (1996:33 [1557:Pt. 1, Ch. 9]) for his account of this event.

166. It is worth noting that when Polo de Ondegardo found the mummy of Pacha-

cuti Inca Yupanqui, the major shrine of the Chancas was found beside it (Polo de Ondegardo 1990:86 [1571]).

167. Location unknown.

168. For a review of Inca astronomy and a critical analysis of this description by Sarmiento, see Bauer and Dearborn (1995).

169. See Chapter 11.

170. This is a reference to Pachacuti's vision at Susurpuquiu; see Chapter 27.

171. Many of the most important shrines of the empire were given lands, flocks, and attendants to maintain them.

172. These are the principal mountains in the Cuzco Basin. They are listed in order starting in the south with Huanacauri and moving clockwise to Anaguarqui, Yauira (modern Picchu), Sinca (modern Huaynacorcor), Picol (modern Pilco), and Pachato-pan (modern Pachatusan).

173. This took place around the time of the December solstice.

174. This ritual took place in August or September, before the heavy rains begin in the highlands.

175. This took place around the time of the June solstice.

176. Other chroniclers mention this rope, including Molina (1943 [ca. 1575]) and Cieza de León (1976 [1554]).

177. Location unknown.

178. Location unknown.

179. Betanzos (1996:87 [1557:Pt. 1, Ch. 19]) also mentions this custom of making prisoners dress in fringe-covered robes in his description of the defeat of the Soras.

180. In an interview that took place on 5–6 September 1571, Spanish authorities met with Gonzalo Cusi Roca, the son of Tocay Capac. He is described as the para-mount lord of all Ayarmaca and as being more than one hundred years old (Levillier 1940:168).

181. There are various Guanancanchas in the Cuzco region. The definitive location of this battle site is currently not known.

182. Cabello Balboa (1951 [1586]), Murúa (1987 [1590]), and Santa Cruz Pachacuti Yamqui Salcamayhua (1950 [ca. 1613]) also describe this attack on Inca Yupanqui.

183. For additional information on the Cuyo, see Covey (2003).

184. Ruiz de Navamuel adds a footnote here stating that " 'eleven' is highlighted."

185. This wound may have been seen later on the mummy of Pachacuti by Acosta (1986:423 [1590:Bk. 6, Ch. 21]).

186. Various other writers mention this fire, including Albornoz (1984 [1582]) and Murúa (1946 [1590]). Cobo (1990:55 [1653:Bk. 13, Ch. 13]), however, provides the fullest description.

. . . Nina [fire], which was a brazier made of a stone where the fire for sacrifices was lit, and they could not take it from anywhere else. It was next to the Temple of the Sun; it was held in great veneration, and solemn sacrifices were made to it.

187. Remains of such a drainage system have been found in a plaza area on the Island of the Sun (Bauer and Stanish 2001).

188. See Cobo (1979:139–140 [1653:Bk. 12, Ch. 13]) for a slightly different telling of the Inca-Colla war.

189. Other chroniclers also describe Andean leaders drinking from the skulls of their vanquished enemies.

190. The Llaxaguasi was a building in which the Inca kept war trophies. It is reported that the skins of the fallen Chanca leaders were also displayed in this building (Cieza de León 1998:317 [1554:Pt. 3, Ch. 69]).

191. The Sancaguaci was a prison within Inca Cuzco. It was most likely located north of the Coricancha (Bauer 1998:137).

192. Here and elsewhere we have translated Sarmiento's word *montañas* as "forests" rather than "mountains," since he is referring to the densely forested area of the eastern Andean slopes.

193. Amaru Topa Inca was the eldest son of Pachacuti Inca Yupanqui, who was passed over as crown prince in favor of his younger brother Topa Inca Yupanqui. Although he did not succeed his father as ruler, Amaru Topa Inca did retain considerable power. For example, it is believed that he was in charge of Cuzco while his brother Topa Inca Yupanqui was away on military campaigns.

194. During the January 1572 meeting for the verification of the painted cloths, Ruiz de Navamuel (1882:256–257 [1572]) recorded that, years earlier, Polo de Ondegardo had found the mummy of Amaru Topa Inca but that it had been sent to Lima along with three or four others. Although he may never have been the principal ruler of the Inca Empire, Amaru Topa's high social position in imperial Cuzco is unquestionable, and there is every reason to believe he would have been mummified at the time of his death.

For information on Amaru Topa Inca, see Cabello Balboa (1951:334 [1586:Pt. 3, Ch. 18]), Sarmiento de Gamboa (1906:77, 84–86 [1572:Ch. 37, Chs. 42–43]), Santa Cruz Pachacuti Yamqui Salcamayhua (1950:245–246 [ca. 1613]), and Cobo (1964:83, 171, 173, 175 [1653:Bk. 12, Ch. 13; Bk. 13, Chs. 13–14]).

195. Now called Huánuco Pampa Viejo.

196. Andrés Hurtado de Mendoza, the Marquis of Cañete, was the third viceroy of Peru (1556–1561).

197. For additional information on Guzmanco, see Watanabe (2002).

198. These were *Spondylus* shells gathered in the warm waters of Ecuador.

199. *Capac cochas* included the offering of young children to the gods.

200. Note that Topa Inca Yupanqui was already mentioned in Chapter 38.

201. That is to say, "as king."

202. After his death, the mummy of Pachacuti was kept in Patallacta. This house is most likely the ruins now called Kenko (Bauer 1998).

203. Here Sarmiento suggests that the Inca visited the various Houses of the Sun in a specific order, like the Stations of the Cross.

204. *Inti raymi* was held near the time of the June solstice.

205. There is broad agreement among the chroniclers concerning the names of the four divisions for the Inca Empire.

206. Modern Cuenca, Ecuador.

207. Pisar Capac was a cacique of the Cañaris. There was also an *ayllu* named Pisar Capac in Cuzco during the Colonial Period, which may have been relocated there after the northern conquest of the Incas.

208. At this point in the manuscript, Ruiz de Navamuel has added a footnote stating that "the word '*cinchis*' is highlighted."

209. For additional information on the Incas in Ecuador, see Bray (2003).

210. Cabello Balboa (1951:323 [1586:Pt. 3, Ch. 17]) also mentions the discovery of the islands of Avachumbi and Niñachumbi.

211. Urco Guaranga is not listed among the signatories of this document. However, an Orco Varanca is mentioned by Titu Cusi Yupanqui (2005:124 [1570]) as being a general of Manco Inca.

212. Lope García de Castro was then the president of the Audiencia of Lima.

213. This recalls Mendaña's discovery of the Solomon Islands. For additional information on this voyage, see Mendaña (1901 [1568]) and Sarmiento de Gamboa (1895, 1988, 2000).

214. Also see Cabello Balboa (1951:333 [1586:Pt. 3, Ch. 18]).

215. Betanzos saw the mummy of Pachacuti Inca Yupanqui while it was still in Patallacta:

Only the body [of Pachacuti Inca Yupanqui] is in Patallacta at this time, and, judging by it, in his lifetime he seems to have been a tall man. (Betanzos 1996:139 [1557:Pt. 1, Ch. 32])

216. This was the mourning ritual of the Incas.

217. Betanzos provides a very similar description of Pachacuti Inca Yupanqui's death, suggesting a shared informant. Betanzos writes that Pachacuti Inca Yupanqui

raised his voice in a song that is still sung today in his memory by those of his generation. The song went as follows: "Since I bloomed like the flower of the garden, up to now I have given order and justice in this life and world as long as my strength lasted. Now I have turned into earth." Saying these words of his song, Inca Yupanqui Pachacuti expired . . . After he was dead, he was taken to a town named Patallacta, where he had ordered some houses built in which his body was to be entombed. (Betanzos 1996:138 [1557:Pt. 1, Ch. 32])

218. In a statement recorded on 6 September 1571, Diego Cayo and Alonso Tito Atauchi provide, based on readings of *quipus* and a [painted] board, very different ages for Pachacuti Inca Yupanqui, Topa Inca Yupanqui, and Huayna Capac than those given in Sarmiento's *History of the Incas* (Levillier 1940:173).

219. The mummy of Mama Anaguarqui was kept in Pumamarca, near Cuzco (Cobo 1990:67 [1653:Bk. 13, Ch. 14]; Bauer 1998).

220. Diego Cayo was present in Cuzco for the viewing of the painted cloths (14 January 1572) as well as for the reading of Sarmiento's *History of the Incas* (29 February–1 March 1572).

221. Juan Quispe Cusi was present for the reading of Sarmiento's *History of the Incas* (29 February–1 March 1572).

222. Francisco Chaco Rimache was present for the reading of Sarmiento's *History of the Incas* (29 February–1 March 1572).

223. Juan Illac was present in Cuzco for the viewing of the painted cloths (14 January 1572).

224. The most likely location for the mummy in Tococache was in the temple of Inti Illapa.

225. Acosta (2002:364 [1590:Bk. 6, Ch. 21]) provides a full description of Pachacuti Inca Yupanqui's mummy, which he saw after it was sent to Lima by Polo de Ondegardo:

> The body [of Pachacuti Inca Yupanqui] was so well preserved, and treated with a certain resin, that it seemed alive. The eyes were made of gold leaf so well placed that there was no need of the natural ones; and there was a bruise on his head that he had received from a stone in a certain battle. His hair was gray and none of it was missing, as if he had died that very day, although in fact his death had occurred more than sixty or eighty years before. This body, along with those of other Incas, was sent by Polo to the city of Lima under orders from the viceroy, the Marqués de Cañete, for it was necessary to root out the idolatry of Cuzco; and many Spaniards have seen this body, along with the others, in the hospital of San Andrés, founded by the aforesaid viceroy, although by now they are very much abused and in poor condition.

226. Pachacuti Inca Yupanqui's mummy was among those that Polo de Ondegardo sent to Lima in 1559 (Hampe Martínez 1982; Bauer 2004). For additional descriptions of his mummy, see Polo de Ondegardo (1990:86 [1571]), Ruiz de Navamuel (1882:256–257 [1572]), Calancha (1981:212 [1638:Bk. 1, Ch. 15]), and Cobo (1990:51 [1653:Bk. 13, Ch. 13]).

227. Paytite was the legendary area of a golden city lost in the jungles of Peru.

228. See Garcilaso de la Vega (1966:440–442 [1609:Pt. 1, Bk. 7, Ch. 16]) for an account of failed Spanish expeditions into the area of the Chuncho.

229. Cobo (1979:143 [1653:Bk. 12, Ch. 14]) and Cabello Balboa (1951:335 [1586:Pt. 3, Ch. 18]) also tell of this revolt by the Collas.

230. Sic; in Quechua, piscachunga is "fifty."

231. Similar descriptions of the counting system of the Incas can be found in Toledo's inspection report (Levillier 1940:21, 26).

232. As Sarmiento correctly states, cacique is Carib for "leader" or "chief," and curaca is the Quechua term with the same meaning.

233. See Cobo 1979:150 [1653:Bk. 12, Ch. 15) for very different information on the Yanayaco.

234. There is no evidence that Sarmiento ever completed this "book of laws."

235. The junction of the two rivers that flow through Cuzco is called Pumachupa (puma tail).

236. In 1536, the city of Cuzco was burned in a revolt against Spanish rule led by Manco Inca. After this, and a brief civil war between the Pizarros and Diego de Almagro, much of Cuzco was rebuilt following the canons of European architecture. The destruction of Sacsayhuaman is noted by a number of chroniclers (Dean 1998; Bauer 2004).

237. Andrés Topa Yupanqui was present in Cuzco to view the painted cloths (14 January 1572) as well as for the reading of Sarmiento's History of the Incas (29 February–1 March 1572).

238. Cristóbal Pisac Topa was present in Cuzco to view the painted cloths (14 January 1572) as well as for the reading of Sarmiento's History of the Incas (29 February–1 March 1572).

239. García Vilcas was present in Cuzco to view the painted cloths (14 January

1572) as well as for the reading of Sarmiento's *History of the Incas* (29 February–1 March 1572).

240. The names Don García Ayache and Don García Pilco have been inserted into the document. Ruiz de Navamuel adds a footnote stating that these two names were added when the manuscript was read and that "the witnesses said [both men] are alive and are said to be from that *ayllu*."

241. Garcilaso de la Vega (1966:306–307 [1609:Pt. 1, Bk. 5, Ch. 28]) states that he saw the mummy of Topa Inca Yupanqui. However, it is believed that he was mistaken (Bauer 2004).

242. Calispuquio was located near Sacsayhuaman (Bauer 1998).

243. Cobo provides a similar description:

> He died in the city of Cuzco, and his body, embalmed and well preserved, was kept intact until his grandson Huascar Inca was imprisoned. At that time the body was burned by Atahualpa's captains Quizquiz and Chalcochima. Tupac Inca had an idol named Cuxichuri which was much honored by the Indians, along with his ashes that they kept in a jar. (Cobo 1979:151 [1653:Bk. 12, Ch. 15])

244. Modern Quispicanchi, near the Inca site of Tipón.

245. This statement suggests that the Inca may have had a pilgrimage route that followed the mythical route of Manco Capac from Huanacauri to Cuzco.

246. This plaza is now called Limacpampa and is on the edge of old Cuzco.

247. Huayna Capac's mother, Mama Ocllo, is a well-known figure in Inca history. After her death, her mummy was kept just outside Cuzco in Picchu (Betanzos 1996:172–173 [1557:Pt. 1, Ch. 44]; Cobo 1990:61 [1653:Bk. 13, Ch. 13]). In 1559, Polo de Ondegardo found the mummy of Mama Ocllo and sent it to Lima, along with several others (Ruiz de Navamuel 1882:256–257 [1572]; Acosta 1986:422 [1590:Bk. 6, Ch. 22]; Garcilaso de la Vega 1966:307 [1609:Pt. 1, Bk. 5, Ch. 28]).

248. The Casana was a royal palace on the central plaza of Cuzco (Bauer 2004).

249. For a detailed description of Huayna Capac's *mitimaes* in Cochabamba, see Wachtel (1982).

250. Cobo provides similar information on Huayna Capac's tour of the Collao and the area of Pocona:

> He left the Andes by way of Cochabamba, and, seeing how fertile and abundant with food the valleys of that province were, and that very few people inhabited them, he ordered that some families from the Collao region should go to reside in these valleys; and for this reason now almost all the inhabitants there are *mitimaes*.
>
> From Cochabamba he went on to Pocona, to visit the border there. He gave orders for a fortress to be repaired; it was one that had been built on the orders of his father. (Cobo 1979:154 [1653:Bk. 12, Ch. 16])

251. The source of this information was most certainly the son of Tito Atauchi named Alonso Tito Atauchi. Alonso was an important figure in the early Colonial Period and was present in Cuzco when the painted cloths were shown (14 January 1572) as well as for the reading of Sarmiento's *History of the Incas* (29 February–1 March 1572).

On both occasions, he signed documents stating that he was the leader of Huascar's kin group.

252. This version of Inca history, perhaps provided by Alonso Tito Atauchi, supports Huascar's claim to the Incaship. Huascar is said to have been the offspring of a royal sister-brother marriage between Huayna Capac and Araua Ocllo. The other descendants of Huayna Capac, including Atahualpa, Ninan Cuyoche, Manco Inca, and Paullu Topa, are all specifically referred to as illegitimate children, that is to say, not the offspring of a royal sister-brother marriage. Not surprisingly, Atahualpa's generals challenge this claim (see Chapter 66).

253. On the death of Huayna Capac, Ninan Cuyoche would be considered for the Incaship. However, he, too, would die in the same plague that killed Huayna Capac, so the Incaship was given to Huascar, half brother of Atahualpa. See Chapter 62 for more details.

254. Sarmiento suggests that Atahualpa's mother, Tocto Coca, was Huayna Capac's cousin rather than his sister.

255. Much later, Manco Inca and Paullu Topa would compete against each other for the Incaship during the early years of Spanish rule in the Andes.

256. Cobo provides a similar description of the conquest of the Pastos. For example, he writes:

> . . . he turned this expedition over to four of the bravest ones: Mollo Cauana, of the Lupaca nation, a native of the town of Hilaui; Mollo Pucara, a native of Hatuncolla; and two others from the province of Condesuyu who were called Apu Cauac Cauana and Apu Cunti Mullu. And besides the soldiers from various nations that were going to this war, he gave two thousand *orejones*, knights of Cuzco, and, as their captains, his brother Auquituma and Collatupa, a brave captain of the lineage of Viracocha Inca. . . . (Cobo 1979:155–156 [1653:Bk. 12, Ch. 16])

257. Cobo (1979:157 [1653:Bk. 12, Ch. 17]) also tells of the rescue, ". . . the king fell to the ground, and if the captains Cusi Tupa Yupanqui and Guayna Achache had not helped him and removed him from danger, he would have died at the hands of the enemies." Also see Cabello Balboa (1951:370 [1586:Pt. 3, Ch. 21]).

258. Cobo (1979:157–159 [1653:Bk. 12, Ch. 17]) provides much of the same information concerning the Inca's war against the Cayambes.

259. Cabello Balboa (1951:380–382 [1586:Pt. 3, Ch. 23]) also provides a detailed account of the Inca's siege of the fortress of the Cayambes.

260. *Sic*; Cayambes.

261. *Taqui* = "dance."

262. Also see Cabello Balboa (1951:383 [1586:Pt. 3, Ch. 23]).

263. See Chapter 64 for additional information on the shrine of Catiquilla.

264. The encounter with these natives is also described by Cabello Balboa (1951:385–386 [1586:Pt. 3, Ch. 23]).

265. *Spondylus* shell.

266. Cabello Balboa (1951:392 [1586:Pt. 3, Ch. 24]) and Cobo (1979:159 [1653:Bk. 12, Ch. 17]) also tell of this visit to the island of Puna.

267. For the death of Huayna Capac, see Cabello Balboa (1951:392–393 [1586:Pt. 3, Ch. 24]).

268. Thus, the tragedy of the Spanish invasion is revealed.

269. European diseases spread southward from Panama, killing a vast number of Native Americans even before Spain had established direct contact with the Incas.

270. Diego Viracocha Inca was present in Cuzco for the viewing of the painted cloths (14 January 1572). He was also a signer of Sarmiento's document, but he is listed only as a witness rather than as a member of the Tomebamba Ayllu.

271. Loarte threatened García Inguil Topa with torture during Toledo's 1572 purge of the Inca nobility (Hemming 1970:454).

272. At the time of this report, Don Carlos, son of Paullu Topa and grandson of Huayna Capac, had been appointed Inca by the ruling Spaniards.

273. This date is problematic, since Sarmiento later states that Huayna Capac was alive when Pizarro first made contact with the Inca Empire during his second voyage of exploration, in 1526–1527.

274. The body of Huayna Capac disappeared from view sometime after the conquest. Betanzos (1996:190 [1557:Pt. 2, Ch. 1]), writing in 1557, specifically states that it had not been seen for many years. Cobo describes the events that led to the discovery of Huayna Capac's remains by Polo de Ondegardo two years later:

> After the Spaniards entered this land, they made every effort to discover his body, and they even resorted to violence many times, because it was widely believed that he had a great treasure and that it would be buried with his body or in the places he frequented the most during his lifetime, since this was an ancient custom among them. At last, owing to the great diligence that was taken, it was found, at the same time as the bodies of the other Incas, on the road to the fortress, in a house where the body seems to have been taken the night before, since the Spaniards were on the right track and catching up with it, the Indians who took care of it would move it to many different places, and although they took it in such a rush, unexpectedly moving it from one place to another, they always took it in the company of five or six idols, for which they showed great veneration, because they were convinced that these idols helped guard the body of the Inca. (Cobo 1979:161–162 [1653:Bk. 12, Ch. 19])

Thus, like the bodies of all the other kings of Cuzco, the mummy of Huayna Capac was hunted down and found in 1559 through the tireless efforts of Polo de Ondegardo.

275. A García Suma Yupanqui, who lists himself as "Principal Inca lord of Cuzco," signed a 1562 testimonial of Mancio Sierra de Leguizamo's past services to the king. Suma Yupanqui is listed as being seventy years old (Stirling 1999:178).

276. Located on the shore of Lake Lucre.

277. Here Huascar kills the members of Inca Yupanqui's lineage, knowing that they sided with Atahualpa, since Atahualpa's mother, Tocto Coca, was from that lineage.

278. Cabello Balboa (1951:398 [1586:Pt. 3, Ch. 25]) also describes Huascar's separation from Hanan Cuzco.

279. Sarmiento states that an individual with the same name, Urco Guaranga, was a witness to the reading of the document; see Chapter 42.

280. Sarmiento crossed the Río Pampa on his journey to Cuzco. Perhaps he was shown the fields at that time.

281. At this point in the manuscript Ruiz de Navamuel adds a footnote stating that "the name 'Guanca Auqui' is highlighted."

282. This would be the last victory gained by the luckless Guanca Auqui.

283. Cobo (1979 [1653]) provides a condensed version of the many battles that took place between Huascar's and Atahualpa's forces. Also see Betanzos (1996 [1557]) and Cabello Balboa (1951 [1586:Pt. 3, Ch. 30]).

284. See Betanzos [1996:256 [1557:Pt. 2, Ch. 22]) for a similar description of the Inca's use of an intermediary.

285. This was the shrine of Catiquilla that is described by a number of chroniclers. See Topic, Topic and Melly Cava (2002) for more information on this shrine.

286. A very similar description is found in Betanzos, suggesting that he and Sarmiento shared an informant. Betanzos writes:

> When they arrived, [Atahualpa] ordered his warriors to surround the *guaca*'s hill and mountaintop so the idol would not escape. When the hill was surrounded, Atahualpa himself, in person, climbed to the *guaca* where the idol was. Atahualpa gave the idol such a blow in the neck with a battle-ax he carried that he cut off the head. They then brought there the old man, who was held as a saint and who had given the idol's reply to the messengers. Atahualpa also beheaded him with his battle-ax.
>
> When this had been done, he ordered fire brought and he had a great amount of firewood that was around the *guaca* piled on the idol and on the old man. He had them set fire to the idol. (1996:231–232 [1557:Pt. 2, Ch. 16])

287. This is the Pampaconga pass on the Cuzco side of the bridge. It is the site of numerous battles in Inca history.

288. This Huánuco Pampa (department of Apurimac, province of Qotabamba) should not be confused with the better-known Inca provincial center also called Huánuco Pampa (department of Huánuco). Also see Betanzos (1996:229 [1557:Pt. 2, Ch. 15]).

289. Titu Cusi Yupanqui (2005:66 [1570]) also noted that this battle occurred near a place called Huánuco Pampa.

290. Cabello Balboa (1951:459 [1586:Pt. 3, Ch. 31]) describes the capture of Huascar.

291. Cobo (1979:167 [1653:Bk. 12, Ch. 19]) writes "Quipaypampa," and Betanzos (1996:244 [1557:Pt. 2, Ch. 19]) writes "Quicpai." Fernández (1963 [1571:Pt. 2, Bk. 3, Ch. 15]) writes "Quipaipan." Garcilaso de la Vega (1966:619 [1609:Pt. 1, Bk. 9, Ch. 37]) takes exception to the latter's spelling and provides a more complete description of this place: "The name of the battlefield which he [Fernández] gives is a corruption: it should be Quepaipa, and is the genitive meaning "out of my trumpet," as though that was the place where Atahualpa's trumpet sounded loudest, according to the Indian phrase. I have been in this place two or three times with other boys who were fellow pupils of mine . . ."

292. Betanzos (1996:228–230 [1557:Pt. 2, Ch. 15]) also describes this final battle and Chalco Chima's ruse with Huascar's litter.

293. This is the hill just outside Cuzco now called Picchu.

294. Also see Cabello Balboa (1951:460–462 [1586:Pt. 3, Ch. 31]) for an account of this meeting.

295. *Infanta* is the Spanish term for a royal princess, equivalent to the French *dauphine*.

296. This is the road that leads from Cuzco to Anta.

297. Betanzos provides a similar description of the killing of Huascar's wives, suggesting that he and Sarmiento may have used the same informant:

> When this was done, he ordered Huascar's wives separated. When this was done, he commanded that those who were pregnant have their babies torn alive from the womb, and some of them had other children of Huascar. Cusi Yupanqui ordered these women opened alive also. These and the rest of Huayna Capac's daughters were hanged from the highest of those stakes. And the babies taken from their wombs were attached to the hands, arms, and feet of their mothers, who were already hanging on the stakes. (Betanzos 1996:244 [1557:Pt. 2, Ch. 19])

298. Paullu Topa would later befriend the Spaniards, and in July of 1537 he was selected, along with his wife, Catalina Usica, to rule the indigenous people of Spanish-controlled Cuzco.

299. A similar description of Paullu Topa's escape is recorded by Betanzos, suggesting that these authors may have used the same informant. Betanzos writes:

> [Paullu Topa] escaped from the imprisonment because he proved that he had been mistreated by Huascar because he had shown himself to be a friend of Atahualpa's. This was a lie. Huascar had ordered him captured because he had been found with one of Huascar's wives. Huascar had him thrown in jail, where he was kept tied and was to die by slow starvation, what we call "to eat by ounces."
> When Chalcochima and Quizquiz entered Cuzco, they found this Paulo in jail and, since he told them he had been imprisoned because he was a friend of Atahualpa's, they released him. When Cuxi Yupanqui arrived, they recaptured Paulo and when he proved to the captains that he had been imprisoned for being a friend of Atahualpa's, Cuxi Yupanqui ordered him released. (Betanzos 1996:243–244 [1557:Pt. 2, Ch. 19])

300. It appears that the Chachapoyas and the Cañaris attempted to take advantage of the dynastic war and rebel against their Inca overseers. Likewise, they would later ally themselves against the Inca with the invading forces of Francisco Pizarro.

301. Don Carlos, son of Paullu Topa and Catalina Usica, was the Spanish-appointed ruler of Cuzco when Sarmiento was in the city. It is also worth noting that Francisco de Toledo baptized the first child of Carlos and his European-born wife, María de Esquivel, Melchor Carlos Inca, on 6 January 1572 (Ocampo 1907:207 [1610]).

302. Cobo writes, ". . . also able to escape were some important women, daughters of great lords, who later became Christians; among them were Elvira Quechonay, Beatriz Caruay Mayba, Juana Tocto, Catalina Usoca, mother of Carlos Inca, and many others" (Cobo 1979:169 [1653:Bk. 12, Ch. 19]), suggesting that these two authors shared a common source for this passage.

303. Similar descriptions of the Tallane messengers reporting Pizarro's arrival to Atahualpa are provided in Betanzos (1996:235 [1557]) and in Titu Cusi Yupanqui (2005:60, 63 [1570]).

304. The third part of Sarmiento's work was never finished.

305. See Chapter 7.

306. The most complete description of the conquest of Peru is provided in Hemming (1970).

307. Before any conquest began, the Spaniards were required to offer the indigenous people an opportunity to convert to Christianity and to recognize the king of Spain as their ruler. Given Sarmiento's political agenda in writing *The History of the Incas*, it was important that he specifically mention that this requirement was offered to Atahualpa.

308. Also see Cabello Balboa (1951:472 [1586:Pt. 3, Ch. 32]).

309. Alonso Tito Atauchi was present in Cuzco for the viewing of the painted cloths (14 January 1572) as well as for the reading of Sarmiento's *History of the Incas* (29 February–1 March 1572).

310. The political agenda of Sarmiento's work is reiterated in this statement.

311. This is to say that their rule was not sanctioned by God.

312. Manco Inca was killed in the Vilcabamba region by rebel Spaniards in 1544.

313. As part of a peace agreement between the Spaniards and the Incas, Diego Sayre Topa left the Vilcabamba region in 1557 and settled on an estate in the Urubamba Valley. He died soon afterward, however, and the conflict between those of Vilcabamba and the Spanish in Cuzco began anew.

314. Sayre Topa died in 1560. In his will, Sayre Topa provided funds for a chapel to be built at the site of the Coricancha and requested that he be buried there (Morales 1944).

315. Tito Cusi Yupanqui was the son of Manco Inca and the brother of Diego Sayre Topa and Tupac Amaru. In 1570, while in exile in Vilcabamba, Tito Cusi Yupanqui dictated a letter to King Philip II describing the life of his father and requesting that he be compensated for the losses that he had suffered (Titu Cusi Yupanqui 2005 [1570]). He died under mysterious circumstances the following year.

316. Unbeknown to Sarmiento, Tito Cusi Yupanqui had recently died, and Tupac Amaru had already taken power in Vilcabamba.

317. This individual is more commonly called Tupac Amaru. The Spanish captured him soon after this document was written.

318. At the time that this document was written, Carlos' holdings included the *encomiendas* of Pinahua, Yauri, and Mohina (Toledo 1975).

319. Soon after Sarmiento finished his *History of the Incas*, Toledo sent Felipe to Lima.

320. Soon after Sarmiento finished his *History of the Incas*, Toledo sent Alonso Tito Atauchi to Lima.

321. Emperor of the Byzantine Empire (565–578).

322. Pope John III (561–574).

323. Pope Paul III (1534–1549).

324.

Maxima Tolleti Proregis gloria creuit,
Dum regni tenebras, lucida cura, fugat.

Ite procul scioli, uobis non locus in istis!
Rex indos noster nam tenet innocue.
(Translation by Bill Hyland)

325. "Audiencia" refers to a Spanish colonial governing body that combined administrative and judicial functions.

326. Now Lima.

327. Now Ayacucho.

328. Diego Cayo Hualpa was present in Cuzco for the viewing of the painted cloths (14 January 1572).

329. Alonso Puscón was present in Cuzco for the viewing of the painted cloths (14 January 1572).

330. Juan Tambo Usca Mayta was present in Cuzco for the viewing of the painted cloths (14 January 1572).

331. Francisco Antihuallpa was present in Cuzco for the viewing of the painted cloths (14 Jan 1572).

332. Domingo Pascac was present in Cuzco for the viewing of the painted cloths (14 January 1572). During an interview with Toledo on 28 June 1571, we learn that Domingo's father had been a captain of Topa Inca Yupanqui and Huayna Capac (Levillier 1940:141).

333. Juan Cuzco was present in Cuzco for the viewing of the painted cloths (14 January 1572).

334. Francisco Sayre was present in Cuzco for the viewing of the painted cloths (14 January 1572) but is listed as being in the kin group of Topa Inca Yupanqui.

335. Cobo (1979:171 [1653:Bk. 12, Ch. 19]) mentions that Francisco Ninan Coro's bother, Juan Ninan Coro, was still living in Cuzco when he was there in 1606.

336. Juan Apanca was present in Cuzco for the viewing of the painted cloths (14 January 1572).

337. Diego Viracocha Inca was present in Cuzco for the viewing of the painted cloths (14 January 1572).

338. The name Gómez has been inserted in the document, and Ruiz de Navamuel has added a footnote stating, " 'Gómez' is written between the lines."

339. Starting with Chapter 6.

Glossary

Quechua terms are indicated with a (Q) after the word.

Aclla (Q): *See mamacona.*

Almagro, Diego: Partner of Francisco Pizarro in the conquest of the Incas.

Amaru Topa Inca: The older brother of Topa Inca Yupanqui and the eldest son of Pachacuti Inca Yupanqui.

Antisuyu (Q): The northeast quadrant of the Inca Empire.

Apu (Q): Lord.

Atahualpa: The Inca ruler captured and killed by Francisco Pizarro in 1532.

auca **(Q):** Warrior; traitor.

ayllu **(Q):** Kin group, clan, lineage, community.

ayuscay **(Q):** Birth rite.

calpa **(Q):** Divination conducted by inflating the lungs of sacrificed animals.

Cañari (pl., Cañaris): An ethnic group of Ecuador.

cancha **(Q):** Enclosure; neighborhood; quarter.

capac cocha **(Q):** A ritual held at a time of great need; it often included child sacrifice.

capac **(Q):** Royal, rich.

capac raymi **(Q):** December solstice celebration.

Capactoco (Q): Rich window; the cave from which the first mythical Incas emerged.

Capac Yupanqui: The fourth Inca.

Carmenca (Q): Suburb of Cuzco, now called Santa Ana.

Cayocache (Q): Suburb of Cuzco, now called Belén.

Chachapoya: Ethnic group of the northern Peruvian Andes.

chasqui **(Q):** Runner.

Chinchaysuyu (Q): The northwest quadrant of the Inca Empire.

chuco **(Q):** Headdress.

cinchi **(Q):** Warrior, leader.

Cinchi Roca: The second Inca.

coca **(Q):** *Erythroxylon coca;* the leaves of this plant contain a mildly narcotic substance.

cocha **(Q):** Sea, lake, or large body of water.

Collasuyu (Q): The southeast quadrant of the Inca Empire.

Coricancha (Q): The Temple of the Sun located in the center of Cuzco.

corregidor: Spanish governor of natives.

coya (Q):   Sister-wife of an Inca.

Cuntisuyu (Q):   The southwest quadrant of the Inca Empire.

curaca (Q):   Local lord.

duho (Q):   Seat, bench, stool.

encomienda: Grant of native labor that was initially given to Spaniards to
   encourage them to settle permanently in Peru.

hanan (Q):   Upper.

hanansaya (Q):   Upper side.

huaca (Q):   Shrine, sacred location or object.

Guamanga (Q):   Modern Ayacucho.

Huanacauri (Q):   Highest mountain peak of the Cuzco Valley and a shrine of
   the Incas.

guarachico (Q):   Male initiation rite of the Incas; it usually included having the ears
   pierced.

huayna (Q):   Young.

Huayna Capac: The eleventh Inca and the last to rule over a united empire.

hurin (Q):   Lower.

hurinsaya (Q):   Lower side.

Inca Roca: The sixth Inca.

inti (Q):   Sun.

Inticancha (Q):   The sun temple in Cuzco; also called the Coricancha.

inti raymi (Q):   June solstice celebration.

League: The average distance a man on a horse can ride in an hour; a distance
   equal to about 5.5 km.

llayto (Q):   Headdress.

Lloqui Yupanqui: The third Inca.

lloqui (Q):   Left.

mamacona (Q):   Holy woman, chosen woman (also called *aclla*).

Manco Capac: The first Inca.

mascapaycha (Q):   Royal tassel of the Inca.

Mayta Capac: The fifth Inca.

michocrima (Q):   Garrison.

mitima (Q; pl., *mitimaes*):   Colonist, settler.

moroy urco (Q):   A multicolored rope that was used in the most important rituals
   of Cuzco.

mullu (Q):   Colored *Spondylus* shell that was highly valued by Andean people.

napa (Q):   A white llama used as an insignia of the royal Incas.

ojota (Q):   Sandal.

Pacariqtambo (Q):   Origin place of the Incas.

pachacuti (Q):   To overturn.

Pachacuti Inca Yupanqui: The ninth Inca, traditionally believed to be responsible
   for the initial expansion of the empire.

pampa (Q):   Plain.

pillaca llayto (Q):   Headdress of the Inca.

Pizarro, Francisco: Leader of the Spanish Conquest forces.

purucaya (Q):   Mourning ritual of the Incas.

guauqui (Q): "Brother" idol of a royal Inca.

Quechua: Language of the Incas; it is still widely spoken in parts of Ecuador, Peru, Bolivia, and Chile.

quicochico (Q): Female initiation rite performed when a woman had her first period.

quipu (Q): A knotted cord used for encoding information.

raymi (Q): Festival.

rutuchico (Q): A rite held at the time of the first hair cutting of any Inca.

Sacsayhuaman (Q): Large fort outside of Cuzco.

Santo Domingo: The church built on the location of the Temple of the Sun in Cuzco.

situay (Q): A ritual cleaning of the city of Cuzco, held in September.

sunturpaucar (Q): Royal banner of the Inca.

suyu (Q): A division or region of the Inca Empire.

suyuyoc apu (Q): Lord of a *suyu*.

Tambotoco (Q): The cave from which the first Inca emerged.

taqui (Q): Dance.

Tiahuanaco: An ancient city on the southern shore of Lake Titicaca (ca. AD 500–1000).

toco (Q): Cave or window.

Topa Capac: Brother of Topa Inca Yupanqui who led an unsuccessful rebellion against the latter.

Topa Inca Yupanqui: The tenth Inca.

topayauri (Q): Scepter of the Inca.

tucurico (Q): Regional governor.

Tupac Amaru: The last heir to the Inca Crown; he was captured and executed in Cuzco under the orders of Viceroy Toledo in 1572.

unu (Q): Water.

unu pachacuti (Q): Refers to a mythical flood that destroyed the world in ancient times.

Vilcabamba (Q): Mountainous area to the northwest of Cuzco where the Incas waged a war against the Spaniards (1536–1572).

Viracocha: The creator god of the Incas; also called Viracocha Pachayachachi and Ticci Viracocha.

Viracocha Inca: The eighth Inca.

yahuar (Q): Blood.

Yahuar Huacac: The seventh Inca.

yanacona (Q): Servant of the Inca.

yanayaco (Q): See *yanacona*.

yauri (Q): Scepter.

Bibliography

MANUSCRIPT SOURCES

Archivo General de Indias (AGI), Sevilla, Spain

Indiferente 739, No. 317, 1, 1, 1581

En quanto al memorial de Pedro Sarmiento ... opinión del Consejo de Indias acerca del manuscrito de Sarmiento.

Justicia: Leg. 465, 1575

Contra el doctor Luarte, por el proceso que hizo en 1572 a los incas por su intento de hacer inca capac al hijo de Carlos Inca. Cuzco, 4 dic. 1575/13 enero 1576, folios 2515–2842v.

Lima 28B, 1572

Un tomo encuadernado en pergamino con 213 fojas utiles que comprende las ynformaciones hechas por el virrey del Perú don Francisco de Toledo en averiguación del origen y gobierno de los incas.

Lima 110, 1552–1699

Cartas del cabildo secular del Cuzco.

Patronato 294, No. 6, 1571

Información de las idolatrías de los incas e indios y de cómo se enterraban (Yucay).

PUBLISHED SOURCES

Acosta, José de
1986   *Historia natural y moral de las Indias* [1590]. Edited by José Alcina Franch. Madrid: Historia 16.
2002   *Natural and moral history of the Indies* [1590]. Edited by Jane E. Mangan, with an introduction and commentary by Walter D. Mignolo. Translated by Frances López-Morillas. Durham: Duke University Press.

Albornoz, Cristóbal de
1984   Instrucción para descubrir todas las guacas del Pirú y sus camayos y haziendas [ca. 1582]. In "Albornoz y el espacio ritual andino prehispánico," edited by Pierre Duviols. *Revista Andina* 2(1):169–222.

Arciniega, Rose
1956   *Pedro Sarmiento de Gamboa, el Ulises de América*. Buenos Aires: Editorial Suamericana.

Barnes, Monica
1996   A lost Inca history. *Latin American Indian Literatures Journal* 12(2):117–131.
Bauer, Brian S.
1991   Pacariqtambo and the mythical origins of the Inca. *Latin American Antiquity* 2(1):7–26.
1996   The legitimization of the Inca state in myth and ritual. *American Anthropologist* 98(2):327–337.
1998   *The sacred landscape of the Inca: The Cuzco ceque system.* Austin: University of Texas Press.
2004   *Ancient Cuzco: Heartland of the Inca.* Austin: University of Texas Press.
Bauer, Brian S., and R. Alan Covey
2002   State development in the Inca heartland (Cuzco, Peru). *American Anthropologist* 10(3):846–864.
Bauer, Brian S., and David S. P. Dearborn
1995   *Astronomy and empire in the ancient Andes.* Austin: University of Texas Press.
Bauer, Brian S., and Charles Stanish
2001   *Ritual and pilgrimage in the ancient Andes: The Islands of the Sun and the Moon.* Austin: University of Texas Press.
Betanzos, Juan de
1987   *Suma y narración de los incas* [1557]. Prólogo, transcripción y notas por María del Carmen Martín Rubio; estudios preliminares de Horacio Villanueva Urteaga, Demetrio Ramos y María del Carmen Martín Rubio. Madrid: Atlas.
1996   *Narrative of the Incas* [1557]. Translated and edited by Roland Hamilton and Dana Buchanan from the Palma de Mallorca manuscript. Austin: University of Texas Press.
Bray, Tamara L.
2003   *Los efectos del imperio incaico en la frontera septentrional: Una investigación arqueológica.* Quito: Abya-Yala Press.
Burns, Kathryn
1999   *Colonial habits: Convents and the spiritual economy of Cuzco, Peru.* Durham, N.C.: Duke University Press.
Cabello Balboa, Miguel
1951   *Miscelánea antártica, una historia del Perú antiguo* [1586]. Edited by L. E. Valcárcel. Lima: Universidad Nacional Mayor de San Marcos, Instituto de Etnología.
Calancha, Antonio de la
1981   *Corónica moralizada del Orden de San Agustín en el Perú* [1638]. Edited by Ignacio Prado Pastor. Lima: Universidad Nacional Mayor de San Marcos, Editorial de la Universidad.
Cieza de León, Pedro de
1976   *The Incas of Pedro Cieza de León* [Part 1, 1553, and Part 2, 1554]. Translated by Harriet de Onís and edited by Victor W. von Hagen. Norman: University of Oklahoma Press.
1998   *The discovery and conquest of Peru* [1554]. Edited and translated by Alexandra Parma Cook and Noble David Cook. Durham, N.C.: Duke University Press.
Cobo, Bernabé
1964   *Historia del Nuevo Mundo* [1653]. Biblioteca de Autores Españoles (continuación), vols. 91–92. Madrid: Ediciones Atlas.

1979   History of the Inca Empire: An account of the Indians' customs and their origin together with a treatise on Inca legends, history, and social institutions [1653]. Translated and edited by Roland Hamilton. Austin: University of Texas Press.

1990   Inca religion and customs [1653]. Translated and edited by Roland Hamilton. Austin: University of Texas Press.

Covey, R. Alan

2003   The Vilcanota Valley (Peru): Inka state formation and the evolution of imperial strategies. Ph.D. dissertation, University of Michigan, Department of Anthropology.

Dean, Carolyn S.

1998   Creating a ruin in Colonial Cusco: Sacsahuaman and what was made of it. Andean Past 5:161-183. Edited by Monica Barnes, Daniel H. Sandweiss, and Brian S. Bauer. Ithaca, N.Y.: Cornell University Latin American Studies Program.

Decoster, Jean-Jacques

2002   La sangre que mancha: La iglesia colonial temprana frente a indios, mestizos e ilegítimos. In Incas e indios cristianos: Elites indígenas e identidades cristianas en los Andes coloniales, edited by Jean-Jacques Decoster, pp. 251-294. Cuzco: Centro Bartolomé de Las Casas/IFEA/Kuraka.

Dorta, Enrique Marco

1975   Las pinturas que envió y trajo a España don Francisco de Toledo. Historia y Cultura 9:67-75.

Espinoza Soriano, Waldemar

1974   El hábitat de la etnia Pinagua, siglos XV y XVI. Revista del Museo Nacional (Lima) 40:157-220.

Esquivel y Navia, Diego de

1980   Noticias cronológicas de la Gran Ciudad del Cuzco [1749]. Edición, prólogo y notas de Félix Denegri Luna con la colaboración de Horacio Villanueva Urteaga y César Gutiérrez Muñoz. Tomos 1 y 2. Lima: Fundación Augusto N. Wiese, Banco, Wiese Ltdo.

Fernández, Diego

1963   Primera y segunda parte de la historia del Perú [1571]. In Crónicas del Perú, edited by Juan Pérez de Tudela Bueso. Biblioteca de Autores Españoles (continuación), vols. 164-165. Madrid: Ediciones Atlas.

Garcilaso de la Vega, Inca

1966   Royal commentaries of the Incas and general history of Peru, Parts 1 and 2 [1609]. Translated by Harold V. Livermore. Austin: University of Texas Press.

González Carré, Enrique

1981   La ciudad inca de Vilcashuamán. Ayacucho, Peru: Universidad Nacional de San Cristóbal de Huamanga.

Guaman Poma de Ayala, Felipe

1980   El primer nueva corónica y buen gobierno [1615]. Edited by John V. Murra and Rolena Adorno. Translated by Jorge I. Urioste. 3 vols. Mexico City: Siglo Veintiuno.

Hampe Martínez, Teodoro

1982   Las momias de los incas en Lima. Revista del Museo Nacional (Lima) 46:405-418.

Hemming, John

1970   The conquest of the Incas. New York: Harcourt Brace Jovanovich.

Iwasaki Cauti, Fernando
1986   Panacas del Cuzco y la pintura incaica. *Revista de Indias* 46(177):59–74.
Julien, Catherine
1999   History and art in translation: The *paños* and other objects collected by Francisco Toledo. *Colonial Latin American Review* 8(1):61–89.
2000   *Reading Inca history.* Iowa City: University of Iowa Press.
Landín Carrasco, Amancio
1945   *Vida y viajes de Pedro Sarmiento de Gamboa: Descubridor de las islas Salomón, poblador y capitán general del estrecho de Magallanes, almirante de Indias.* Madrid: Instituto Histórico de Marina.
Levillier, Roberto
1918–1922   La Audiencia de Charcas. Correspondencia de presidentes y oidores, documentos del Archivo de Indias, edited by Roberto Levillier. 3 vols. Colección de Publicaciones Históricas de la Biblioteca del Congreso Argentino. Madrid: Imprenta de J. Pueyo.
1921   Carta del Virrey por d. Francisco de Toledo anunciando a S. M. el envío de algunos paños de los que usaban los naturales y como quisiera algunos pintores indios [1 March 1572: Cuzco]). In *Gobernantes del Perú*, edited by Roberto Levillier, 3:542–544. Madrid: Sucesores de Rivadeneyra (S. A.).
1924   Carta del Virrey Toledo a S. M. dando cuenta de cuantas medidas creía oportunas para evitar nuevas rebeldías y delitos por parte del inca y su gente [8 May 1572]. In *Gobernantes del Perú*, edited by Roberto Levillier, 4:363–376. Madrid: Sucesores de Rivadeneyra (S. A.).
1940   *Don Francisco de Toledo, supremo organizador del Perú.* Vol. 2, Sus informaciones sobre los incas (1570–1572). Buenos Aires: Espasa-Calpe.
1942   *Don Francisco de Toledo, supremo organizador del Perú.* Vol. 3, La historia de los incas de Sarmiento de Gamboa que él mandó escribir cotejada con los comentarios de Garcilaso y otras crónicas. Buenos Aires: Espasa-Calpe.
Loaisa, Francisco de
1943   Introduction to *Relación de las fábulas y ritos de los incas* [1575], edited by Francisco de Loayza. Los Pequeños Grandes Libros de Historia Americana. Lima: Librería e Imprenta D. Miranda.
Marcoy, Paul
1875   *Travels in South America: From the Pacific Ocean to the Atlantic Ocean.* London: Blackie & Son.
2001   *Viaje a través de América del Sur* [1875]. 2 vols. Translated to Spanish by Edgardo Rivera Martínez. Lima: IFEA, BCRP, PUCP, CAAP.
Markham, Clements R.
1895   Introduction to *Narratives of the voyages of Pedro Sarmiento de Gamboa to the Straits of Magellan* [1586]. London: Hakluyt Society.
1999   Introduction to *History of the Incas by Pedro Sarmiento de Gamboa*, Mineola, NY: Dover. [Reprint of *History of the Incas by Pedro Sarmiento de Gamboa and The Execution of the Inca Tupac Amaru by Captain Baltasar de Ocampo*. Translated with notes and introduction by Sir Clements Markham, The Hakluyt Society (1907). Cambridge: Cambridge University Press.]
McEwan, Colin, and Maarten Van de Guchte
1992   Ancestral time and sacred space in Inca state ritual. In *The ancient Americas: Art*

from sacred landscapes, edited by Richard F. Townsend, pp. 359–371. Chicago: The Art Institute of Chicago.

Means, Philip Ainsworth

1928 Biblioteca Andina: The chroniclers, or, the writers of the sixteenth and seventeenth centuries who treated of the pre-Hispanic history and culture of the Andean countries. *Transactions of the Connecticut Academy of Arts and Sciences* 29:271–525. New Haven: Connecticut Academy of Arts and Sciences.

Medina, José Toribio

1952 *Historia del Tribunal del Santo Oficio de la Inquisición en Chile* [1890]. Prólogo de A. Almeyda. Santiago, Chile: Imprenta Ercilla.

Mena, Cristóbal de

1929 *The conquest of Peru, as recorded by a member of the Pizarro expedition* [1534]. Translated by Joseph H. Sinclair. New York: New York Public Library.

Mendaña, Alvaro de

1901 *The Discovery of the Solomon Islands by Alvaro de Mendaña in 1568.* Introduction, edited and notes by Lord Amherst of Hackney and Basil Thomson. Vol. 1. London: The Hakluyt Society.

Molina, Cristóbal de

1913 *Relación de las fábulas y ritos de los Incas* [ca. 1575]. In *Las crónicas de los Molinas* [ca. 1575], edited by Carlos A. Romero, Raúl Porras Barrenechea, and Francisco A. Loayza, 4:7–84. Los Pequeños Grandes Libros de Historia Americana, 1st ser. Lima: Imprenta D. Miranda.

1989 *Relación de las fábulas i ritos de los Ingas* [ca. 1575]. In *Fábulas y mitos de los incas,* edited by Henrique Urbano and Pierre Duviols, pp. 47–134. Crónicas de América. Madrid: Historia 16.

Morales, Ambrosio

1944 Documentos para la historia del Cuzco: Tumbas de los incas Sairi Tupac, D. Felipe Tupac Amaru, . . . y de la coya doña María Cusihuarcay. *Revista del Instituto Americano de Arte* (Cuzco) 3(1):13–21.

Murúa, Martín de

1946 *Historia del origen y genealogía real de los reyes incas del Perú* [1590]. Introduction and notes by Constantino Bayle. Biblioteca "Missionalia Hispánica," vol. 2. Madrid: Instituto Santo Toribio de Mogrovejo.

1987 *Historia general del Perú* [1590]. Edited by Manuel Ballesteros-Garbrois. Crónicas de América. Madrid: Historia 16.

2004 *Historia y genealogía de los reyes incas* [1590]. Madrid: Testimonio Compañía Editorial.

Ocampo Conejeros, Baltasar

1907 *Account of the Province of Vilcapampa and a narrative of the execution of the Inca Tupac Amaru* [1610]. Translated by Clements Markham, 22:203–247. London: The Hakluyt Society.

Pease, Franklin

1995 *Las crónicas y los Andes.* Lima: Fondo de Cultura Económica Lima.

Pizarro, Pedro

1921 *Relation of the discovery and conquest of the kingdoms of Peru* [1571]. Translated and edited by Philip Ainsworth Means. New York: The Cortés Society.

Polo de Ondegardo, Juan
1965   On the errors and superstitions of the Indians, taken from the treatise and investigation done by Licentiate Polo [1585]. Translated by A. Brunel, John Murra, and Sidney Muirden, pp. 1–53. New Haven, Conn.: Human Relations Area Files.
1990   Notables daños de no guardar a los indios sus fueros [1571]. In *El mundo de los incas*, edited by Laura González and Alicia Alonso, pp. 33–113. Madrid: Historia 16.
Porras Barrenechea, Raúl (ed.)
1986   *Los cronistas del Perú (1528–1650)*. Lima: Imprenta DESA.
Rowe, John H.
1944   *An introduction to the archaeology of Cuzco*. Papers of the Peabody Museum of American Archaeology and Ethnology, vol. 27, no. 2. Cambridge, Mass.: Harvard University.
1980   Relación de las guacas del Cuzco [1653]. In "An account of the shrines of ancient Cuzco," translated and edited by John H. Rowe. *Ñawpa Pacha* 17(1979):2–80.
1985   La constitución inca del Cuzco. *Histórica* 9(1):35–73.
1986   Probanza de los incas nietos de conquistadores. *Histórica* 9(2):193–245.
Ruiz de Navamuel, Alvaro
1882   La fe y testimonio que va puesta en los cuatro paños . . . [14 enero 1572]. In *Informaciones acerca del señorío y gobierno de los ingas hechas por mandado de don Francisco de Toledo*, edited by Marcos Jimenez de Espada, 16:245–252. Colección de Libros Españoles Raros y Curiosos. Madrid: Imprenta de M. Ginesta.
Salazar, Antonio Baptista de
1867   De vireyes y gobernadores del Perú [1596]. In *Colección de Documentos Inéditos, relativos al descubrimiento, conquista y organización de las antiguas posesiones españolas*, transcribed by Luis Torres de Mendoza, 8:212–293. Madrid: Imprenta de Frías y Compañía. (Formerly attributed to Tristán Sánchez.)
Salomon, Frank, and George L. Urioste (trans. and eds.)
1991   *The Huarochirí Manuscript: A testament of Ancient and Colonial Andean religion* [1608]. Austin: University of Texas Press.
Sancho de la Hoz, Pedro
1917   *An account of the conquest of Peru* [1534]. Translated by Philip A. Means. Documents and Narratives Concerning the Discovery and Conquest of Latin America, no. 2. New York: The Cortés Society.
Santa Cruz Pachacuti Yamqui Salcamayhua, Juan de
1950   Relación de antigüedades deste reyno del Perú [ca. 1613]. In *Tres relaciones de antigüedades peruanas*, edited by Marcos Jiménez de la Espada, pp. 207–281. Asunción, Paraguay: Editora Guaranía.
Sarmiento de Gamboa, Pedro
1895   *Narratives of the voyages of Pedro Sarmiento de Gamboa to the Straits of Magellan* [1586]. Translated and edited with notes and an introduction by Clements R. Markham. London: The Hakluyt Society.
1906   *Segunda parte de la historia general llamada Índica* . . . [1572]. In *Geschichte des Inkareiches von Pedro Sarmiento de Gamboa*, edited by Richard Pietschmann. Abhandlungen der Königlichen Gesellschaft der Wissenschaften zu Göttingen, Philologisch-Historische Klasse, Neue Folge, vol. 6, no. 4. Berlin: Weidmannsche Buchhandlung.
1964   *La "Historia Índica" de Pedro Sarmiento de Gamboa* [1906]. Nota preliminar de

Alberto Tauro. Colección Comentarios del Perú 2. Lima: Universidad Nacional Mayor de San Marcos. [Traducción española por Federico Schwab de la introducción a *Geschichte des Inkareiches von Pedro Sarmiento de Gamboa*. Berlin: Weidmannsche Buchhandlung.]

1988   *Los viajes al estrecho de Magallanes* [1586]. Introduction, transcriptions, and notes by Justina Sarabia Viejo. Madrid: Alianza Editorial.

2000   *Los viajes al estrecho de Magallanes* [1586]. Edited by Juan Batista González Las Rozas. Madrid: Daston.

Schjellerup, Inge

1997   *Incas and Spaniards in the conquest of the Chachapoyas: Archaeological and ethnohistorical research in the northeastern Andes of Peru.* Göteborg, Denmark: Göteborg University/National Museum of Denmark.

Sillar, Bill, and Emily Dean

2002   Identidad étnica bajo el dominio inka: Una evaluación arqueológica y etnohistórica de las repercusiones del estado inka en el grupo étnico canas. *Boletín de Arqueología PUCP* 6:205–264.

Stirling, Stuart

1999   *The last conquistador.* Sutton, England: Thrupp.

Titu Cusi Yupanqui, Diego de Castro

2005   *An Inca account of the conquest of Peru* [1570]. Translated, introduced, and annotated by Ralph Bauer. Boulder: University Press of Colorado.

Toledo, Francisco de

1975   *Tasa de la visita general de Francisco de Toledo* [1573]. Introducción y versión paleográfica de Noble David Cook, y los estudios de Alejandro Málaga Medina and Thérèse Bouysse Cassagne. Lima: Dirección Universitaria de Biblioteca y Publicaciones, Universidad Nacional Mayor de San Marcos, Seminario de Historia Rural Andina.

Topic, John, Theresa Lange Topic, and Alfredo Melly Cava

2002   Catequil: The archaeology, ethnohistory, and ethnography of a major provincial huaca. In *Andean archaeology 1: Variations in sociopolitical organization*, edited by William H. Isbell and Helaine Silverman, pp. 303–336. New York: Kluwer Academic.

Urbano, Henrique

1989   Introduction to *Fábulas y mitos de los incas*, edited by Henrique Urbano and Pierre Duviols, pp. 9–41. Crónicas de América. Madrid: Historia 16.

Valera, Blas

1950   De las costumbres antiguas de los naturales del Pirú [ca. 1585]. In *Tres relaciones de antigüedades peruanas*, edited by Marcos Jiménez de la Espada, pp. 135–203. Asunción, Paraguay: Editorial Guaranía.

Villanueva Urteaga, Horacio

1982   *Cuzco 1689: Economía y sociedad en el sur andino.* Cuzco: Centro de Estudios Rurales Andinos "Bartolomé de Las Casas."

Wachtel, Nathan

1982   The *mitimas* of the Cochabamba Valley: The colonization policy of Huayna Capac. In *The Inca and Aztec states, 1400–1800: Anthropology and history,* edited by George A. Collier, Renato I. Rosaldo, and John D. Wirth, pp. 199–235. New York: Academic Press.

Watanabe, Shinya

2002 El reino de Cuismancu: Orígenes y transformación en el Tawantinsuyu. *Boletín de Arqueología PUCP* 6:107–136.

Xérez, Francisco de

1985 *Verdadera relación de la conquista del Perú* [1534]. Edited by Concepción Bravo. Crónicas de América 14. Madrid: Historia 16.

Zimmerman, Arthur Franklin

1938 Francisco Toledo, fifth viceroy of Peru, 1569–1581. Caldwell, Idaho: Caxton Printers.

Index